Delphi Programming with COM and ActiveX

DELPHI PROGRAMMING WITH COM AND ACTIVEX

V. PONAMAREV

CHARLES RIVER MEDIA, INC.
Hingham, Massachusetts

Acquisitions Editor: Brian Sawyer
Production: A-List Publishing
Cover Design: The Printed Image

CHARLES RIVER MEDIA, INC.
20 Downer Avenue, Suite 3
Hingham, Massachusetts 02043
781-740-0400
781-740-8816 (FAX)
info@charlesriver.com
www.charlesriver.com

This book is printed on acid-free paper.

V. Ponamarev. *Delphi Programming with COM and ActiveX.*
ISBN: 1-58450-254-1

Printed in the United States of America
02 7 6 5 4 3 2 First Edition

Table of Contents

Introduction

Among developers of software for Windows, the Borland Delphi rapid application development environment is popular worldwide. This popularity is no doubt due to its simplicity, as well as the ease with which it can be learned and used.

Many people who make their careers in the area of software development don't think that Delphi can be taken seriously when it comes to creating professional applications. In my opinion, this is a huge mistake, and one of the reasons I decided to write this book. In the following pages, I'll show you the capabilities of Delphi that are often simply overlooked and not used at all by professional developers. I know a number of programmers who have no idea how to create COM objects using Delphi. These developers write software in Delphi, but work with OCXs that they write themselves in other programming environments. These situations and others like them occur due to the fact that programmers simply aren't acquainted with the powerful programming tools that Delphi provides.

As a whole, this book is dedicated to using and creating VCL Delphi components and COM objects. The majority of examples included in the book were done in Delphi 5 Enterprise.

Throughout the book, I assume that the reader has access to a version of Delphi that has been installed on a computer. I also recommend that, while going through the book, you perform each example on your own computer.

INTENDED AUDIENCE

This book was written mainly for developers who create serious commercial products, for component developers, and also for the following types of readers:

- Developers who use and build automation elements and other COM objects
- Students who are in the process of learning Delphi
- Mid-level programmers who want to improve their skills

I have tried to write this book so that the reader needn't refer to any additional literature. However, even the biggest book can't cover all possible problems and issues that might arise, and so at the end of the book I give a list of recommended literature to which the reader can refer for additional information. I would be most grateful to my readers for informing me of possible errors they might come across in this book and, I certainly welcome any comments and critical observations from my audience.

THE STRUCTURE OF THE BOOK

This book consists of three parts.

Part I is dedicated to a discussion of the Delphi integrated development environment. The user interface provided by Delphi is also described, and we go into the principles of object-oriented programming as well. This part also explains Delphi exceptions and interfaces. One of the chapters in this part deals with the creation of multithreaded applications. Finally, the last chapter briefly touches on the subject of the Windows API.

Part II concentrates on VCL Delphi libraries, as well as creating your own components. Here we'll look at most of the properties, methods, and events inherent in VCL Delphi component architecture. From the last few chapters of this part, you can learn how to create a component on your own, how to add properties, methods, and events to it, and how to register the new component in the Component palette.

The third and final part of the book will give you the basics of COM technology. The material in this part teaches you how to create simple COM objects, servers, and automated control managers. Chapters 12 and 13 show you how to use ActiveX controls in your applications, and how to create an ActiveX control from VCL Delphi components and forms. The last chapter deals with creating Microsoft Transaction Server objects.

TYPOGRAPHIC CONVENTIONS

This book uses the following typographic conventions:

- `Monospaced type` is used for the text of code listings, identifiers, names of functions, variables, classes, commands, etc.; basically, any text that you might see on your screen.
- *Italics* is used to highlight new terms when they are introduced for the first time, as well as to emphasize the most important terms and concepts.
- **Boldfaced** words in the text represent names of interface elements, windows, menu items, tabs, icons, etc.
- The material that is most essential for understanding is given in the form of notes.
- Key captions are enclosed in angle brackets, for example, <F1>; the + character is used throughout the text to define a shortcut key, for instance, <Ctrl>+<Alt>+<O>.

PART I Programming in Delphi

1 Using Object Pascal and VCL to Develop Windows Applications

As you probably know, Delphi was originally developed based on Object Pascal. The advantages and most powerful features of this skillfully designed language were universally recognized and highly appreciated by the developing community. Therefore, it seemed quite reasonable to adapt Object Pascal for use on a Microsoft Windows platform. Thus, Delphi was created to facilitate development of applications for Windows in Object Pascal. The most important feature of Delphi is its use of visual design technology. Borland introduced this feature in the special *Visual Component Library (VCL)*.

In this chapter, we will explore the wide range of Delphi's capabilities in quickly and effectively developing applications for Windows. You will learn the basics of Delphi IDE and familiarize yourself with standard Delphi components. We will also show you how to create a simple Delphi application. We'll cover the concept of objects and discuss their inner structure, as well as the principles of creating and deleting objects. Next, we will take a look at the `TObject` parent class. And finally, we will briefly discuss the basic concepts on which Object Oriented Programming is based: encapsulation, inheritance, and polymorphism.

FEATURES THAT DEVELOPERS WILL FIND IN DELPHI 5/6

The following technologies and capabilities were introduced into Delphi 5:

- *ADO (ActiveX Data Object)*: This technology was designed to serve as an alternative to BDE (Borland Database Engine), and allows you to access data in various formats.
- The *Data Module Designer*: Lets you create and manage data modules.
- *InterBase Express* components: Enables you to take advantage of InterBase servers in a most convenient way, without using BDE.
- The *MIDAS* extension: In this new Delphi version, the enhanced MIDAS technology supports stateless remote data modules.
- Changes introduced to *CORBA (Common Object Request Broker Architecture)*: CORBA can now work with VisiBroker for C++ ORB3.32. These changes substantially reduce message traffic between CORBA clients and servers.
- Advanced debugging: The built-in debugger is enhanced by adding a huge number of powerful features, including debug options for various processes.
- VCL (Visual Component Library) extensions: The VCL contains a number of new objects, properties, and events, including newly designed components for working with the Web and for establishing an Internet connection.
- *Frames*: A frame is a special type of form that can be embedded into another form or frame.
- Customizable desktop settings: You can configure your desktop settings and save several concurrent configurations.
- *To-Do lists*: Contains a schedule of tasks to be performed to complete a given project.
- Property categories in the *Object Inspector*: The Object Inspector now allows filtering of properties and events by category.
- Images in drop-down lists of the Object Inspector: The Object Inspector has been further enhanced with the capability of having small images such as cursors appear in drop-down lists.
- Advanced *Project Manager*: The Project Manager facilitates the process of managing a project. Now you can easily work with files from different projects, rearrange them as you wish, and add a new file to a project. Prior to being added to a project, resource files are compiled into files with the RES extension.
- Extended functionality of ActiveX: Importable COM servers can be employed as components for visual development.
- New, efficient wizards: Two new wizards let you create console-based applications and applications for Windows Control Panel.
- Advanced editing: Editing preferences are now centralized and can be called by a separate command: Tools/Editor Options.

- *Project Browser*: A new window for viewing a project.
- **The ability to save form files as text files:** Form files (DFM) now are saved as text files—as opposed to binary—by default. However, you can still save them as binary files if you so choose.
- **New capabilities for automatic form creation:** In earlier Delphi versions, as soon as a form was created it was placed automatically (with certain rare exceptions) into the **Autocreated Forms** list of automatically created forms. In this new Delphi version, a developer is able to choose whether he wants to place newly created forms in this list, or, alternatively, into the **Available Forms** list, in which case only the main form of a given project will be placed into the **Autocreated Forms** list.
- **IDE command line settings:** In this new Delphi version you can start IDE directly from its command line using a number of new parameters that are particularly helpful during a debugging session. For example, some of these parameters can show you the amount of free space in the main memory at the moment, record all messages in a log file, etc.
- **New capabilities for international development:** A new toolkit—*Integrated Translation Environment*—was introduced to further simplify application localization and simultaneous development of multi-language application versions.
- *NetMaster* **components:** NetMaster components are located in a separate tab of the *Component palette*, FastNet.

Delphi Enterprise has all the above features, some of which are absent in other versions. Now let's discuss some of these novelties in more detail.

The new **Data Module Designer** is used as a means for visualizing application development. A data module is a complete presentation of all sample data being used in the application under development (Figure 1.1). The **Data Module Designer** can be called via the main menu by selecting **File/New/Data Module.**

If you take a look at the **Data Diagram** page, you will see a diagram very similar to an "entity-relationship" diagram, which is normally used when developing databases with CASE technology. The **Data Module Designer** provides a developer with a very simple and effective visual tool for designing databases. More specifically, when you join components derived from the `TDataset` parent class by dragging them together, the new required components will be automatically added (such as `TDataSource`); also, values will be assigned to the properties in order to provide this relationship. You can specify the type of this relationship by clicking the proper button on the vertical toolbar to the left of the diagram. Besides `TDataset` components, other components can be shown on the **Data Diagram** page as well; you manipulate them in the same manner.

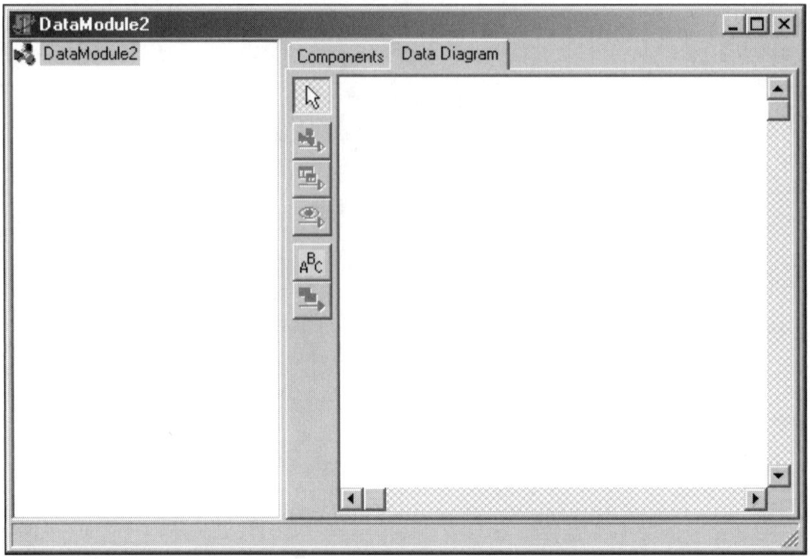

FIGURE 1.1 A **Data Module** editor.

Starting with Version 5, Delphi supports a so-called To-Do list, which is simply a list of tasks that need to be accomplished to complete a given project.

Tasks included in a To-Do list may relate not only to the whole project, but also to some individual unit. You can view your current To-Do list by selecting the View/To-Do List command in the main menu, which will result in the corresponding window appearing on your screen (Figure 1.2). Here you are able to add new tasks to the list, check those tasks that have already been completed, edit them, and change priority settings.

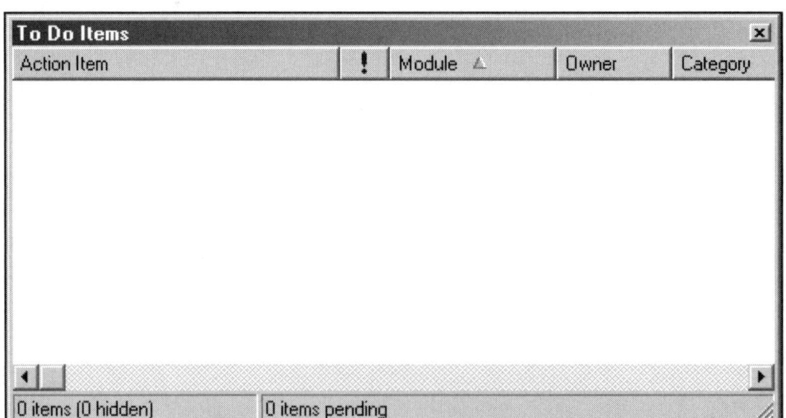

FIGURE 1.2 A sample To-Do list.

You can add a new task to the list either by using a pop-up menu or with the <Ctrl>+<Shift>+<T> shortcut key. Both these operations call a window for creating a new task (Figure 1.3).

Tasks included in the To-Do list that relate to an individual module are saved as comments in the original text of this module:

```
{ TODO 1 : Change the name of the OK button}
```

Tasks scheduled for the whole project are stored in a file with the To-Do extension. These two types of tasks are represented by different icons in a To-Do list. If the module to which a given task is related is not uploaded in the **Code Editor**, the task in question is highlighted in gray color. Each task can have a priority, the name of the person to whom it is assigned, a category, textual content, and status notification:

```
{ DONE 1 : Change the name of the OK button }
```

A To-Do list can be filtered by all the aforementioned settings.

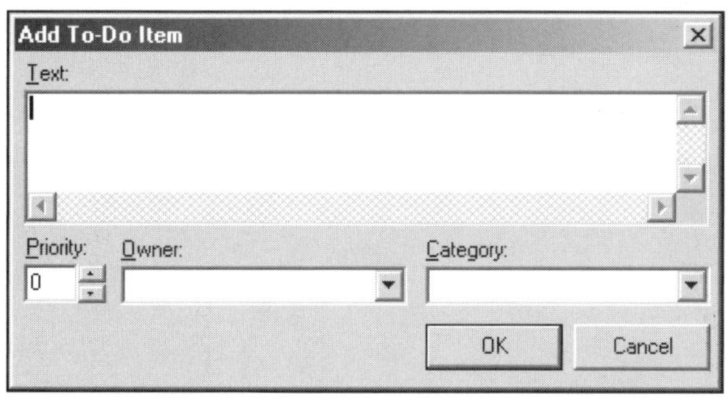

FIGURE 1.3 Adding a new To-Do item.

The new version supports the development of multi-language applications. Most importantly, you can do this concurrently, for instance, simultaneously create English and Russian versions of the same application. Let's see how this can be done with Delphi's new feature, *Integrated Translation Environment*. First, you need to create a new project containing only one form with two buttons. Then, by selecting **Project/Languages/Add** from the Delphi main menu, start the wizard (Figure 1.4), which will bring up a sequence of dialog windows in which you select the languages to be supported by your application—in this case we want English (USA) and Russian.

The **Translation Manager** will then start automatically (Figure 1.5).

This Manager is essentially an editor for dealing with string resources that can be present in a form. The **Translation Manager** is supplied with information on those properties of interface elements that sometimes tend to vary, depending on the language of a given version. These can be not only such properties as `caption` or `text`, but also other visual characteristics. Now, you need to set the button captions (`Button1.Caption` and `Button2.Caption`). In the English version set them to "Yes" and "No," and in the Russian version to "Да" and "Нет," respectively. After that, change the form name (`Form1.Caption`) to "Приложение" in the Russian version. Lastly, issue the **Project/Language/Set Active** command from the Delphi main menu and select Russian and English. Compile your project and you will get both language versions (Figure 1.6).

Some major changes have also been introduced to the Visual Component Library framework. Among them are:

- The **`TApplicationEvents`** component: In earlier Delphi versions you had to create a procedure and then assign the name of this procedure to the handler of the `TApplication` event in order to create an event handler for the `TApplication` object. Delphi 5 introduced a new non-visual component that can be placed in an application form. As a result, you will be able to process all `TApplication` events directly from the **Object Inspector** window (the **Object Inspector** will be discussed later in this chapter) in much the same manner as you do with other Delphi components.
- The **`TAppletApplication`** class: Expressly for developing applications for the Windows Control Panel (with the extension CPL), a new class, `TAppletApplication`., has been introduced into Delphi 5. An application of this type can contain several modules derived from the `TAppletModule` class, and each descendant module will be represented on the Windows Control Panel. If you need to build such an application, simply select **File/New/Control Panel Application (Module)** from the Delphi main menu.

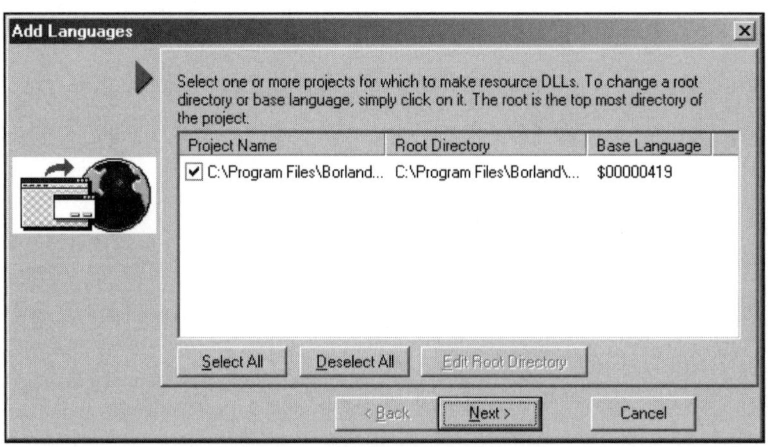

FIGURE 1.4 The **Add Languages** wizard allows for developing multi-language applications.

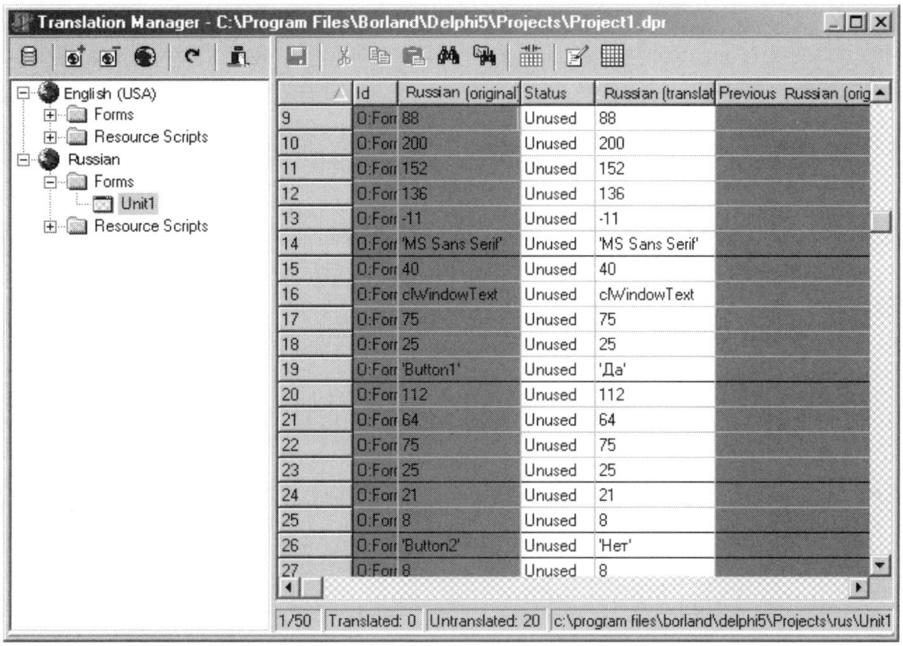

FIGURE 1.5 The **Translation Manager** window.

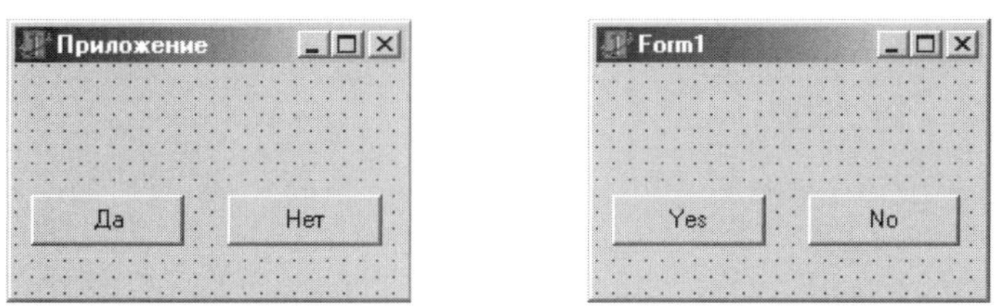

FIGURE 1.6 Two versions of the same application written in different languages.

- New events for the **`TToolBar`** and **`TListView`** components: A number of events related to these components have been added (`OnAdvancedCustomDrawItem`, `OnAdvancedCustomDraw`, etc.). Handlers for these events now have an extra setting for specifying the exact stage of the redrawing of an image in which a given event should occur.
- New container-type classes have been introduced: These classes are descendants of the `TList` class: `TObjectList`, `TComponentList`, and `TClassList`. These classes were developed specifically for storing references to objects, components, and classes, respectively. Delphi 5 also features such new classes as `TObjectQuery` and `TObjectStack`, which are designed for storing references to objects in the form of queries and stacks.

One of the highly useful novelties among those introduced into Delphi 5 is the concept of a *frame*. Frames are essentially visual containers with various components placed within their borders (much as working with forms) that can subsequently be used in forms. You can build a frame by selecting **File/New Frame** from the Delphi main menu. As soon as you create all the necessary frames, they can be placed in various forms of your application by using the **Frames** component included in the standard Component palette. The important factor to be remembered in these matters is that, when you embed a frame into any form, Delphi automatically creates a descendant of the chosen frame class. That is to say, when you introduce any changes to the components included into a parent frame, the very same changes automatically occur in the descendant frames. If you so choose, you can add the frame that you use most frequently to the Component palette. To do this, just follow the standard procedure.

The Delphi development environment was originally designed for working primarily with databases. Naturally, with every new version, old technologies aimed at working with databases have been updated and improved, and new and more sophisticated ones have been appearing. Delphi 5 and 6 provide a much-extended set of components which were developed exclusively for manipulating databases. The Component palette now includes a new tab where the components are grouped, **InterBase Express**, which allows you to access the *IB Database* server (starting with Version 5.5 and higher). Another good thing is that all the components of this tab use its client API, which means that you can now do without BDE.

ActiveX Data Objects (ADO) is another new feature designed for handling databases. ADO components are also grouped together in a separate tab of the Component palette. ADOs are actually COM servers that use OLE DB to work with data. COM servers are provided with many Microsoft products. ADO components are not BDE-oriented either. Introducing ADO support to Delphi 5 brought about new descendant classes of the `TFields` class in order to support those data types associated with ADO.

Quite understandably, certain changes had to be introduced to the components that support BDE. Since the Delphi 5, the `TDatabase` component has a new method, `Execute`, which lets you perform SQL queries without using the component specially designed for this, `TQuery`.

While working on all these improvements, Delphi's creators could simply not overlook COM technology. When importing type libraries, Delphi 5 allows you to add COM servers to the Component palette. The resulting components are directly derived from the `TOLEServer` class and have the same event as the given object. This enables a developer to build event handlers for COM servers using the **Object Inspector**. The COM server's properties are available only at runtime; that's why the properties in question are not featured in the **Object Inspector**. COM server support will be discussed in more depth in Part III.

THE DELPHI INTEGRATED DEVELOPMENT ENVIRONMENT (IDE)

A convenient development environment is a very important, possibly the most important, factor in the work of every programmer. It factors in both the software product's quality and the speed of its development. The Delphi development environment is relatively handy for quick and effective application creation. Delphi designers have put much time and effort into perfecting the environment in question. Another important aspect in these matters is the possibility of customizing your development environment to meet your requirements. Delphi enables the developer to customize the environment as he chooses.

In the next section, we will discuss the basic elements of the Delphi development environment.

The Main Parts of the Delphi IDE

The Delphi IDE includes four essential parts (windows) which are displayed as soon as you launch the environment:

- The main window
- Form Designer
- Object Inspector
- Code Editor

The main window is the most important part of IDE (Figure 1.7). It resembles a standard Windows window and contains three main areas: the menu, six toolbars, and the Component palette.

The menu in the main window includes the set of items standard for any software. The menu is located on the uppermost string of Delphi's main window. By using the menu you can manipulate files, projects, and forms. You can configure the whole Delphi environment by customizing various options, and perform a whole host of other operations. The menu allows you to create new components and import various external development tools, for instance. You can also use shortcut keys to execute certain Delphi commands. For example, the **Open Project** command can be executed via the <Ctrl>+<F11> shortcut.

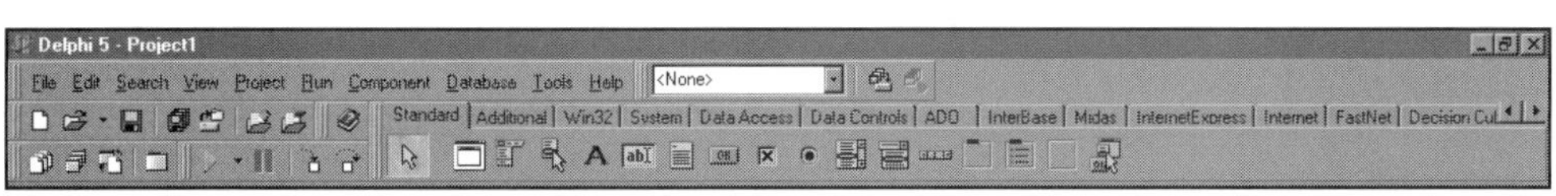

FIGURE 1.7 Delphi's main window.

There are six toolbars in Delphi, which are located under the menu (except for the Desktop bar to the right of the menu) and include a number of buttons that replicate some commands available from the menu of the main window. The elements contained in these bars are logically grouped together by type.

- The Standard bar includes buttons for manipulating project files and enables the user to create, save, and delete them.
- The View bar facilitates working with forms and the textual content of programs.
- The Debug bar allows you to start and debug your application.
- The Custom bar is designed for a developer's own use.
- The Desktop bar keeps you informed about which windows are active at the moment and where exactly they are located on the screen. Such information is referred to as the Delphi *desktop configuration.* Delphi allows for creating and saving different desktop configurations. Additionally, you can specify a default desktop configuration which will automatically start when you run in debug desktop mode and stop when you switch to another mode. To do this, you can use the following buttons: Save current desktop and Set debug desktop. All the saved environment configurations are stored in the Delphi\Bin directory in files with the DST extension.

Using the Customize dialog window, you can specify the buttons to be included into the bars according to your own preferences (Figure 1.8). This window can be called either from a pop-up menu, by right-clicking within the toolbars area, or with View/Toolbars/Customize.

The window contains three tabs: Toolbars, Commands, and Options.

- The Toolbars tab (Figure 1.8) shows or hides toolbar tabs.
- The Commands tab (Figure 1.9) includes commands logically grouped into categories. You can select any command by first clicking its name, and then clicking the desired toolbar. The new button will appear on the chosen toolbar. In order to remove a button, simply click and drag it outside the toolbars area. The Commands tab is a very convenient tool for adding almost any command to the toolbars in order to speed up access to it.
- The Options tab (Figure 1.10) lets you choose the manner in which you want to use pop-up tooltips when working with any toolbar.

You can use the Show tooltips command to enable or disable the appearance of tooltips when you place your cursor on any toolbar button. You can also have the tooltips show the shortcut key for a button.

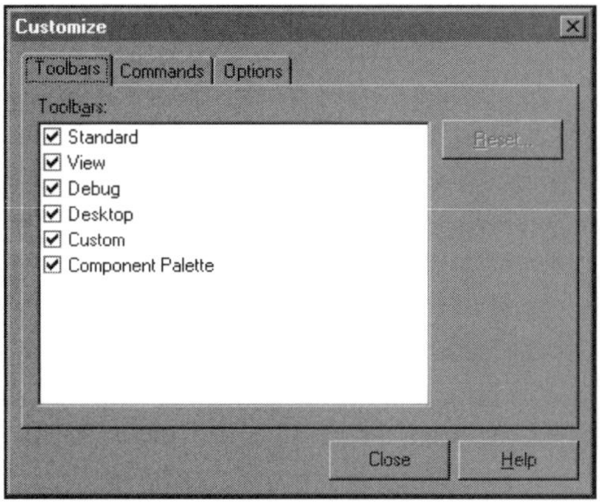

FIGURE 1.8 The **Toolbars** tab.

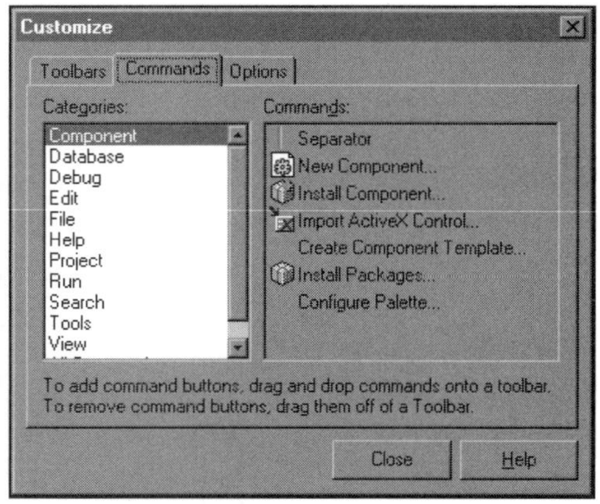

FIGURE 1.9 The **Commands** tab.

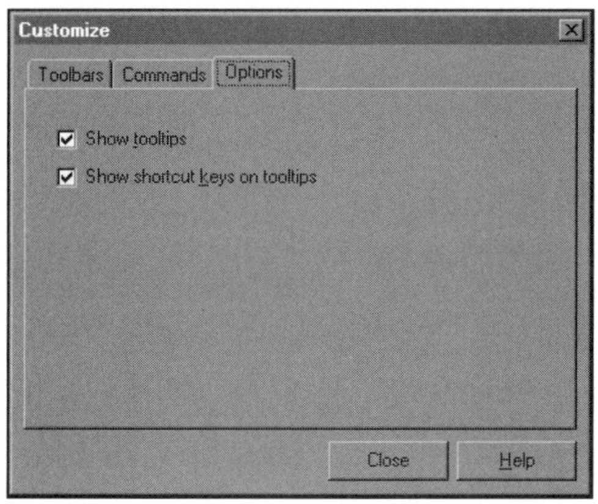

FIGURE 1.10 The **Options** tab.

Upon first installing Delphi, the Component palette contains 19 or more tabs (depending on the version of Delphi) where components are stored, each component being represented by its icon. All the components are grouped by type. You can customize the Component palette as you choose by using the **Palette Properties** window. This window can be activated either via a pop-up menu, by right-clicking in the Component palette, or by selecting **Component/Configure Palette** from the main menu. The Component palette features the following tabs:

- **Standard:** The standard components, such as buttons, captions, etc.
- **Additional:** Additional components, such as a drawing, input masking, etc.
- **Win32:** Access to the 32-bit Windows interface.
- **System:** System components such as the timer, the media player, etc.
- **Data Access:** Access to the contents of database applications through BDE.

- Data Controls: Controls the data stored in database applications.
- ADO: Access to the contents of database applications through ActiveX.
- InterBase: Access to the InterBase database.
- Midas: Working with distributed databases.
- InternetExpress: Builds applications which combine the functions of a Web server and a distributed database.
- Internet: Creates components for working on the Internet.
- FastNet: Provides a number of protocols for accessing the Internet.
- Decision Cube: Multi-dimensional analysis of database application data.
- QReport: Visual development of reports for database applications.
- Dialogs: The components used in standard Windows dialog windows, such as Save, Open, Print, etc.
- Win 3.1: The components of various Windows 3.1 controls give a program a Windows 3.1 look and feel.
- Samples: Sample components that can be built by a developer.
- ActiveX: ActiveX components.
- Servers: Components for regular COM servers.

All the above components are subdivided into two large groups: *visual* and *non-visual.*

Obviously, visual components are visible on a form at runtime. Non-visible components are represented by small icons on the form at design time, but are hidden while running the application.

When Delphi starts, the *Form Designer* (Figure 1.11) looks like an ordinary bare Windows window without any elements. This window is referred to as a Form. A developer places the necessary components on a form simply by dragging them from the Component palette. Using your mouse, you can modify the shape and size of a form, as well as its location on the screen. Any application under development can contain several forms (see Figure 1.6).

If you need to customize properties, methods and events related to specific components, use Object Inspector (see Figure 1.12).
Object Inspector performs the following basic operations:

- Setting properties for the components placed on a form
- Facilitating navigation and creation of event handlers
- Filtering properties and events

Object Inspector includes an object list, along with two tabs: Properties and Events.

An *object list* lets you quickly navigate your objects, and is represented by a drop-down list containing all the components of the current form. The currently active component is at the top of the list. In the sample object list shown in Figure 1.12, Form1 itself is the active component.

FIGURE 1.11 The Form Designer.

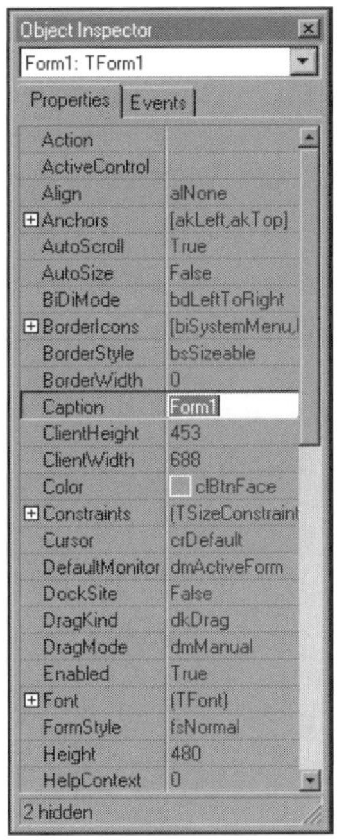

FIGURE 1.12 The Properties tab of the **Object Inspector** window.

The **Properties** tab allows you to set the necessary properties for an active component at design time. Such design time settings determine the initial properties for a given object during runtime. All properties are listed in the left part of the **Properties** tab, and all their values are given in the right part. Some properties might have a '+' sign to the right of the property's name. As soon as you click it, you see a list of the subproperties included in this particular property, and '+' will be replaced by '-'.

In order to reset the property to its initial state (with the plus sign), simply click '-'. If a property can be assigned a value through a dialog box, then the "......" button appears next to the property value. By clicking this button, you activate the dialog box in question. This same dialog box is also called when you double-click the property's value.

If the values of a property are limited, as soon as you select this property, a button with a downward arrow will appear, and after clicking it you will see a drop-down list with all the possible values that can be assigned to the property in question. A property is selected simply by clicking it.

Due to the improvements that have been introduced by the Delphi creators into API, and specifically to the part responsible for creating properties, some properties are accompanied by a small rectangle with a relevant drawing. For example, next to the **Color** property, you will see a rectangle of the corresponding color. While developing your own components, you can specify what should be drawn in the **Object Inspector** when you define a certain property for your component.

You can also arrange properties by category. In order to do this, just right-click one and select **Arrange/by category** from the drop-down menu. The **Properties** tab then will look like the window shown in Figure 1.13.

You can view the properties of any category simply by clicking the '+' sign to the left of the category's name. Also, you can show or hide certain groups of properties: just right-click a property or a group of properties and select **View** from the pop-up menu. Those groups that are checked will be visible on your screen. By default, the **Legacy** group is hidden.

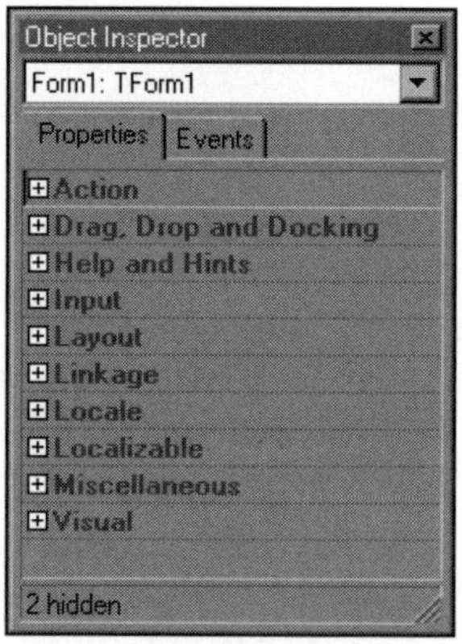

FIGURE 1.13 Properties arranged in categories.

Notice that properties can vary substantially for different objects. Delphi enables you to select multiple objects on a form (by holding down <Shift> while clicking each desired object on the current form). As you are doing this, **Object Inspector** will show those properties which are common to all objects being selected. If you change a property's value, you automatically assign this value to this property for all selected objects.

The **Events** tab (Figure 1.14) contains a list of events, both system and custom, that may occur with the object that has been chosen in the window for selecting objects. An event list varies depending on the object. Event names are given in the left column of the **Events** tab.

Every event name begins with the `On` prefix.

In order to attach a desired event handler to any given event, double-click the left part of the tab, next to the selected event. In doing this, you activate the **Code Editor** window. Later in this chapter, while developing a simple application, we will discuss the problem of creating event handlers.

As soon as you select any event, a drop-down list appears on its right, which contains all available event-handlers for this particular event; the developer is free to choose any of them. This functionality is a great help when assigning the same handler to several events.

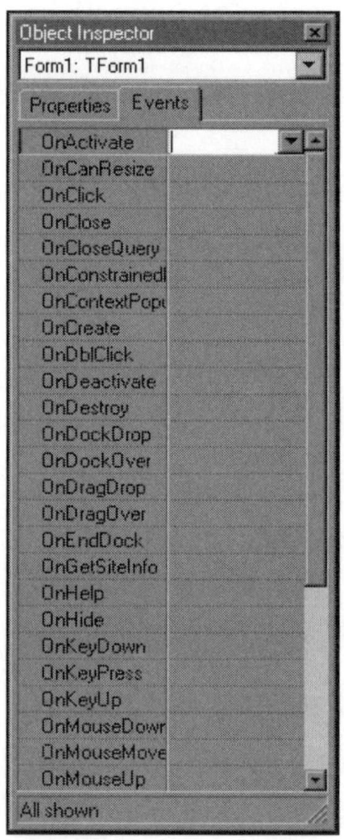

FIGURE 1.14 The **Events** tab.

Code Editor is a full-fledged text editor that includes a number of extra functions:

- Style editing
- Syntax check and command highlighting
- Additional functions, the most widely used of which are code completion and templates

Most commands available in this editor can be found in its context menu. In order to customize Code Editor, select Tools/Editor Options from the main menu.

As soon as a developer begins a new project, Delphi adds a new page (unit) to Code Editor for the main form. The default name of this page is `Unit1`.

If your project contains several forms, a separate unit is added to Code Editor for each form (Unit2, Unit3, etc.). You can add new units yourself by selecting File/New/Unit from the main menu. It is important to remember that Delphi automatically creates a separate unit for each form; that is to say, each form is necessarily associated with some unit of the given project. Any unit created manually by a developer is independent and is not associated with any form in a given project. Such a unit is very handy for storing subroutines, which are used by different units in the project or by different projects. Code Editor consists of two parts: the Code Browser window and the Code Explorer window.

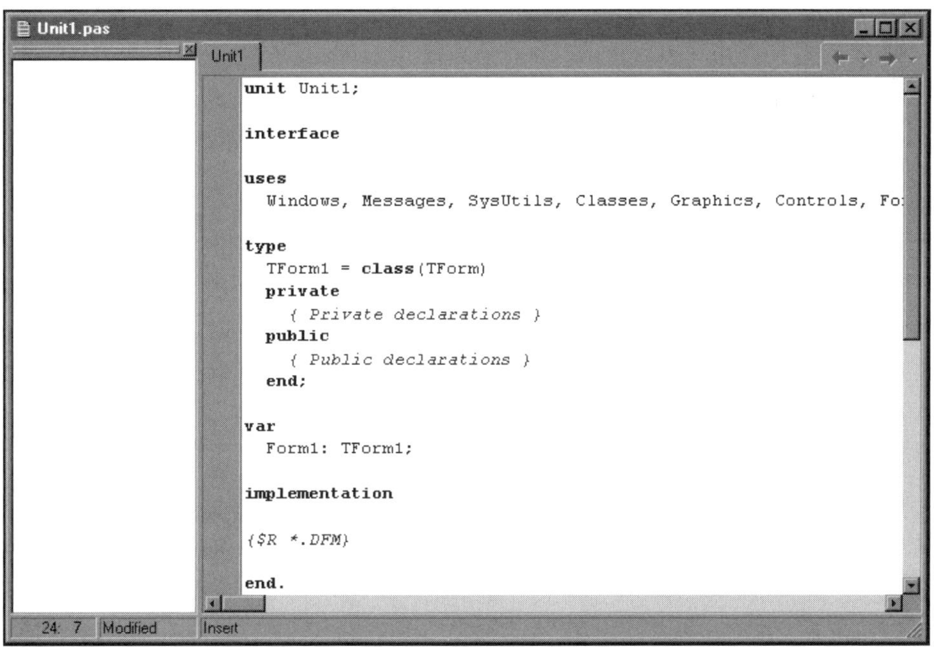

FIGURE 1.15 Code Editor.

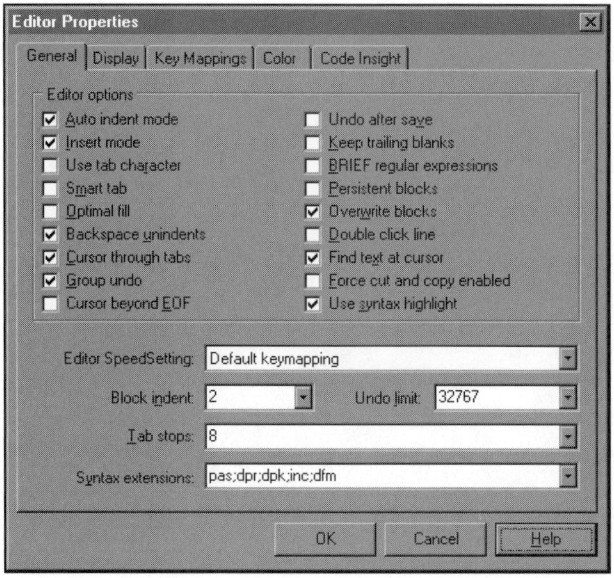

FIGURE 1.16 The **Editor Properties** window.

Code Editor shows all the program code associated with the current unit. This window allows you to validate the syntax of input commands "on the fly"; it can also provide you with relevant tips. You can customize the Code Editor window as you like by selecting Tools/Editor Options from the Delphi main menu. As soon as you have done this, the Editor Properties window will be displayed (Figure 1.16). This window contains five tabs: General, Display, Key Mappings, Color, and Code Insight.

In the Editor Properties window, you can customize practically all settings that determine text representation in Code Browser, including syntax checking.

The Code Explorer window is designed to facilitate navigating units in a given project. You can close this window by clicking its top right corner. If need be, you can activate this window later by selecting View/Code Explorer from the main menu.

The Code Explorer window contains the Diagram Tree; the diagrams in question present all the types, classes, properties, methods, global variables, and globals that are declared in a given unit. This window shows other units as well, listed after the `uses` command.

The following icons are conventionally used in the Code Explorer window (Figure 1.17).

In order to toggle back and forth between the Code Explorer window and the Code Editor window, you can use the <Ctrl>+<Shift>+<E> shortcut key. In the Code Explorer window you can implement a step-by-step search.

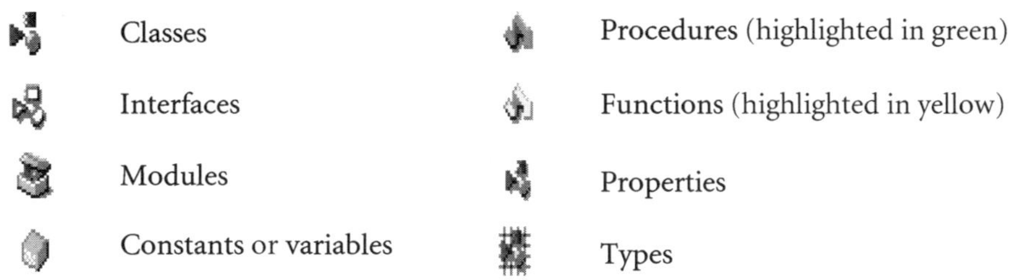

FIGURE 1.17 The icons used in the Code Explorer window.

If you need to find any class, property, method, variable, or routine (procedure or function), just type its name. The Code Explorer window and the Code Editor window are directly related. When you select any object in the Code Explorer window, the cursor in the Code Editor window immediately moves to the `Implementation` section of a given object.

If you wish to add an object to the Code Explorer window (or rename it), simply right-click the relevant node and select New/Rename from the context menu.

The Code Explorer window can also be customized in the Environment Options window (Figure 1.18). The latter is brought up when you select Tools/Environment Options from the main menu.

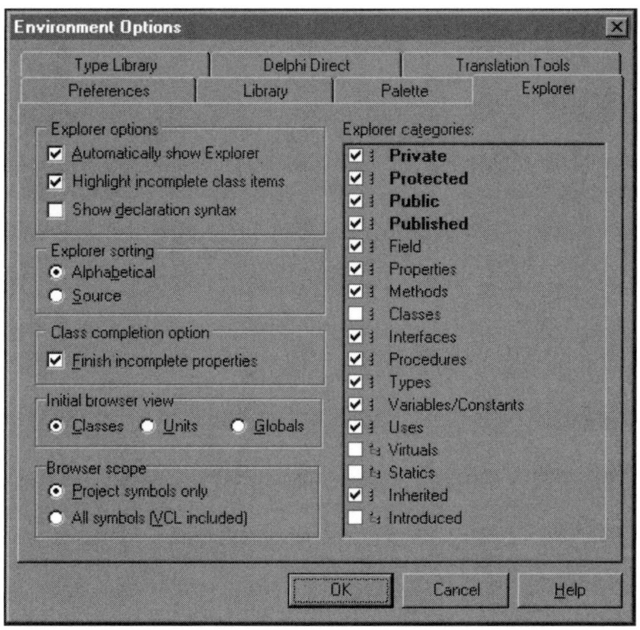

FIGURE 1.18 The **Environment Options** window.

GENERATING SOURCE CODE: DEVELOPING A SIMPLE APPLICATION

When you work with components in the Form Designer window, the corresponding Object Pascal code is automatically generated. The simplest and most effective way to familiarize yourself with this Delphi feature is to start a new project. In order to do this, select File/New Application from Delphi's main menu. This operation will result in a new form appearing in the Form Designer window. In the Code Editor window you will see a code already generated, which is intended to serve as the "skeleton" for a future program written in Object Pascal (Listing 1.1).

LISTING 1.1

```
unit Unit1;
interface
uses
  Windows, Messages, SysUtils, Classes, Graphics, Controls, Forms, Dialogs;
type
  TForm1 = class(TForm)
    private
      {Private declarations}
    public
      {Public declarations}
  end;
var
  Form1: TForm1;
implementation
{$R *.DFM}
end.
```

Let's take a closer look at Listing 1.1. It presents the skeleton for a new unit. In this case, the unit's name is `Unit1`. This unit contains elements that can be used in this routine or other units. Delphi provides a number of standard units, such as `System`, `SysUtils`, etc. Upon completing a unit's compilation, Delphi saves it in the DCU (Delphi Compiled Unit) file for this unit.

As a rule, any unit consists of a unit name and four sections (Listing 1.2).

LISTING 1.2

```
unit UnitName;
interface
{the interface section}
```

```
uses
{list of the units used};
const
{list of constants};
type
{type specifications};
var
{variable declarations};
{headers for procedures included in this unit};
{headers for functions included in this unit};
implementation
{the implementation section}
uses
{list of the units used};
const
{list of constants};
type
{type specifications};
var
{variable declaration};
{procedure declaration};
{function declaration};
{preprocessor directives};
initialization
{the initialization section}
{statements, commands};
finalization
{the finalization section}
{statements, commands};
end.
```

The first section, `interface`, introduces a given unit. It contains descriptions of those units used in a given unit. Additionally, it is here that all the types, constants, variables, functions, and procedures are declared, and where the identifiers to be reused in all the units and routines that use the given unit are described. Notice that functions and procedures are represented in this section only by their headers—their actual declaration is given later in the implementation section.

The second section, `implementation`, in addition to specifications of functions and procedures, provides declarations of all the types, constants, and variables being used, along with a description of those units utilized only in this module.

Also, this section contains *preprocessor directives*, or development environment commands, for example:

```
{$R *.DFM}
```

Preprocessor directives instruct the Delphi compiler as to what operations should be performed. They are written in the `{$ directive}` form. All preprocessor directives fall into one of two categories: *global* and *local*. *Global directives* pertain to the whole file being compiled, and *local* ones execute only locally, starting with the point at which they were issued, and ending when the cancel directive appears.

All in all, there are three types of directives: *key directives*, *setting directives*, and *conditional directives*. The first two types of directives are set by default. You can configure them yourself on the **Compiler** tab of the **Project Options** dialog window, which is available via **Project/Options** of the main menu. In order to view the default settings for these directives, use the <Ctrl>+<O> shortcut, and then press the <O> key when you are in the **Code Editor** window. This operation will insert all the present values for preprocessor directives at the beginning of a given unit (Listing 1.3).

LISTING 1.3

```
{$A+,B-,C+,D+,E-,F-,G+,H+,I+,J+,K-,L+,M-,N+,O+,P+,Q-,R-,S-,T-,U-,V+,W-,X+,Y+,Z1}

{$MINSTACKSIZE $00004000}

{$MAXSTACKSIZE $00100000}

{$IMAGEBASE $00400000}

{$APPTYPE GUI}
```

The following is the list of all the main types of preprocessor directives:

- Conditional directives
- Assertion checking directives
- Input-output checking directives
- Stack size specifying directives
- Type information directives
- Overflow checking directives for operations with integers
- The resource linkage directive
- Range checking directives
- A directive for creating console-based applications

Conditional directives enable you to manage the process of compiling the source code. There are two ways to specify the conditional compilation:

```
{$If Statement}
{code being compiled};
{$EndIf}
```

and

```
{$If Conditional Statement}
{code being compiled};
{$Else}
{code being compiled};
{$EndIf}
```

In both cases, provided that the condition specified in the `$If` string is fulfilled, the code that follows `$If` is compiled. Otherwise, when using the first method it is ignored and not included into the resulting compiled file, and when using the second method the code that follows the `$Else` directive is executed.
Now let's discuss the conditional directives themselves. The first one is:

```
{$IfDef a conditional identifier}
```

This directive checks whether the conditional identifier specified in it has been declared. If so, the code that follows this directive will be compiled. Otherwise, if there was no directive that specified this conditional identifier, or such a directive was cancelled, then the code that follows a given conditional directive will not be compiled.
In order to set a conditional identifier, the following directive is utilized:

```
{$Define a conditional identifier}
```

In order to cancel the declaration of a conditional identifier, use the following directive:

```
{$UnDef a conditional identifier}
```

There is also a directive that cancels the `$IfDef` directive: `$IfNDef`.It resets the true value if the conditional identifier specified in it has not been declared.

This type of directive is very useful during a debugging session. For instance, a programmer is often forced to introduce various intermediate variables and objects, which are necessary for debugging, but redundant in the complete application. A very handy construct exists specifically for such an occasion:

```
{$IfDef Debug}
  debug statements
{$EndIf}
```

If you issue the following directive in the beginning of a routine:

```
{$Define Debug}
```

then debug statements will be compiled and implemented. But as soon as you either remove this directive, or comment it out:

```
//{$Define Debug}
```

or introduce the following directive immediately after it:

```
{$Undef Debug}
```

then all the debug statements will be removed from the routine.

Assertion checking directives authorize or forbid checking a given assertion. They affect the implementation of the `Assert` procedure, which is used for debugging routines. The `Assert` procedure is designed to validate assertions which originally were intended to be true, but could become invalid due to errors. If the assertion being checked happens to be false, the procedure stops executing the program and generates the `EAssertionFailed` exception and an error message.

> **NOTE** *Exceptions and methods of handling them are discussed in Chapter 2.*

Assertion checking directives are local directives and generally look like the following:

`{$C+}` or `{$ASSERTIONS ON}`

and

`{$C-}` or `{$ASSERTIONS OFF}`

Regardless of its location in a file, this directive is valid for the whole file.

Input-output checking directives serve to start and stop checking operations with files. These directives have the following syntax:

`{$I+}` or `{$IOCHECKS ON}`

and

`{$I-}` or `{$IOCHECKS OFF}`

When file input-output check is running (either the `{$I+}` directive or the `{$IOCHECKS ON}` directive) and an input-output error occurs, the `EInOutError`.exception is generated. However, this doesn't happen if either the `{$I-}` directive or the `{$IOCHECKS OFF}` directive has been issued.

Directives that determine stack size are required for defining the minimum and maximum amount of basic memory space to be allocated to a given stack. All the local variables used in functions and procedures are stored in the application stack. As soon as any procedure or function is called, its local variables are placed into the stack. When a function or procedure stops, its local variables are removed from the stack. The following preprocessor directives

```
{$M minimum stack size, maximum stack size}
```

or

```
{$MINSTACKSIZE minimum stack size}
{$MAXSTACKSIZE maximum stack size}
```

specify the minimum and maximum stack size. Windows guarantees that the amount of space required for the stack (the minimum size) will be allocated. If the space allotted from main memory is not large enough to accommodate a given stack, Windows will generate an error message as soon as you attempt to run your application.

The minimum value for a stack size should fall within the range between the integers 1024 and 2,147,483,647. The maximum value should fall within the range between the minimum value and 2,147,483,647.

If the stack experiences a memory shortage at runtime, its size grows by 4 KB if it doesn't exceed the maximum value by doing so. If the stack size exceeds the acceptable value, the `EStackOverflow` exception is generated.

Type information directives turn on and off runtime type information (RTTI). Their syntax is:

`{$M+}` or `{$TYPEINFO ON}`

and

`{$M-}` or `{$TYPEINFO OFF}`

Overflow checking directives for operations with integers turn on and off checking for overflow when you perform arithmetical operations with integers (`+`, `-`, `*`, `Abs`, `Sqr`, `Succ`, `Pred`, `Inc`, and `Dec`). The syntax of these directives is as follows:

`{$Q+}` or `{$OVERFLOWCHECKS ON}`

and

`{$Q-}` or `{$OVERFLOWCHECKS OFF}`

When the `{$Q+}` directive is issued, the result of calculation is checked for overflow. If the overflow is registered, the `EIntOverflow` exception is generated. The directives at their issuance check only the results of arithmetical operations. By default, this directive is deactivated, since it tends to significantly increase the size of the application and slow down its work. Obviously, the most reasonable solution is to run these directives during a debugging session.

NOTE

If this directive is turned off, calculation errors may occur, and without any error messages.

Resource linkage directives are used for linking resource files to the executing unit. Its syntax is:

`{$R resources}` or `{$RESOURCE resources}`,

where `resources` is a filename or a file template.

This directive specifies those resource files having the DFM or RES extension, and which are to be linked to the executing unit. Notice that while generating a skeleton for a form unit, (see Listing 1.1), Delphi automatically adds the `{$R *.dfm}` string, which enables the compilation of a form's resource file.

NOTE

Never remove or change the `{$R *.dfm}` *string. If you do, Delphi will fail to find the form's resource file and will generate the* `EResNotFound` *exception.*

Range check directives are designed for turning the range check for integers and indexes on and off. These directives have the following syntax:

`{$R+}` or `{$RANGECHECKS ON}`

and

```
{$R-} or {$RANGECHECKS OFF}
```

These directives start and stop validation of the range for integers and indexes. If you run the `{$R+}` directive, all the indexes of arrays and strings, along with all the values assigned to scalar variables and variables with a limited range of values, are checked in order to see if they fall within the necessary range. If the requirements imposed by a specified range are not met, or the value being assigned exceeds the maximum acceptable value, then the `ERangeError` exception is generated. Similar to the overflow check directive, the `{$R+}` directive also slows down the application's operation and increases its size. It is mostly used during a debugging session.

The directive for creating console-based applications is aimed at informing the compiler that a given application is supposed to run under DOS. This implies that all the forms and visual objects should be removed. The directive's syntax is as follows:

```
{$APPTYPE CONSOLE}
```

NOTE

*Alternatively, you can create a console-based application by selecting Project/Options from Delphi's main menu and specifying the **Generate Console Application** setting in the **Linker** tab.*

The last two sections are optional. The `initialization` section contains the commands and statements that should execute at the startup of the program running these units. If the unit includes the `initialization` section, then it may contain the `finalization` section as well. The latter includes the commands and statements that execute when the program stops running.

Your First Delphi Application

Now it's time to create your first application in a Delphi environment. Begin by dragging the `Button1` object from the Component palette (the **Standard** tab) on the form. As a result, the button with the name `Button1` with a caption of the same name appears on the form. Always keep in mind the difference between the connotation of these terms:"name" and "caption." A *name* of any object (including a button) indicates how this particular object will be subsequently referenced. Usually, Delphi assigns its own default names to all newly created objects, which can be (and often should be) changed. The default name and the default caption of any object are also usually identical—in our case they have a default value of `Button1`. You can change the name and the caption of any object by modifying the settings for either its `Name` property or its `Caption` property in the **Object Inspector** window. Let's change the caption of the button to `Open`. As soon as you introduce any modifications to this property in the **Object Inspector** window, the button caption on the form is automatically changed to a new value; the same is true for other properties of the button. You will be able to visually observe all the changes by watching the button on the form (provided you are modifying visual properties).

Let's now take a look at the **Code Editor**. First, a new record, `StdCtrls` (standard controls), has appeared in the list of units being used (`uses`). Units start running automatically and are not destroyed if a developer chooses to destroy an object from the form (try to destroy your newly created `Button1` button). Second, one more string has appeared in the **Code Editor**:

```
Button1: TButton;
```

This indicates that the button you just created is an instance of the `TButton` class (descriptions of objects will be provided later in this chapter). Additionally, the declaration of this instance is included in the `TForm1` form specification, thereby specifying the relationship between them: this button belongs to this form. If you need to reference this button while working with this form or one from another unit, you will have to use the reference where the name of this form is indicated: `Form1.Button1`. The code string where this button is declared will be automatically removed as soon as you remove the button from the form.

For the button to perform any operations, code needs to be written for an event. This is generally done by selecting the event from the **Events** tab in the **Object Inspector**. Events that might be triggered by the button are listed here. We are interested in the `OnClick` event. Double-click this item, and Delphi will automatically generate the skeleton for this event handler and move you to the edit window (you can also double-click within the form). Add the code for closing `Form1` to the skeleton:

```
Form1.Close;
```

In order to make sure that you program can run, start it either by pressing the <F9> key, or by selecting **Run/Run** from the menu. Now click the only button on the form and it (the form) will close.

OBJECT-ORIENTED PROGRAMMING

Delphi uses Object Pascal as its development language. The crucial difference between Object Pascal and Pascal resides in the fact that Object Pascal deals with objects. The Visual Component Library (VCL) is based on the hierarchy of classes written in Object Pascal and organized in a single architecture in the Delphi integrated development environment (IDE). Developers can design their own objects and classes and share them with one another. This makes for faster and more effective application development. By using the Component palette and **Object Inspector**, a developer is able to place components on forms and change the properties of these components *without bothering to write a single string of code.*

So what exactly do we mean by an object? A class is a data type that combines data and various routines for operating on this data, and an object is an instance of some class. To put it differently, a class is a generic description (a type), and an object is an entity that was created on the basis of this description. Before the era of *object-oriented programming,* data and the operations performed with it were regarded as different elements. If you happened to work with records in Pascal, the concept of an object will seem rather simple to you. Records consist of areas, and each area is designated for storing data of a particular type. Records were designed in order to facilitate handling elements containing data of different types.

Objects also serve as repositories for data of various types. Object data—which is referred to as *fields,* is essentially identical to record fields. But unlike records, objects also possess procedures and functions that are valid for the fields of a given object. Such procedures and functions are called *methods.* In addition, object fields can be modified by changing the values of the *properties* of these objects. Every object property in Delphi is represented by a field and several

Every object property in Delphi is represented by a field and several methods; the latter enable setting and reading the value of the field (so-called access methods). Object properties can be modified in the process of development by using **Object Inspector**, a tool that saves you the trouble of writing any code specifically for this purpose. If such fields can be accessed from outside only by using access methods, this object architecture is referred to as *encapsulation.* Besides encapsulation, object-oriented programming involves two more basic principles: *inheritance* and *polymorphism. Inheritance* is the concept according to which newly created objects inherit their properties and methods from other objects (the latter are called ancestors). Descendant objects inherit from their ancestors all properties, methods, and fields, which can either be saved as they are or can be modified to change the behavior of the new objects. Descendant objects can also have extra fields, methods, or properties. *Polymorphism* implies that a method of an ancestor can always be replaced by the method of a descendant with the same name, and the method of the object actually used will be invoked (and, certainly, these methods may differ significantly).

Objects in Delphi dynamically take up blocks of memory whose structure is determined by the object's class. Every object is a unique instance of its class, and possesses all methods pertaining to this class.

Typically, a new class declaration looks like the following:

```
type Class name = class (ancestor class)
   {class structure}
 private
   {private declarations}
 protected
   {protected declarations}
 public
   {public declarations}
 published
   {published declarations}
end;
```

where `class name` is any correct name (which is chosen arbitrarily); `ancestor class` is the name of the class from which the newly designed class was derived. `class structure` includes the properties and methods of the new class. You can set a different *degree of visibility* for every class element by choosing one of four keywords: `private`, `protected`, `public`, or `published`. The *visibility* of any class element determines whether other units or code can access the element.

Minimum visibility is specified by the `private` keyword. The `protected` keyword sets an average degree of visibility, and `public` and `published` choose the highest degree of accessibility. For example, the following string

```
published property Color: TColor read GetColor write SetColor;
```

sets the `Color` property for a *published* class, which is one that has the highest degree of visibility.

If the declaration of some class instance is not preceded by a keyword determining its visibility, then the default visibility of this instance is the same as that of the preceding instance of this class, for example:

```
published property Color: TColor read GetColor write SetColor;

property BackColor: TColor read GetBackColor write SetBackColor;
```

In the above example, both properties, `Color` and `BackColor`, are published. Let's now discuss these four keywords in more detail:

- **`private`**: Defines those elements of a class that are not visible outside the unit where the class containing the elements in question was declared. In other words, private methods cannot be called from other units, and private fields or properties cannot be read or changed from other units. Descendant classes cannot use private elements in an ancestor class.
- **`protected`**: Defines those elements of a class which are visible only inside the unit where the class containing the elements in question was declared, and inside the units where descendant classes derived from the class are present.
- **`public`**: Defines those elements of a given class which are visible from any place in the program and from any unit from which you can see the class itself.
- **`published`**: Defines those elements of a given class which belong to the same scope of visibility as `public` elements. The only difference is that published elements generate runtime type identification information (RTTI). On the basis of this information, Delphi can identify the class of a given object's element. Delphi uses RTTI to access values of properties when saving and loading various form files (*.DFM) in order to show these properties in the Object Inspector window and associate certain properties with certain methods. All methods can be published except for the `overload` methods, which have the same names.

Besides properties and methods, a new class declaration may include a list of interfaces supported by the class in question (for further information about interfaces refer to *Chapter 2*).

Delphi uses the concept of an *abstract class.* An abstract class cannot be instantiated. It is used for declaring certain fundamental properties and methods of those object instances derived from this abstract class. Every class in Delphi is derived from the `TObject` root. The `TObject` class is the ancestor of many classes.

It incorporates the basic functions common to all Delphi objects. The `TObject` class allows for:

- Creating, destroying, and managing object instances, as well as allocating the necessary memory space for a given object and freeing it up as soon as the object in question has been destroyed
- Support of information on objects and types
- Support of message processing

So you now know that every class in Delphi is a descendant of the `TObject` class. A class is called a *direct descendant* of `TObject` if it has been derived directly from the `TObject` class. And if a given class has been derived from a class which itself is a direct or indirect descendant of the `TObject` class (that is to say, from some intermediate class), then it is referred to as *an indirect descendant* of the `TObject` class.

NOTE *Other sources sometimes use the terms child class and descendant class. In this book, "direct descendant" means "child class," and "indirect descendant" refers to "descendant class."*

If the parent class is not specified when a new class is being created (for more detail about creating classes, refer to Part II), then the default parent is the `TObject` class.

All VCL components are created from the `TComponent` abstract class. These components are objects with certain properties—and the properties in question can be easily modified while an application is being developed. The `TComponent` class incorporates the most fundamental properties and methods such as:

- The capability to place a component in the Component palette and subsequently use this component while developing an application
- The capability to own other components and to be owned by them
- The capability to exchange data with external files and threads
- The capability to serve as a shell for ActiveX elements and other objects

Visual components (that is, those components which are shown on a screen during runtime) such as `TForm` and `TSpeedButton`, are called *controls* and their ancestor is the abstract component named `TControl`.

Figure 1.19 presents a simplified diagram of the VCL hierarchy. This diagram includes several components that are controls derived from the same `TControl` component.

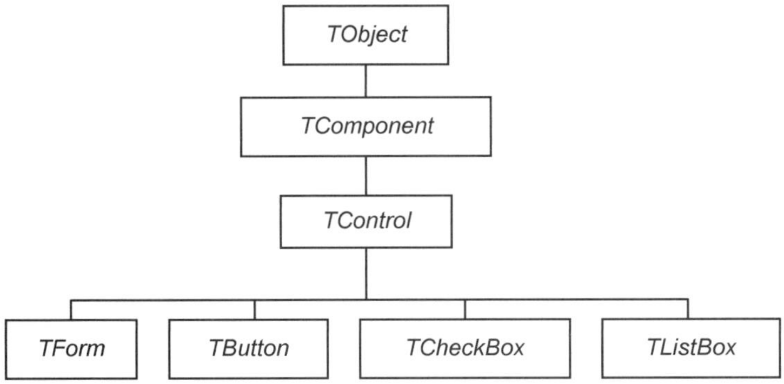

FIGURE 1.19 A simplified diagram of the Delphi Visual Component Library (VCL) hierarchy architecture.

In spite of its name, the VCL framework consists, for the most part, of non-visual components. A developer is able to place non-visual components on forms at design time (they are not visible at runtime) and modify their properties in the same manner as with visual components.

In addition to above classes, Delphi uses the following base classes: `TWinControl`, `TCustomEdit`, and `TBaseArray`.

The *scope of object visibility* is one of the most essential concepts incorporated into the Delphi object model. The scope of visibility for an object defines the Object Pascal code where the properties and methods of this object are available, without explicitly specifying the object in question. When you write the code, which is located within the scope of visibility of a given object, you need not indicate the name of the object in order to get access to its properties and methods. For example, when you place a new button on a form, you can reference the properties and methods of the form in the event handlers for this button without defining the form's name (Listing 1.4).

LISTING 1.4

```
procedure TForm1.Button1Click(Sender: TObject);
begin
  Color := clGray;
  Button1.Color := clTeal;
end;
```

NOTE *In the above template (Listing 1.4), the code string that specifies the color of the* `Button1` *button may fail to work in some Delphi versions. This code has been successfully tested in Delphi 5 and 6 Enterprise.*

In the `OnClick` event handler included in Listing 1.4, the string

```
Color := clGray;
```

is tantamount to the following string

```
Form1.Color := clGray;
```

You needn't specify the name of the form, since the `Button1Click` method is contained in the `TForm1`object.

The second code string in Listing 1.4 changes the property of the `Button1` object, leaving the corresponding property of the form unchanged, which means that you should define the name of the object.

Delphi creates a separate unit file for each form. Therefore, in order to access an object from another unit, you need to specify the full name of a given object, for example:

```
Form2.Button1.Color := clTeal;
```

In a similar manner, you can call the methods of objects contained in another form (in some other unit), for instance:

```
Form2.Edit1.Clear;
```

Finally, in addition to these considerations, in order to use the objects contained in the `Form2` (`Unit2`) unit in the `Form1` (`Unit1`) unit, you will need to register `Unit2` in the `uses` section of `Unit1`:

```
implementation

uses Unit2;
```

CREATING AND DESTROYING OBJECTS

While taking advantage of all those standard components which are provided by Delphi, you may want to create your own objects in order to fine-tune the work of your application.

For an example of how to build your own objects, let's take an object representing a company employee and name this object `TEmployee`. Suppose your object includes such properties as name, position in the company, and salary; let's name these properties `Name`, `Title`, and `Salary`. Let's also add the `CalculateSalary` method for calculating the salary. As a result, your object will be declared in a manner similar to the one presented in Listing 1.5.

LISTING 1.5

```
type
  TEmployee = class(TObject)
```

```
private
  FName: string;
  FTitle: string;
  FSalary: Double;
public
  property Name: string read FName write FName;
  property Title: string read FTitle write FTitle;
  property Salary: Double read FSalary write FSalary;
  function CalculateSalary: Double;
end;
```

The first string of code informs you that the object is a descendant of the `TObject` class, which implies that all the methods and properties pertaining to the `TObject` instance are inherited by the `TEmployee` object. Now you can embed the code of Listing 1.5 into one of two sections of the unit, the `interface` section or the `implementation` section. After that, in order to design the `TEmployee` object, you will need to call the `Create` method inherited by your new object from the basic `TObject` object:

```
var
  Employee: TEmployee;
begin
  Employee := TEmployee.Create;
end;
```

The `Create` method invokes the object's `constructor`, which allocates the memory space required for the object under construction and returns the reference to this newly built instance.

NOTE

Components included in a form are automatically created and destroyed by the programming environment. When you choose to design your own objects, you will also have to take care of their destruction, if need be.

To destroy an object that you have created, and to deallocate the corresponding memory space, you need to invoke the `Destroy` method, which is also inherited from the parent `TObject` object. In this example, the string for destroying the object will look like this:

```
Employee.Free;
```

DELPHI STANDARD COMPONENTS

When familiarizing yourself with the Component palette, you got a general idea about the most important Delphi components and how they are grouped together. Each group is designated for solving a certain problem and is located in a separate tab of the Component palette. We've already briefly touched on the content of each of these tabs. Here we will take a closer look at the standard Delphi components contained in some of them.

- The Standard tab (Figure 1.20) contains the following elements:
  - `Frames`: Opens the dialog box which lists the frames of a given project, if any.
  - `MainMenu`: Creates the main menu of your form. In order to add new elements to the main menu and to create event handlers for the main menu elements, place the MainMenu component on your form and double-click it, thereby invoking the Menu Designer.
  - `PopupMenu`: Creates a pop-up menu, which appears at runtime when a user right-clicks any component or area on the screen. The process of adding elements to a pop-up menu is similar to that of adding elements to the main menu.
  - `Label`: Shows text that cannot be edited by a user at runtime.
  - `Edit`: Shows the edit box where a user can enter or change one string of text.
  - `Memo`: Shows an editable field for a user to enter or edit several strings of text.
  - `Button`: Creates a button that can be clicked by a user in order to perform some operation.
  - `CheckBox`: Provides a check box that can assume one of two possible states: "checked" or "unchecked." A user is able to check a number of check boxes simultaneously.
  - `RadioButton`: Creates a radio button, which operates in much the same way as a check box does, except that a user can enable only one radio button in a form or other container.
  - `ListBox`: Shows a list box.
  - `ComboBox`: Creates an element that combines the features of an edit box and a list box. A user can enter the necessary data in the edit box or select an element from the list.
  - `ScrollBar`: Creates a tool for scrolling a visible area in a form or a list.
  - `GroupBox`: Creates a container for components which subsequently will be grouped together in a single category.
  - `RadioGroup`: Creates a group for radio buttons. This allows you to have multiple groups of radio buttons on one form.

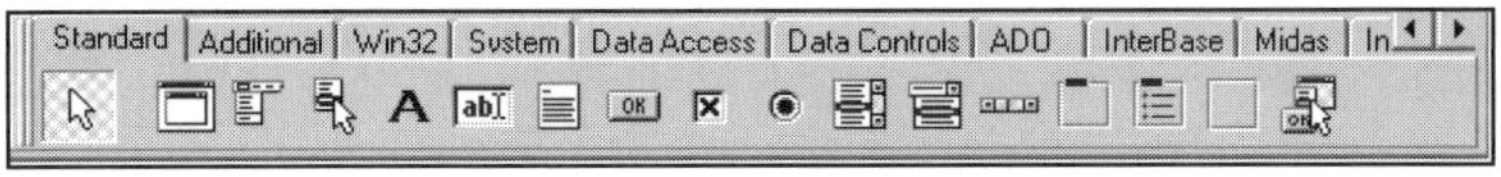

FIGURE 1.20 The **Standard** tab.

FIGURE 1.21 The **Additional** tab.

- `Panel`: Creates a panel that can contain various components. Panels are designed for building status panels or toolbars.
- `ActionList`: Creates a list of actions that centralize responses to a user's actions.

■ The Additional tab (Figure 1.21) includes the following components:

- `BitBtn`: Creates a button that can contain an image.
- `SpeedButton`: Creates a button that can contain only an image (without text). Such buttons can be placed in a panel that will be used for building a toolbar.
- `MaskEdit`: Creates a control that enables a user to enter data in the same manner as when working with an edit box, except that here the user is provided with an input mask (input using a predefined template).
- `StringGrid`: Builds a grid that can contain text strings.
- `DrawGrid`: Creates a grid for displaying data.
- `Image`: Shows the content of files containing images, icons, or metafiles.
- `Shape`: Draws geometric objects (ellipses, circles, rectangles, squares, and squares with rounded corners).
- `Bevel`: Creates a 3D string or square (convex or concave).
- `ScrollBox`: Creates a box that can change its size. A scroll box automatically displays scrollbars if necessary.
- `CheckListBox`: Shows a scrollable list, which resembles a usual list with the exception that here there is a check box next to each of the items.
- `Splitter`: Shows the delimiter between two adjusted controls, which allows the user to modify the size of each control during runtime by clicking the splitter and dragging it.
- `StaticText`: A component very similar to a label, except that the given component (static text) has its own handler.
- `ControlBar`: The component for building a floating toolbar.
- `ApplicationEvents`: The component which manages application events
- `Chart`: A graphic analog of a table.

FIGURE 1.22 The **Win32** tab.

- The Win32 tab (Figure 1.22) contains the following components:
  - `TabControl`: Allows you to include several switchable pages each including components of various types (Delphi palettes are implemented in the form of tabs, for example).
  - `PageControl`: Creates multi-page dialog windows (for instance, the Delphi Project Options window).
  - `ImageList`: Creates a group of indexed images which have the same size.
  - `RichEdit`: Creates a memo field which serves as a full-fledged RTF (Rich Text Format) editor. In addition to text itself, this editor includes controls and font properties; for example, size, type, color, etc.
  - `TrackBar`: The bar for visually manipulating a variable magnitude; it can move both vertically and horizontally.
  - `ProgressBar`: Creates a rectangular bar which is filled from left to right in order to show the task's progress.
  - `UpDown`: Creates buttons for manipulating a variable magnitude.
  - `HotKey`: Creates hotkeys.
  - `Animate`: Creates a window for displaying a soundless video AVI clip (Audio Video Interleaved).
  - `DateTimePicker`: Creates an element that enables the user to set the time or date by selecting it or typing it in.
  - `MonthCalendar`: Shows the calendar for only one month. A user can choose a date if necessary.
  - `TreeView`: Shows a list in the form of a tree.
  - `ListView`: Shows a list.
  - `HeaderControl`: Shows headers for columns that contain text or numbers.
  - `StatusBar`: Creates a bar for displaying information on the system status.
  - `ToolBar`: Creates the element which allows for buttons and other tools to be placed on it, automatically adjusting their sizes and arrangement.
  - `CoolBar`: Shows the collection of controls. This is similar to a toolbar, but the controls can have different shapes and sizes.
  - `PageScroller`: Defines the element that contains client area objects, which can be scrolled vertically and horizontally.

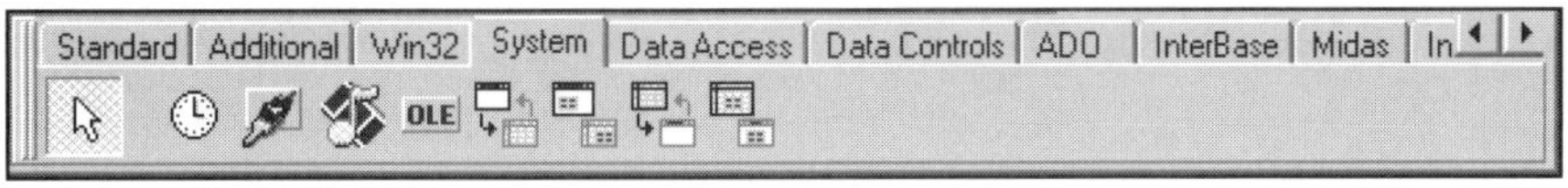

FIGURE 1.23 The **System** tab.

- The System tab (Figure 1.23) includes:
  - **`Timer`**: A non-visual component which periodically generates the `OnTimer` event
  - **`PaintBox`**: Places a box in which a user can draw using the Delphi graphic tools
  - **`MediaPlayer`**: Shows the panel for playing and recording audio and video files
  - **`OleContainer`**: Creates an OLE client
  - **`DdeClientConv`**: Connects a client to the Dynamic Data Exchange (DDE) server
  - **`DdeClientItem`**: Specifies the DDE client profile that should be passed to the server
  - **`DdeServerConv`**: Connects a server to a DDE client
  - **`DdeServerItem`**: Specifies the DDE server profile that should be passed to the client

The functions provided by the rest of the tabs (except for those containing the components for handling databases) will be discussed in *Chapter 4*, which introduces the techniques of handling certain components.

THE BASIC PROPERTIES OF DELPHI VISUAL COMPONENTS

Component properties allow you to manage a component's appearance and behavior. Almost every manipulation with component properties is done with Object Inspector. Let's now get acquainted with the most common properties of visual components.

NOTE

The standard properties of components are discussed in more detail in Chapter 6. This section deals only with a few basic properties that are characteristic of most visual components.

- The properties which define the location and size of a component are as follows (these properties are not supported by non-visual components):
  - **`Height`**: Specifies the vertical size of a component
  - **`Width`**: Specifies the horizontal size of a component

  - **`Top`**: Defines the vertical coordinate of the top left corner of a component
  - **`Left`**: Specifies the horizontal coordinate of the top left corner of a component
- The properties which determine the visual representation of a given component on a screen are:
  - **`BorderStyle`**: Specifies the style of the border around a component
  - **`Color`**: Specifies the background color of the component
  - **`BevelKind`**: Specifies the bevel kind of a component (concave or convex) if a given component supports a bevel
  - **`Font`**: Specifies the font which is used in the text and captions of a given component, specifically, the font color, type, and size
- Parent properties: These are those properties inherited from the component containing the given component. The names of such properties begin with the word `Parent`, such as `ParentFont`, `ParentShowHint`, `etc`. Let's consider, for example, the `Button` button on the `Form` form. The default `ParentFont` property of this button is set to `true`. This means that as soon as you somehow change the `Font` property of the form, identical changes will be automatically introduced to the same property of the `Button` button. If you modify the `Font` property of the button, then the font of the button caption will be changed, and the `ParentFont` property of the button will be automatically set to `false`.
- Navigation properties: These properties specify the navigation techniques that can be employed by a user to move components around during runtime:
  - **`Caption`**: Contains a text string that marks a component. In order to underline any letter in a caption, you can put the ampersand character (&) immediately before it. By doing so, you enable the user to select a given component by pressing <Alt>+<the underlined letter>.
  - **`TabOrder`**: This property specifies the ordinal number of a given component while you navigate around components on a form with the <Tab> key. This property is activated only if the `TabStop` property is set to `true`.
  - **`TabStop`**: Determines whether or not navigation using the <Tab> key is enabled. If this property is set to `true`, by pressing the <Tab> key, you will be able to move around the components on a form in the order defined by the `TabOrder` properties of the components.
- Drag-and-drop properties: The properties that allow you to move components using the mouse:
  - **`DragMode`**: Specifies how to begin dragging a component. The default value of this property is set to `dmManual`. In order to start dragging a component, you need to invoke the `BeginDrag` method. Alternately, if you set the `DragMode` property to `dmAutomatic`, the dragging starts as soon as you click a component.
  - **`DragCursor`**: Specifies the appearance of the cursor when dragging a component.

2 Exceptions and Interfaces in Delphi

Most developers who work with Delphi create rather sophisticated applications, which in turn implies complex interactions between those applications and the operating system and its applications. Any such interactions may be terminated incorrectly. The examples illustrating this are numerous: from the trivial error of division by zero, to the attempt to open a non-existent file. Multiple testing and debugging can be a partial solution. But obviously there is no way to foresee all possible emergencies that might happen in an application in the course of its interaction with the operating system, other applications, or the user. It is in order to deal with such emergencies that the concept of structured exception handling has been introduced and implemented. Originally, this concept was geared towards those developers who created applications for Windows NT, but structured exception handling was later given support in Windows 9x operating systems. Most modern programming environments for developing applications intended to run in Windows, including Delphi, support structured exception handling. The exception handling functionality was first introduced with Delphi 1.0, but only since Delphi 2.0 were exceptions integrated with the Win32 API.

In this chapter, you will learn what an exception is and how Delphi can handle it. Additionally, we will discuss RTL exceptions and the use of the `TApplicationHandleException` method for handling exceptions. We will provide you with the necessary information about interfaces and, by way of illustration, present a detailed description of the `IUnknown` interface. Finally, we'll briefly introduce you to the issue of using interfaces in distributed applications.

EXCEPTIONS: WHAT THEY ARE AND HOW TO HANDLE THEM

By the word *exception*, we mean any emergency that can affect the otherwise smooth running of a given routine.

When handling such a situation, Delphi, as usual, works with objects. From the point of view of a Delphi compiler, an exception is an object. In order to deal with an object of this type, the following language constructs have been introduced in Delphi (or rather in Object Pascal): `try .. except` and `try .. finally`.

Let's discuss these language constructs in more depth.

The `try .. except` construct has the following syntax:

LISTING 2.1

```
try
   {Execute Code};
except
   on Exception1 do {code executed if Error 1 occurs};
   on Exception2 do {code executed if Error 2 occurs};
   ...
else
   {code that handles all errors that were not caught earlier};
end;
```

If any exception is generated while the code in the `try` block is being processed, the execution of this block terminates, and execution of the code in the `except` section begins. The `except` section can be used in two ways. First, it could include any statements other than exception handlers, which have the `on` prefix, for instance: error message statements, statements that provide release of system resources, and other statements and commands. Second, the `except` section could be used exclusively for handling exceptions. In this case, it can contain *only* exception handlers. If the handler for the exception that has occurred is found, then the statement of this handler starts executing, the exception in question gets destroyed, and execution passes to the code that follows the `on Exception do` statement. The block that follows the `else` keyword deals with all the exceptions that were not declared in the `except` section. This section is optional. If the handler for some particular exception is not found, the system exception handler will be invoked.

Consider a simple example of handling the exception that occurs when something is divided by zero (Listing 2.2).

LISTING 2.2

```
try
   a:=10;
   b:=0;
   c:=a/b;
except
   On EZeroDivide do MessageBox (0,'improper Division!','Error', MB_OK);
```

As you can see from Listing 2.2, there are different handlers for processing different types of exceptions. Let's discuss the `on .. do` exception handler. The handler in question is located within the `except` block, and can have one of two possible syntax patterns (Listing 2.3).

LISTING 2.3

```
  on <Exception Class> do <Statement>;
```

or

```
  on <Name>: <Exception Class>
     do <Statements that can use exception properties>;
```

This handler processes only the exception class specified in it. If a parent (base) class is defined, then all the classes derived from this ancestor class will also be dealt with. In order to ensure the processing of every exception class, you should specify a parent class for all exceptions: `Exception`. As soon as an exception is handled, it is destroyed. The second form of the same `on .. do` handler differs from the first one in that a given exception can be assigned a temporary name, and you will subsequently be able to reference the properties of this exception. In order to reference the exception's properties, use the `<Name>.<Property Name>` construct. Take a look at Listing 2.4.

LISTING 2.4

```
try
  ScrollBar1.Max := ScrollBar1.Min-1;
except
  on E: EInvalidOperation do
    MessageDlg('Ignore Exception: ' +
    E.Message, mtInformation, [mbOK], 0);
   end;
```

In the Listing 2.4, the temporary name of `E` has been assigned to the `EInvalidOperation` exception. Then the default error message, `E.Message`, which is generated by Delphi if no localized handler is found, is output on the screen.

NOTE

Never destroy a temporary exception object. Exception handlers automatically do this after processing. If you destroy an exception object manually, an access error may be returned.

Sometimes it is necessary to call a standard exception handler as soon as the exception in question has been processed by the local code. For instance, should a particular error occur, you want your application to generate a specific message for a user, and only after that execution is passed to a standard exception handler. As you already know, an exception is destroyed as soon as it has been processed by the local code. You can get around this problem by *regenerating the exception.* Use the `raise` command to do this. Look now at Listing 2.5.

LISTING 2.5

```
try
  {Statements}
except
  on <Exception Class> do
  begin
    {Exception Handlers}
    raise;   // Exception raising
  end;
end;
```

As soon as the local exception handlers have processed the exception, the `raise` command executes, raising the exception. After that, execution jumps to a standard exception handler.

If a given exception has successfully passed all the `try` blocks in the application code, the `HandleException` method is invoked. It calls the error dialog window. You can invoke this method as follows.

LISTING 2.6

```
try
    {Statements}
  except
    Application.HandleException(Self);
end;
```

The next construct to be discussed here, `try .. finally`, is used for guarding the code of the `finally` portion from those exceptions that can be raised in the `try` section. The syntax of this construct is presented in Listing 2.7.

LISTING 2.7

```
try
      {statements that can generate an exception};
finally
      {protected statements that must be executed in any case};
end;
```

The statements located in the `finally` section of the code will always execute, regardless of whether or not an exception was generated. If an exception was raised in the `try` block, execution immediately passes to the `finally` section. And the `finally` portion will get executed even if no exception in the `try` part has been generated—that is to say, under any circumstances, including a situation when an error occurs in the `finally` section itself. The `try .. finally` construct doesn't process exceptions; its function is to ensure that memory resources are freed up files not required at the moment are closed, and to perform other operations associated with freeing up resources. This means that you will need this construct when working with files, memory, Windows resources, and objects.

An exception handling code can be divided into blocks: `try .. except .. end` and `try .. finally .. end`. These blocks can be nested (see Figure 2.1).

While developing applications with Delphi, as often as not, a programmer will not need to process exceptions; his task is just to terminate the routine execution as soon as an error manifests itself. In order to do this, so-called *silent exceptions* are used. Silent exceptions are descendants of the standard `EAbort` exception. By default, a VCL Delphi exception handler displays the error dialog window for every exception except `EAbort` descendants.

NOTE

When you develop console-based applications, error messages are generated for unprocessed `EAbort` *exceptions as well.*

If you need to generate a silent exception, you can invoke the `Abort` procedure. It will automatically raise the `EAbort` exception, which will terminate the current routine without any error messages being displayed. Now let's consider the following example. Let's say that a form contains an empty list box (`ListBox1`) and a button (`Button1`). Let's write the following code for the `OnClick` event handler:

LISTING 2.8

```
procedure TForm1.Button1Click(Sender: TObject);
var
  I: Integer;
begin
  for I := 1 to 10 do {loop 10 times}
  begin
   ListBox1.Items.Add(IntToStr(I));  {add item to the list}
   if I = 7 then Abort;  {stop adding items after adding the seventh item}
  end;
end;
```

As the result, the above routine will get executed as soon as you press the `Button1` button, and seven strings, with numbers from 1 to 7, will be added to the list.

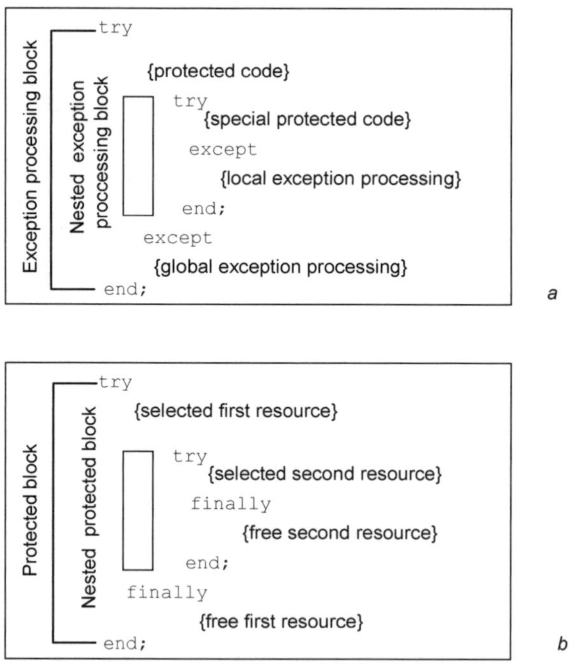

FIGURE 2.1 Nested blocks of the Exception Handler (a) and of the Code Protecting Construct (b)

HANDLING RTL EXCEPTIONS; EXCEPTION HIERARCHY

RTL (real time library) exceptions are declared in the Delphi `SysUtils` module, and descend from the basic `Exception` class.

There are several types of RTL descendant exceptions (Table 2.1).

TABLE 2.1 The Classes of Exceptions Raised by RTL

Exception class	***Diagnosis***	***Explanation***
Input/output exceptions	An access error which occurs when you try to access a file or an input/output device	Most input/output errors are due to the error code returned by Windows when you reference a file.
Heap exceptions	A dynamic memory error	Heap errors occur when there is a memory shortage or some pointer in an application indicates a memory area outside the heap.
Integer math exceptions	Incorrect operation with an integer	This type includes exceptions for thedivide by zero error, overflow, exceeding the specified range, etc.
Floating-point math exceptions	Incorrect operation with a floating-point number	Errors that occur in operations with floating-point numbers can be generated either by a co-processor or by a program emulator. Such errors can be due to invalid instructions, division by zero, overflow, etc.
Typecast exceptions	Improper use of the as operation when working with object classes	These exceptions occur when an object is not cast to a compatible type.
Conversion exceptions	Improper conversion	Type conversion functions (IntToStr, StrToInt, etc.) generate this error if a given conversion is impossible.
Hardware exceptions	A system fault	Hardware errors indicate that either a user or the processor has generated an access error, stack overflow, or some other error of that type.
Variant exceptions	Improper use of the Variant type	An error occurs in expressions in which the Variant type cannot be used.

Now let's discuss the hierarchy of exception classes in more detail:

`Exception`	the base exception class
`EAbort`	exception raised without generating an error message dialog
`EAbstractError`	invalid attempt to call an abstract method
`EAccessViolation`	unauthorized access to memory
`EArrayError`	improper handling of arrays
`EAssertionFailed`	invalid assertion check
`EBitsError`	invalid access to the `TBits` array of Boolean values
`ECacheError`	cache building error when using a decision cube
`EComponentError`	invalid registration or renaming of a component
`EControlC`	user pressed the <Ctrl>+<C> shortcut while a console-based application was running
`EConvertError`	string (object) conversion error
`EDatabaseError`	base class for database exceptions
`EDBClient`	client data set error
`EReconcileError`	invalid `TClientDataset` update
`EDBEngineError`	BDE error
`ENoResultSet`	generated by the `TQuery` component when the attempt is made to run a query without the `Select` statement
`EUpdateError`	invalid `TProvider` update
`EDateTimeError`	invalid date/time value
`EDimensionMapError`	dimension format error
`EDimIndexError`	invalid dimensional index
`EExternalException`	unknown external exception
`EInOutError`	input/output error when managing a file
`EIntError`	the base integer math exception class
`EDivByZero`	division by zero error
`ERangeError`	value or index that doesn't fall within the specified range
`EIntOverflow`	overflow error
`EIntfCastError`	invalid conversion with `as` types to an interface
`EInvalidGraphic`	invalid graphic file
`EInvalidGraphicOperation`	improper operations with graphics
`EInvalidGridOperation`	improper handling of a grid
`EInvalidOperation`	invalid operation on a component
`EInvalidPointer`	improper handling of a pointer
`EListError`	improper handling of a list
`ELowCapacityError`	insufficient memory capacity when using a decision cube
`EMathError`	the base class for floating-point exceptions
`EInvalidArgument`	invalid argument
`EInvalidOp`	invalid operation
`EOverflow`	overflow error

`EUnderflow`	underflow error
`EZeroDivide`	division by zero error
`EMCIDeviceError`	improper access to devices through the Media Control Interface (MCI) driver
`EMenuError`	improper handling of menu elements
`EOleCtrlError`	improper linkage between an application and an ActiveX element
`EOleError`	OLE low-level error
`EOleSysError`	OLE `IDispatch` interface error
`EOleException`	OLE error associated with a method or a property
`EOutlineError`	improper handling of `TOutline`
`EOutOfMemory`	memory allocation error
`EOutOfResources`	creates a Windows handler error
`EPackageError`	exception generated when loading or using a package
`EParserError`	improper conversion of text format into binary format
`EPrinter`	printer error
`EPrivilege`	invalid processor instruction due to insufficient privilege
`EPropReadOnly`	invalid attempt to write via OLE when there is a read-only property value assigned
`EPropWriteOnly`	invalid attempt to read via OLE when there is a write-only property value assigned
`EPropertyError`	invalid value for a given property
`ERegistryException`	improper operation with the Windows registry
`EReportError`	an invalid server type (the `TReport` component cannot connect to a database)
`EResNotFound`	improper resource file loading (*.DFM `or` *.RES) at design time
`EStackOverflow`	stack overflow
`EStreamError`	the base class for stream exceptions
`EFCreateError`	error when creating a file
`EFOpenError`	error when opening a file
`EFilerError`	the base class of file stream exceptions
`EReadError`	invalid reading of a specified number of bytes
`EWriteError`	erroneous recording of a specified number of bytes
`EClassNotFound`	stream being read mentions a class not linked to the application
`EInvalidImage`	invalid reading of a resource file
`EMethodNotFound`	method not found
`EStringListError`	erroneous access to a string list
`EThread`	multithreaded application error
`ETreeViewError`	index error that occurs when you work with `TTreeView`

`EVariantError`	improper operation with the `Variant` data type
`EWin32Error`	Windows system error

So now you know that the `Exception` class is the base class for all Delphi exceptions. All of these classes are directly or indirectly derived from the `Exception` class. If you want to create your own exceptions, you will need to use the `Exception` class as the parent class. Only in this case can you be sure that Delphi will always identify and process your new class as an exception class. In turn, the `Exception` class is a direct descendant of the basic `TObject` class, and consequently, all the functions of the latter are inherited by the `Exception` class. Unlike other classes, object names of the exception class begin with the `E` character (and not the `T` character). When you create your custom exception classes, you are free to name them as you choose, and not necessarily beginning with `E`. The above conventions were developed by the Delphi team; it was considered good program style.

CREATING CUSTOM EXCEPTIONS

In order to create your own exceptions, you have to know how to declare an exception instance type and how to raise it in your routine.

Any exception is a Delphi object; therefore, to declare it is as easy as declaring any object instance with a new type. Theoretically, you can call any object and treat it as an exception object—but the problem is that standard exception handlers can process only those objects which descend from `Exception` or `Exception` descendants.

By way of example, let's take a look at the following declaration:

```
type

  EMyException = class(Exception);
```

Now if you raise the `EMyException` exception without previously designing the handler to process it, the standard exception handler for `Exception` will be automatically invoked. This standard handler for `Exception` displays the name of the exception that has been raised, which means that you will be able to see the name of your new exception instance.

Use the `raise` command if you need to raise your newly created exception. Let's look at the typical task of validating a password that has been entered by a user:

```
type

  EPasswordInvalid = class(Exception);
```

As soon as you have declared your new `EPasswordInvalid` exception, you can raise the exception in question anywhere in your program:

```
if Password <> CorrectPassword then
  raise EPasswordInvalid.Create('You have entered an invalid password');
```

In order to raise a new exception, you need to use its name.

INTERFACES AND COMBINED USE OF THEM BY VARIOUS CLASSES

The Delphi keyword `interface` allows you to create and use interfaces in your applications. *Interfaces* are actually an extension of the VCL inheritance pattern, because they enable a single class to belong to several interfaces. They also make it possible for a number of classes that descend from different base classes to share a common interface or functionality. Using interfaces is very effective when operation sets such as threads, for example, are used by multiple objects.

In other words, interfaces are tools which serve to provide interoperability for various objects.

Interfaces are also the basis for such technologies as COM and CORBA.

Interfaces are much like abstract classes that contain only abstract methods and explicit declarations of their functions. An interface method declaration includes variables and their types, a returned type, and expected behavior. Interface methods are semantically and logically associated with a given interface designation. There is a general agreement about interfaces, which states that each interface should be named in accordance with the task it is designed to solve. For instance, the `IMalloc` interface was created for the purpose of distributing, deallocating, and managing memory. Likewise, the `IPersist` interface can be used as the basic interface for unrelated classes, each one of which determining specific methods for loading and saving object states in memory, in a file, or in a thread. Consider a simple example of an interface declaration (Listing 2.9).

LISTING 2.9

```
type
IEdit = interface
  procedure Copy; stdcall;
  procedure Cut; stdcall;
  procedure Paste; stdcall;
  function Undo: Boolean; stdcall;
end;
```

NOTE

To those readers who have only a vague idea as to how to create components and new classes, I would recommend that you refer to Part II, which discusses the subject of creating custom interfaces and modifying existing components.

You cannot instantiate an interface. In order to get an interface instance, you will need to declare a class that the given interface implements. Therefore, you will have to identify the class that has the interface in question by its parent (Listing 2.10).

LISTING 2.10

```
TEditor = class(TInterfacedObject, IEdit)
    procedure Copy; stdcall;
    procedure Cut; stdcall;
    procedure Paste; stdcall;
    function Undo: Boolean; stdcall;
end;
```

As mentioned earlier, using interfaces enables different classes to utilize a common interface, ignoring the requirement of sharing a common base class. It should be remembered that an interface is a type with a manageable life cycle; that is to say, at initialization, it automatically assumes the `nil` value, has a reference counter, and is automatically destroyed as soon as it exceeds the scope of its visibility.

THE *IUNKNOWN* INTERFACE

By analogy with the principle of class inheritance, which is valid for all classes derived from the `TObject` class, all interfaces are either direct or indirect descendants of the `IUnknown` interface. This ancestor interface is declared in the `System` unit as follows (Listing 2.11).

LISTING 2.11

```
type
  IUnknown = interface
  ['{ 00000000-0000-0000-C000-000000000046}']
  function QueryInterface(const IID: TGUID; out Obj): Integer; stdcall;
  function _AddRef: Integer; stdcall;
  function _Release: Integer; stdcall;
end;
```

The syntax used in order to declare an interface is very similar to that for class declaration. However, the fundamental difference lies in the fact that an interface can be associated with a Global Unique Identifier, (GUID).

A GUID is a 128-bit integer which is used as a unique address for an interface. Due to the fact that 128 bits allows for the encoding of many numbers, GUID almost absolutely guarantees the global uniqueness of a given interface identifier. This means that the chance of coincidence between two GUIDs is negligible. The GUID generation algorithm is based on particular features of the computer's hardware (the processor frequency, the network adapter number, etc.). When an algorithm is processed by the special API function, `CoCreateGUID()`, a record of the `TGUID` type is returned. This record can be represented by a string in the following format:

```
'{xxxxxxxx-xxxx-xxxx-xxxx-xxxxxxxxxxxx}'
```

Later on, while discussing COM, we will see that every interface and every COM class has its own unique GUID; for interfaces it is referred to as an Interface ID (IID), and for classes it is a Class ID (CLSID).

In order to create a new GUID in the Delphi environment, press <Ctrl>+<Shift>+<G> in the **Code Editor** window.

The `IUnknown` interface supports three methods, all of which are inherited by all interfaces:

- **`QueryInterface()`**: This method is used for generating a query in order to learn whether a given interface is supported; if it is, the method returns the pointer to the interface in question. For example, suppose there is a certain object, `Object`, that supports several interfaces (`Interface1`, `Interface2`, etc.). If you need to obtain the pointer to `Interface2` of the `Object` object, you have to call the `Interface2.QueryInterface()` method.
- **`AddRef()`**: This method is used after you have obtained a pointer to the interface and intend to work with this pointer. The `_AddRef()` method must always be completed by invoking the `_Release()` method.
- **`Release()`**: This method is used when you have finished working with the interface.

Using interfaces is a fundamental principle of such distributed object models as COM and CORBA.

We will explore the potentials of the `IUnknown` interface in more depth in Part III, while discussing the COM and ActiveX technologies.

The *TInterfacedObject* Class

Delphi VCL contains the `TInterfacedObject` class, which is the base class for interface objects. This class is declared in the Delphi `System` unit as presented in the following listing:

LISTING 2.12

```
type
  TInterfacedObject = class(TObject, IUnknown)
  private
      FRefCount: Integer;
  protected
      function QueryInterface(const IID: TGUID; out Obj): HResult; stdcall;
      function _AddRef: Integer; stdcall;
      function _Release: Integer; stdcall;
  public
      property RefCount: Integer read FRefCount;
  end;
```

As you see, this class descends from the `TObject` class and implements the `IUnknown` interface. The `TInterfacedObject` class allows for rather fast and efficient creation of classes that support interfaces. For instance,

```
type
  TMyObjInterfaced = class(TInterfacedObject, IPaint)
    ...
  end;
```

In this example, the new `TMyObjInterfaced` class is being declared, which is a direct descendant of the `TInterfacedObject` class, and supports the `IPaint` interface.

Using the *as* Operator

Those objects that support interfaces can use the `as` operator to dynamically link to an interface. For example,

```
procedurePaintObjects(P: TInterfacedObject)
var
  X: IPaint;
```

```
begin
  X := P as IPaint;
{Statements}
end;
```

In this example, the variable `P` has the `TInterfacedObject` type. This variable can be declared as the variable `X`, which will serve as the link to the `IPaint` interface. In order to provide such a declaration, a compiler generates the code for invoking the `QueryInterface` method, which is a native method of `P`'s `IUnknown` interface. This declaration is possible even if `P` doesn't support a given interface—that is, the compiler won't return an error.

The running of the preceding code either results in a successfully completed assignment:

```
X:= P as IPaint;
```

or in an exception being generated.

While using the `as` operator, you should conform to the following rules:

- Explicitly specify the `IUnknown` interface as the parent interface when you declare a new interface. Only in this case will you be able to use the `as` operator.
- If you use the `as` operator for an interface, this interface must have a unique IID. As you probably remember, in order to generate a new IID, just press <Ctrl>+<Shift>+<G>.

Using the *implements* Keyword

Many classes declared in Delphi VCL use objects as their properties. However, you can also use interfaces as class properties. If a certain property has an interface type, then the `implements` keyword can help you identify the methods passed to a given object by the interface. By default, the `implements` keyword passes all the native methods of a given interface. However, while performing this operation, you are free to define only those methods that you want to assign to a given object.

Listing 2.13 illustrates an example of using the `implements` keyword for creating a color adapter object, which allows you to convert the 8-bit value of an RGB color.

LISTING 2.13

```
unit cadapt;
interface
uses
  Windows, Messages, SysUtils, Classes, Graphics, Controls, Forms, Dialogs;
```

```
type
  IRGB8bit = interface
      ['{1d76360a-f4f5-11d1-87d4-00c04fb17199}']
      function Red: Byte;
      function Green: Byte;
      function Blue: Byte;
  end;
  IColorRef = interface
      ['{1d76360b-f4f5-11d1-87d4-00c04fb17199}']
      function Color: Integer;
  end;
  TRGB8ColorRefAdapter = class(TInterfacedObject, IRGB8bit, IColorRef)
  private
    FRGB8bit: IRGB8bit;
    FPalRelative: Boolean;
  public
    constructor Create(rgb: IRGB8bit);
    property RGB8Intf: IRGB8bit read FRGB8bit implements IRGB8bit;
    property PalRelative: Boolean read FPalRelative write FPalRelative;
    function Color: Integer;
end;
implementation
constructor TRGB8ColorRefAdapter.Create(rgb: IRGB8bit);
begin
  FRGB8bit := rgb;
end;
function TRGB8ColorRefAdapter.Color: Integer;
begin
  if FPalRelative then
    Result := PaletteRGB(RGB8Intf.Red, RGB8Intf.Green, RGB8Intf.Blue)
  else
    Result := RGB(RGB8Intf.Red, RGB8Intf.Green, RGB8Intf.Blue);
end;
end.
```

USING INTERFACES IN DISTRIBUTED APPLICATIONS

The concept of an interface is a fundamental feature of such distributed object models as COM and CORBA (for more detail on this subject, refer to Part III). Delphi provides base classes for these technologies that extend the potentials of the `TInterfacedObject` object.

Introducing COM classes opens up new prospects of using class factories and class identifiers (CLSID). Class factories produce classes using CLSID. In turn, CLSIDs are used for registering and handling COM classes. The COM classes, which have both a class factory and a class identifier, are named `CoClasses`. `CoClasses` have an advantage over `QueryInterface` in matters concerning support of new versions of interfaces. Every new version of any interface automatically becomes available to client programs. A developer is able to amend code in COM applications in order to improve its performance, without introducing any changes to the client part of a code.

Another distributed object technology is referred to as Common Object Request Broker Architecture (CORBA). A detailed description of the wide range of possibilities provided by CORBA is beyond the scope of this book. It is enough to mention that CORBA allows for creating applications for use on various hardware and software platforms.

3 Threading in Windows Applications

Most developers often face situations where multiple tasks must be executed simultaneously in a single application. In order to help those developers working in the Delphi environment to get around this and some other performance problems, powerful tools enabling so-called *multithreading* were designed. Multithreading is a very effective solution if you need to:

- Circumvent delays incurred by slow processes: When only a single thread is being used, the execution of your application may be suspended until some slow process has been completed (such as accessing a disk, connecting to a remote computer, etc.). This may happen even though the computer's CPU is capable of executing additional commands at that moment. By taking advantage of multithreading, your application can continue running other threads while one of them is waiting for some lengthy process to be completed.
- Organize the behavior of your application more efficiently: Due to multithreading, you are able to manage the various parts of your application as you choose. For example, you can set execution priorities for each of the tasks in the application (provided a separate thread has been allocated to each task). As a result, the task with the highest priority will take more of the CPU's time—which is a very important issue for solving time critical tasks.
- Ensure support of multiprocessing systems: If you run your multithreaded application on a computer which has several processors, you can significantly accelerate performance by directing an individual thread to each processor.

NOTE

Actually, it can by no means be said that every operating system supports multithreading, even if the hardware allows for execution of multiple threads. A good example of such an operating system is Windows 95. This operating system can only emulate multithreading and will use only one CPU, even if more are available.

OVERVIEW OF THREADS: GENERAL CONCEPTS AND DEFINITIONS

A *thread* is an object of an operating system that is enclosed within a process and that performs some particular task. Every Win32 application (or process) has at least one thread, which is referred to as the main thread. Any process can contain a number of threads.

NOTE

You should bear in mind, however, that only 32-bit applications support threading—which means that an application that uses threads will fail to run on 16-bit operating systems.

Multithreading became possible with the introduction of the concept of *preemptive multitasking*. Older 16-bit Windows versions used *cooperative multitasking*.

Cooperative multitasking is the support of concurrent execution of several applications that share one operating system It is characterized by passing the control from one of the applications to the operating system. This type of multitasking happened to be rather ineffective; as soon as one application "froze," the whole system ground to a halt.

Preemptive multitasking, on the other hand, implies that it is the operating system that controls threading. The operating system divides the CPU time among the threads according to their priorities. Following this pattern, if one of the threads "freezes," the operating system will simply continue allocating CPU time among the rest of the threads.

Most applications allow you to use a *thread object*, which allows for threading in your applications. Thread objects encapsulate the fundamental properties and methods required for creating multithreaded applications.

So, to sum up, every thread is an object which is allocated a certain share of the CPU time. Every Windows application, in turn, is an operating system process. Every process consists of at least one thread, which is referred to as the main thread. Generally, Windows imposes no restrictions on the number of threads for each process.

NOTE

Thread objects do not enable you to directly control security properties or determine the stack size of your threads. To manage them, you need to use the `BeginThread` *function.*

If you intend to use thread objects in your application, you have to create descendants of the `TThread` class.

The `TThread` class was introduced to facilitate the process of multithreaded application development. This class ensures compatibility when you work with Delphi VCL.

Generally, while creating multithreaded applications, you need to follow such rules as:

- Avoid creating too many threads. Too many threads may result in an operating system or CPU overload. It is recommended that you limit the number of active threads to 16 threads per process (this applies to a single processor system). Using too many threads can also cause unnecessary overhead.
- Make use of synchronization in situations where several threads are trying to access a single resource.
- Most methods that handle VCL objects and modify the content of forms must either be called from the main VCL thread, or use a synchronization object, `TMultiReadExclusiveWriteSynchronizer`.

The declaration of the `TThread` object is contained in the `Classes` unit and looks like the code in Listing 3.1.

LISTING 3.1

```
TThread = class
  private
    FHandle: THandle;
    FThreadID: THandle;
    FTerminated: Boolean;
    FSuspended: Boolean;
    FFreeOnTerminate: Boolean;
    FFinished: Boolean;
    FReturnValue: Integer;
    FOnTerminate: TNotifyEvent;
    FMethod: TThreadMethod;
    FSynchronizeException: TObject;
    procedure CallOnTerminate;
    function GetPriority: TThreadPriority;
    procedure SetPriority(Value: TThreadPriority);
    procedure SetSuspended(Value: Boolean);
```

```
  protected
    procedure DoTerminate; virtual;
    procedure Execute; virtual; abstract;
    procedure Synchronize(Method: TThreadMethod);
    property ReturnValue: Integer read FReturnValue write FReturnValue;
    property Terminated: Boolean read FTerminated;
  public
    constructor Create(CreateSuspended: Boolean);
    destructor Destroy; override;
    procedure Resume;
    procedure Suspend;
    procedure Terminate;
    function WaitFor: LongWord;
    property FreeOnTerminate: Boolean read FFreeOnTerminate write
             FFreeOnTerminate;
    property Handle: THandle read FHandle;
    property Priority: TThreadPriority read GetPriority write SetPriority;
    property Suspended: Boolean read FSuspended write SetSuspended;
    property ThreadID: THandle read FThreadID;
    property OnTerminate: TNotifyEvent read FOnTerminate write FOnTerminate;
end;
```

As you can see from the Listing 3.1, the `TThread` object is a direct descendant of the `TObject` object, and therefore is a non-visual component. Its `Execute` method is an abstract method, which means that the object itself is an abstract object, and you will not be able to instantiate this class. Thus, in order to provide threading in your application, you need to declare descendant classes of `TThread`.

Creating a descendant of the `TThread` class involves the following steps: First, select File/New from the main menu, and click Thread Object in the displayed dialog window (Figure 3.1).

You will see another dialog window where you should enter a name for your new thread object. These operations will result in Delphi creating a new unit, and a new tab will appear in the Code Editor window.

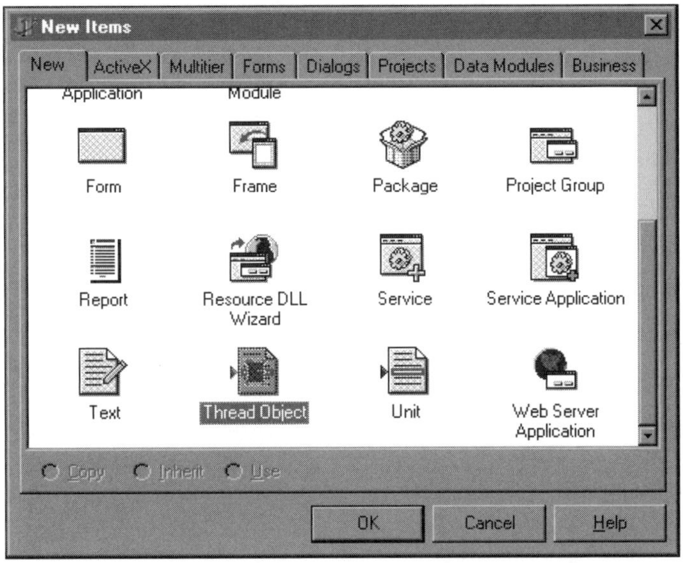

Figure 3.1 An example of adding a new thread object to a project using the **New Items** dialog window.

NOTE

Unlike most IDE dialog windows, which require that you enter the class name, the dialog window for creating a new thread instance does not automatically add the "T" character to the beginning of the name of your newly created class. It is therefore recommended that you give correct names to new threads, for example, `TMyThread`.

If you have successfully completed all the aforementioned actions and named your new object `TMyThread`, Delphi will generate a new unit that will include the code that will serve as a "skeleton" for your new thread object (Listing 3.2).

LISTING 3.2

```
unit Unit2;
interface
uses
  Classes;
type
  TMyThread = class(TThread)
   private
      {Private declarations}
   protected
```

```
    procedure Execute; override;
  end;
implementation
{TMyThread}
procedure TMyThread.Execute;
begin
  {Place thread code here}
end;
end.
```

In this automatically generated unit file, you can:

- Initialize a given thread.
- Create the `Execute` method for your thread by including the necessary functions and procedures.
- Write code to insure the termination of your thread.

INITIALIZING THREADS

If you need to write initialization code for your new thread object, you'll need to add a new constructor to the declaration of your new thread class. When you have done so you'll be able to add the initialization code with the implementation code for this new class. Here you can also specify the *priority* for a given thread, along with its behavior upon completion.

Thread Priorities

Priorities serve to indicate to the operating system the exact share of CPU time that should be allocated to a given thread. The highest priority is set to the most time critical tasks; less important tasks are given a lower priority.

The priority of a thread is a combination of two constituent factors:

- *Priority class*: The priority of the process that gave birth to a given thread
- *Relative priority*: The priority of the thread itself

The priority class of a process can assume one of the four following values: `Idle`, `Normal`, `High`, and `Realtime`, which are expressed numerically from 4 to 24. The default value for any application is `Normal`. Table 3.1 presents the priority classes of processes.

TABLE 3.1 The Priority Classes of Processes

Class value	*Priority*	*Numerical value*
`Idle`	The lowest priority—for performing background tasks	4
`Normal`	The standard priority of most Windows applications	7–9
`High`	High-level priority, which entitles the application to get a more substantial share of CPU time than what is allocated to an application with a priority of Normal.	13
`Realtime`	The highest priority	24

NOTE

When you run your application under Windows NT, you have to have certain privileges set in order to change its priority class. You are free to assign any priority class to your processes, but these priorities can be revoked by the system manager.

Use the `GetPriorityClass` and `SetPriorityClass` functions for identifying the current priority class and specifying the required one, respectively. For example, you can write the following code to assign your application high priority (`High`):

```
If not SetPriorityClass(GetCurrentProcess, HIGH_PRIORITY_CLASS) then
ShowMessage ('Priority class error');
```

NOTE

Try to avoid using `High` and `Realtime`, since this may boost the priority of your application thread to such a level that it'll get more CPU time than the operating system itself, which may cause serious problems.

In order to specify the relative priority value, use the `Priority` property of your threads. A given property can be assigned one of seven values. Thread priority values are listed in Table 3.2.

TABLE 3.2 Thread Priorities

Relative priority value	*Priority*	*Numerical value*
`tpIdle`	The thread executes only when the system is free and no other threads are being processed. Windows will not suspend the work of other threads to process a thread with tpIdle priority.	–15

TABLE 3.2 Thread Priorities (*Continued*)

Relative priority value	***Priority***	***Numerical value***
`tpLowest`	The lowest priority. The thread uses the minimum share of CPU time.	–2
`tpLower`	Low priority. The thread takes up a little more CPU time than a thread with `tpLowest` priority.	–1
`tpNormal`	Normal priority. By default, all threads have `tpNormal` priority.	0
`tpHigher`	High priority. The thread executes at a level of priority higher than normal.	1
`tpHighest`	The highest priority. The thread executes at a level of priority higher than `tpHigher`.	2
`tpTimeCritical`	The time critical priority. A given thread takes up the maximum share of CPU time.	15

NOTE *Using the high and highest priorities may result in a delay in processing other threads. It seems reasonable to assign your threads such priorities only if you urgently need the particular process to be completed as soon as possible.*

The following example illustrates a thread constructor with a priority of idle, which is intended to be used when performing background tasks. These tasks must not affect the execution of the main processes.

```
constructor TMyThread.Create(CreateSuspended: Boolean);
{
 inherited Create(CreateSuspended);
  Priority := tpIdle;
}
```

Thread Completion and Termination

As a rule, a thread is simply set free upon completing its work. However, it is sometimes necessary to coordinate the completion and release of a given thread with the work of other threads. For instance, you may need to obtain some data which is to be returned by one thread in order to start another one.

Implementation of such a scheme requires that the first thread not be freed until the second one obtains the values to be returned by the first thread. There is a special thread property, `FreeOnTerminate`, which helps you manage thread termination. The default value of this property is set to `true`, which means that the given thread is released as soon as it finishes executing. If you assign a value of `false` to this property, you will be able to explicitly terminate the thread's execution yourself.

Besides this, Delphi allows for requested termination of one thread by issuing a command from another thread. When one thread attempts to terminate the execution of any other thread, it invokes the `Terminate` method. In order for this method to work, the thread's code must periodically check the Terminated property. The `Terminate` method sets the Terminated property to `true`, which you can check while the `Execute` method is executing:

```
procedure TMyThread.Execute;
begin
  while not Terminated do
   {perform a certain task};
end;
```

NOTE

In case of system failure, you can forcibly terminate a thread by calling the Win32 API `TerminateThread` function. But bear in mind that this function should be your very last resort, and should only be used only if other attempts to terminate a thread have failed. This function should be considered dangerous, in the sense that it behaves differently with different operating systems. When this function is used in Windows 9x, it releases a thread stack, but when you use this same function in Windows NT, the stack is not released until the process that gave birth to the thread is completed. The second reason to be careful when using this function is that it sometimes tends not to free resources. That is, those files activated by a thread may be left open, and the memory that has been allocated to the thread may not be returned to the heap. In addition, if you are using a Dynamic Link Library (DLL) in a thread that has been terminated with the `TerminateThread` function, you may experience certain problems when you try to unload the DLL.

Creating a Sample Multithreaded Application with Delphi

It's time to try your hand at developing your own multithreaded application.

This section shows you how to create a simple application which comprises three threads. For starters, you need to start Delphi and select File/New/Application from the main menu. After that, place an Edit field, a Progress Bar, and a system Timer on Form1. You will then see a form similar to the one shown in Figure 3.2.

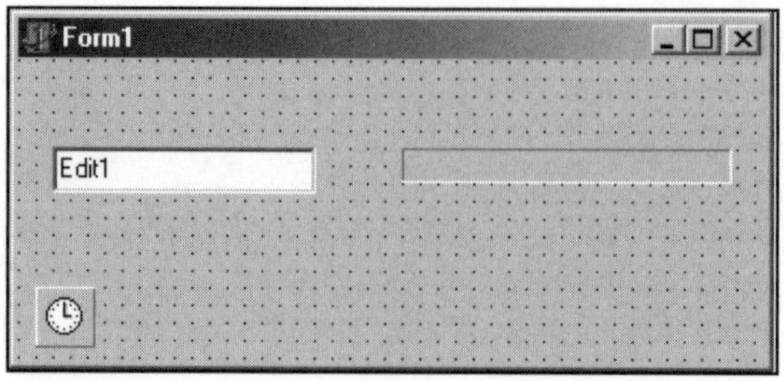

FIGURE 3.2 A sample multithreaded application form.

Now add a new thread object via File/New/Thread Object. Enter a name for this new descendant of the `TThread` class; for instance, `TMyThread1`. Delphi will automatically add `Unit2` to your application. You now need to include the `public` section into the `TMyThread1` object declaration, and declare a global variable with the `count` name in this section. The result will look like this:

```
type
  TMyThread1 = class(TThread)
  private
    {Private declarations}
  protected
    procedure Execute; override;
  public
   count:integer;
  end;
```

The next step will be to write the code that will execute in the thread to the `Execute` method of the `TMyThread1` object. Let's say that it is code which generates random numbers and assigns them to the `count` global variable. In order to provide for permanent generation of random numbers, let's use a "permanent loop:"

```
procedure TMyThread1.Execute;
begin
  while true do
     begin
       count:=random(maxint);
     end;
end;
```

At this point, it's time to create a second thread instance to do the job of filling the Progress Bar, which will indicate the process's progress.

Create the second thread object the same way as you did the first one and name it `TMyThread2`, using Delphi's main menu. In the newly added `Unit3` unit, declare the `prcount` global variable:

```
type
  TMyThread2 = class(TThread)
   private
    {Private declarations}
   protected
    procedure Execute; override;
   public
    prcount:integer;
  end;
```

Then, write the following code to the `Execute` procedure of the `TMyThread2` object, "looping" it in the same manner as in the first instance:

```
procedure TMyThread2.Execute;
begin
  while true do
  begin
    prcount:=prcount+1;
    if prcount>100 then prcount:=0;
  end;
end;
```

Now we'll save the project and units under the names that Delphi suggests (`Project1`, `Unit1`, `Unit2`, `Unit3`).

Add the `Thread1` thread object (a descendant of the `TMyThread1` class) and the `Thread2` thread object (a descendant of the `TMyThread2` class) to the `private` section in the form class declaration in `Unit1`:

```
type
  TForm1 = class(TForm)
    ProgressBar1: TProgressBar;
    Edit1: TEdit;
    Timer1: TTimer;
    procedure FormCreate(Sender: TObject);
  private
```

```
    Thread1:TMyThread1;
    Thread2:TMyThread2;
  public
    {Public declarations}
  end;
```

Next, double-click any free space within Form1. You'll see a skeleton for the form creation method, FormCreate, for building Form1. You need to write the following code in the FormCreate constructor:

```
procedure TForm1.FormCreate(Sender: TObject);
begin
  Thread1:=TMyThread1.Create(False);
  Thread1.Priority:=tpLowest;
  Thread2:=TMyThread2.Create(False);
  Thread2.Priority:=tpNormal;
end;
```

In this code, you've created a thread object using the Create constructor, and you've also set the priorities for the new threads (tpLowest and tpNormal).

NOTE

The only parameter inherited with the Create *method of the* TThread *class is* CreateSuspended. *This parameter can assume one of the two Boolean values* (True, False), *and its function is to indicate whether the thread should be created in suspended state* (True), *or if it should be started as soon as it has been created* (false). *In other words, the* Execute *method will be run automatically and at once if the* CreateSuspended *parameter is set to* False *(as it is in the preceding example). If you need to suspend a given thread for a while, then assign the* True *value to* CreateSuspended *and employ the* Resume *method to invoke the* Execute *method.*

Now you need to include Unit2 and Unit3, which have been used in your routine, into the uses block of Unit1:

```
uses
  Windows, Messages, SysUtils, Classes, Graphics, Controls, Forms,
   Dialogs, Unit2, Unit3, StdCtrls, ComCtrls, ExtCtrls;
```

The last step is to display the results of calculations returned by your threads on the form. In order to do this, create the OnTimer event handler by double-clicking the `Timer1` object. Write the following code to the `OnTimer` event handler:

```
procedure TForm1.Timer1Timer(Sender: TObject);
begin
   Edit1.Text:=IntToStr(Thread1.count);
   Progressbar1.Position:=Thread2.prcount;
end;
```

Congratulations! You have done it! You have created your first application that supports threading. Now you can start it with **Run/Run** from the Delphi main menu to make sure that the two newly built threads really work and at different rates as well (which depends on the priority).

Managing the Thread Schedule

In addition to all the previous methods, which are invoked for starting and terminating threads, you can take advantage of another rather helpful feature of thread objects, namely, the possibility of suspending and resuming their execution. These capabilities are implemented through the `Suspend` and `Resume` methods, respectively.

A single-threaded operating system lets you quite easily determine the time necessary for some of your calculations. To do this, just use the `GetTickCount` function. For example, if you need to determine how long the process of generating a random number in the Delphi environment will take, simply write the following code:

```
Var
   StartTime, Summa: longint;
   R,I: integer;
begin
  StartTime:=GetTickCount;
  for I:=0 to 100000 do
      R:=Random(MaxInt);
      Summa:=GetTickCount-StartTime;
end;
```

A multithreaded operating system makes the same task a bit more complicated, because the processing of your thread can be suspended at any time for the purpose of processing other threads. In order to get around this problem, truly multithreaded operating systems, such as Windows NT, use the `GetThreadTimes` function, which helps you manage the schedule for your thread:

```
function GetThreadTimes (hThread: THandle; var lpCreationTime,
  lpExitTime, lpKernelTime, lpUserTime: TFileTime): BOOL; stdcall;
```

Let's take a closer look at the variables utilized in this function:

- **hThread**: The handle of the thread whose schedule you need to retrieve
- **lpCreationTime**: The time of the thread's creation
- **lpExitTime**: The time of the thread's completion (specified only if the thread's work has already completed)
- **lpKernelTime**: The time the execution of the code has taken in Kernel Mode
- **lpUserTime**: The time the execution of the codehas taken in User Mode

As you can see, the last four parameters have a `TFileTime` type:

```
type
  TFileTime = record
    dwLowDateTime: DWORD;
    dwHighDateTime: DWORD;
end;
```

That is to say, once they are summed up, the `TFileTime`: `dwLowDateTime` and `dwHighDateTime` elements make up a 64-bit number. This number indicates the number of 100-nanosecond intervals that have passed since 1/1/1601.

NOTE

When working with a `TFileTime` type, it is convenient to use the function which converts a given type to the `Int64` type, for example:

```
If Int64(CreationTime) > Int64(ExitTime) then ShowMessage('OK').
```

USING THE MAIN VCL THREAD

The `Execute` method is a thread function. A thread can be thought of as an application run from your application, except for one detail: both your application and a given thread work in the framework of the same process. Building a thread function is a much more challenging task than creating an ordinary application, because you will have to watch that your threads do not interfere with each other when accessing the main memory. On the other hand, if the threads operate in a single process, you can enable sharing of the main memory in order to provide for their interoperability.

When you use VCL objects, or any third-party objects, in your application, you have to take into account that properties and methods of VCL objects cannot guarantee thread safety.

If all objects address their properties and implement their methods in the framework of one thread, you needn't worry about the possible conflicts that may occur among them.

To use the main VCL thread and avoid conflicts, you have to create a particular procedure to perform the necessary operations. Later you will be able to call this procedure from your thread unit (located inside the `Execute` method) by employing synchronization. This suspends your thread and uses the main UCC thread to execute the code. For example:

```
procedure TMyThread.PushTheButton;
begin
  Button1.Click;
end;
procedure TMyThread.Execute;
begin
  ...
  Synchronize(PushTheButton);
  ...
end;
```

The *synchronize* method will protect your application from so-called *race conditions.*

A race condition is when two or more threads are trying to gain access to a shared resource to change its status.

NOTE

The synchronize method cannot be called in console-based applications. In order to ensure safe, concurrent access to VCL objects in such applications, you have to use other methods.

Sometimes you can do without the synchronize method, for example:

- Data access components are thread safe components, provided each thread is accessing a separate database. There is an exception, however: when you try to get access to the Microsoft Access database. Access works with the Microsoft ADO library, which is not thread safe.

NOTE

If you use data access components, you must synchronize when, for example, you set the links between data access components (say, when you are specifying the `DataSet` *property in the* `DataSource` *object). Or, you could avoid synchronization and use the data contained in the database table.*

- Graphics handling objects are thread-safe objects. This type of object is grouped in the following classes: `TFont`, `TPen`, `TBrush`, `TBitmap`, `TMetafile`, and `TIcon`.
- Instead of `List` objects, which are not thread safe, you can use the thread-safe descendant of the `TList` object—`TThreadList`.

COORDINATING THREADS

Because you are still a novice as far as threading is concerned, be prepared for all kinds of bugs and unpleasant surprises. The most irritating errors are usually associated with conflicts between threads trying to access shared resources and global variables. Quite often, you'll need to coordinate the work of your threads—for example, if you need a certain event to occur in one thread as soon as another event has taken place in some other thread. Such a technique is referred to as thread coordination. Let's explore the benefits of this technique in the sense of efficient thread management for solving various practical tasks.

To begin with, let's recall the techniques that Delphi provides for storing local thread variables. There are three of them:

- Storing local variables in a thread stack. Due to the fact that each application thread has a separate stack, it will have its own local variables.
- Storing local variables in an object that descends from the `TThread` class.
- Storing local variables on the operating system level. In this case, the `threadvar` keyword is used in local variable declarations.

The first technique seems to be the simplest and most obvious, as well as the most effective. Local variables stored in a stack are the ones most readily and quickly available.

Let's consider the other two methods of storing local thread variables:

The second approach is less complicated and more powerful than the third one. The following example shows why this is true:

```
type
  TMyThread1 = class(TThread)
   private
    i,j,k,l: integer; // local thread variables of the integer type
    a,b,c: char; // local thread variables of the char type
   ...
  end;
```

The technique that involves storing local variables in a descendant of the `TThread` class is far more serviceable, since access to every object field is very fast in this case (roughly 10–11 times quicker than when you use `threadvar`).

The third way to store local variables (by using `threadvar`) lets you create local replicas of global variables in your threads. Global variables can be used by all the threads in a given application, which may bring about a situation in which, for example, two threads are modifying the same global variable simultaneously. This may cause all sorts of trouble, since the value set by the first thread is eliminated (in this example, an erroneous value of the global variable will be processed by the first thread). In order to prevent such an occurrence, Delphi provides thread-local storage. By using this very powerful tool, you can create local replicas of global variables for every one of your threads. You just need to replace the `var` word with `threadvar` when you declare global variables.

SYNCHRONIZING THREADS

If you intend to take advantage of threading in your applications in the future, you will have to learn how to manage your threads so that they don't interfere with each other. This technique of optimizing the performance of your threads is referred to as *synchronization.*

Waiting for Thread Completion

The fundamental concepts to be considered in reference to the mechanism of thread synchronization are those of a *waitfor function* and a *waitfor object.*

Win32 API provides its users with a number of functions referred to as waitfor functions; they allow you to suspend a thread until the state of some other object of the operating system is modified. The object at issue is called a waitfor object.

The typical waitfor objects of the Win32 API kernel are as follows:

- `Critical section`
- `Events`
- `Mutexes`
- `Semaphores`
- `Timers`

In addition to the above objects, you can also utilize a great variety of other methods: threads, changes that have been made to the file system, console input, etc.

Using the Critical Section

If you work with objects in your application that are not thread safe, Delphi allows you to use *critical sections.*

The critical section is an area in the global memory which can be used by only one thread at any given moment.

The critical section performs the function of "gates," which are closed for all other threads immediately after one thread has entered the gates in question. The critical section ensures that only one thread is permitted access to a given memory area, and then it locks other threads out.

To create a critical section in your application, you should begin with a global instance of the `TCriticalSection` class. This class has several methods, but we are interested only in two of them: `Acquire` (or `Enter`) and `Release` (or `Leave`).

- The `Acquire` (or `Enter`) method links the critical section to the thread that has invoked a certain method, at the same time locking access to this section for all other threads.
- The `Release` (or `Leave`) method revokes the lock and lets another thread enter the critical section.

NOTE

When using the critical section, make sure that all your threads that have access to it use the `Acquire` (`Enter`) method to enter this section. Otherwise, you may face a problem related to sharing a resource.

As an example, let's take a look at a small routine which uses a critical section global variable: `LockXY`. This variable locks access to the `X` and `Y` global variables.

```
LockXY.Acquire; // lock access for other threads
try
  Y := sin(X);
finally
  LockXY.Release;
end;
```

Any other threads that use the `X` or `Y` global variables must contain essentially the same piece of code.

Events

If you intend to use synchronization in your applications, a waitfor object is the simplest solution. An object of the `TEvent` type can assume one of two possible states: *active* or *passive.*

When this waitfor object is set to the active state, it can be referenced by multiple threads simultaneously. This means that you are able to use one object to manage many concurrent threads.

Among other methods, an object of the `TEvent` class has `SetEvent`, which sets this object to the active state, and `ResetEvent`, which resets the state of the object to passive. Additionally, this object includes the `WaitFor` method:

```
type TWaitResult = (wrSignaled, wrTimeout, wrAbandoned, wrError);

function WaitFor(Timeout: DWORD): TWaitResult;
```

This method contains the `Timeout` variable, which specifies the number of milliseconds for the object to wait for the event. This method returns either the `wrSignaled` value if the event has been activated, or the `wrTimeout` value if it hasn't. If you specify the `INFINITE` value for the `Timeout` variable, your object will wait infinitely for a given event to occur.

In order to create the `Event` object, use the `CreateEvent` function:

```
CreateEvent (lpEventAttributes, bManualReset, bInitialState, lpName);
```

where:

- **`lpEventAttributes`**: Specifies the security descriptor for a new event. In a Windows NT implementation, if this variable is set to `NULL`, the given event is assigned a default safety handle. Windows 9x ignores this variable altogether.
- **`bManualReset`**: Specifies either manual or automatic reset for the state of a given event. If the value is `True`, you will have to utilize the `ResetEvent` function in order to manually change the state of a given event to non-signaled. If the value is `False`, Windows will automatically perform the same operation.
- **`bInitialState`**: Determines the initial state for a given event (signaled or non-signaled). If this variable is set to `True`, then the initial state is signaled, and a `False` setting causes the initial state to be non-signaled.
- **`LpName`**: Defines the event name for referencing it from other threads. Any name can include any character except for '\.' These names are case sensitive. If a name repeats the name of an existing event, the existing event will be referenced. If the value of this variable is `NULL`, the event is nameless. If any event name is the same as the name of a semaphore, a mutex, or some other object, then the `ERROR_INVALID_HANDLE` error is returned.

Mutexes (Mutual Exceptions)

This type of waitfor object ensures that only one thread will be able to access it at any given moment. A mutex generates a signal when it is not owned by a thread, and stops signaling as soon as any thread accesses it. When the thread in question exits, another one is enabled to get access to the mutex.

This object is very helpful if several threads need to access the same memory to modify it.

In order to create a mutex object, threads must use the `CreateMutex` function:

```
CreateMutex (lpMutexAttributes, bInitialOwner, lpName)
```

where:

- **`lpMutexAttributes`**: A pointer to the `SECURITY_ATTRIBUTES` construct, which specifies whether the handler can be inherited by descendant threads. If in Windows NT `lpMutexAttributes = NULL`, then the mutex is assigned a default safety handle. Windows 9x doesn't support this variable.
- **`bInitialOwner`**: Specifies the initial owner of a given mutex. If the value is `true`, then the owner is the thread that called the mutex. Otherwise, the owner is not specified.
- **`lpName`**: Sets the mutex name. This name will be used for referencing the mutex from other processes. The mutex's name can include any characters except for '\.' These names are case sensitive. If a name duplicates the name of an existing mutex, the existing event will be referenced. If this variable is set to `NULL`, the mutex is left nameless. If the mutex name is the same as the name of a semaphore, an event, or some other object, then the `ERROR_INVALID_HANDLE` error is returned.

Semaphores

Sometimes you need to limit the number of threads referencing a given waitfor object (there can be more than one). An object of the semaphore type can be set to a value defining the number of threads permitted to access a given semaphore. All those threads that exceed the specified number and try to access the semaphore are suspended. As soon as the threads linked to the semaphore exit, the waiting threads access it.

Semaphores help you control access to shared resources that can support only a limited number of users. For instance, if an application can display only a limited number of windows, you can use a semaphore to set the maximum number of windows for a given application.

Threads use the `CreateSemaphore` function in order to access an object of the semaphore type:

```
CreateSemaphore (lpSemaphoreAttributes, lInitialCount,
                 lMaximumCount, lpName);
```

where :

- **`lpSemaphoreAttributes`**: Specifies the security descriptor for the new semaphore; Windows 9x doesn't support this parameter. If this parameter is `NULL`, a given semaphore is assigned a default security descriptor.

- **lInitialCount**: Sets the initial value for the semaphore access control counter. It must be more than zero and less than or equal to the `lMaximumCount` value.
- **lMaximumCount**: Specifies the maximum value for the semaphore counter (the maximum number of threads). This value must be more than zero.
- **lpName**: Defines the semaphore name. This name can contain any characters except for '\'. It is case sensitive. If a semaphore with the same name has already been declared, this existing semaphore will be accessed. If the `lpName` value is `NULL`, the new semaphore will be created nameless. If a new semaphore is assigned a name that has already been specified for another object (a mutex, etc.), then an error will occur—and if you invoke the `GetLastError` function the `ERROR_INVALID_HANDLE` error will be returned. The reason for this error is quite simple: all these objects share the same namespace.

NOTE

You can reference a semaphore by name from other processes as well.

STARTING AND STOPPING THREADS

While running an application, you can start and suspend threads any time you choose to do so. In order to suspend a thread, call the `Suspend` thread method. If you need to set a given thread on its way again, call the `Resume` thread method. You can use nested calls for these methods due to the fact that the `Suspend` method increases and the `Resume` method, on the contrary, decreases the value of a thread counter. A given thread cannot resume until the counter value is zero—that is to say, if you have invoked the `Suspend` method five times and the `Resume` method four times, then in order to resume the thread you need to call the `Resume` method one more time.

THREADING IN DISTRIBUTED APPLICATIONS

Distributed applications are another pain in the neck for programmers dealing with multithreaded applications. As if worrying about the synchronization of threads within a single application is not enough, their tasks become even more complicated when faced with the problem of ensuring that other external processes do not interfere with the performance of the threads in the application.

Typically, processing distributed threads is the responsibility of a server application. This should be borne in mind if you happen to develop servers.

If every query generated by a client application is contained in an individual thread, then you have to guarantee that different client threads do not interfere with each other.

All these issues will be covered in Part III when we discuss developing COM and ActiveX applications.

4 Working with Packages and Components

Packages are special dynamic-link components (analogous to DLLs) used by Delphi applications and Delphi IDE. (For information on Delphi components and creating them, refer to Part II) All packages can be divided into three major categories by their intended use:

- *Runtime packages*: Such packages include code and components required for running a given application. If an application refers to a non-existent package, it won't work.
- *Design time packages*: Typically, design time packages include various elements which are intended to facilitate developing with Delphi: a wide range of components, property editors, wizards, etc.
- *Packages which combine the features of the two above types* and can work both at runtime and at design time.

In order to draw a distinction between packages and other dynamic-link libraries with the DLL extension, packages use the BPL (Borland Package Library) extension.

Similar to other dynamic libraries, packages contain code that can be invoked by a number of concurrent applications. For example, the VCL50.BPL Delphi 5.0 package is by far the one most popular with users. Almost every Delphi application is created using this package. The Delphi environment itself uses it.

And the most important advantage of using this VCL50.BPL package is that it is enough to have just one copy of it on a given computer, which can be used simultaneously by any number of applications and by Delphi itself.

Certainly, the choice to use packages while developing applications is a matter of taste, but if you are going to enrich your software with custom components, you will have to install a runtime package to contain your newly created objects.

This chapter covers the subjects of potential uses of packages, how to dynamically load them, and how to take full advantage of them in your applications. Also, it provides guidelines for package installation, creation, and editing. And finally, you will learn the basics of package architecture.

WHY USE PACKAGES

As mentioned earlier, design time packages serve to facilitate the problems of arranging and installing packages created by a developer. By definition, using packages in programming provides a number of benefits as compared with conventional programming, and the most appealing of them is a much more compact code. Just consider: all your applications, including the Delphi programming environment, can simultaneously use standard Delphi components placed in a single package. Since your applications now needn't have individual component libraries, their size is substantially decreased. Moreover, compiling with packages takes up much less time, since only the necessary code is compiled for every application.

For your application to use packages, you need to check the **Build with Runtime Packages** check box in the **Project Options** dialog box in the **Packages** window. This window can be opened through **Project/Options.** This approach to compiling an application will make this application much more compact (roughly 8–10 times). Later, however, at the distribution stage, you will have to supply all the packages used by the application (including one as bulky as VCL50.BPL, which takes up almost 2 MB with the application it self.

Let's now discuss the comparative advantages of using packages and DLLs in different situations:

- If you wish to use components which you yourself have created with Delphi, then a package is your solution. Remember, though, that Delphi packages are usable only by applications developed with Delphi or Borland C++ Builder.
- If your purpose is to use a newly designed library in various applications that were developed in different programming environments, you will require a DLL.

Besides the mentioned BPL, packages use a number of other file extensions, which are listed in Table 4.1.

TABLE 4.1 File Types Used in Packages

File extension	*File contents*
DPK	An initial package file that lists all the units of the package. It is created as soon as you start a package editor (its functionality and purpose are similar to those of a Delphi DPR project file).
DCP	A binary file which contains the header of the package and declarations of all DCU files, including the character information necessary for the compiler. Each package includes only one DCP file.
DCU	A binary file which contains the textual content of a package module. Only one file with this extension is created for every individual package module.
BPL	Files of this type are used at runtime. They contain Delphi environment specifications and are analogous to Windows DLL files. If a given package belongs to the runtime category, then you must supply it to your users along with the application file.

USING PACKAGES IN APPLICATIONS

In order to successfully start, your application must have the necessary EXE and BPL files. BPL file paths must be explicitly specified.

NOTE

When developing an application for commercial use, make sure that your users get the correct versions of the BPL files.

If you've decided to use runtime packages in your applications, perform the following procedure:

1. Open an existing project (or create a new one) in the Delphi environment.
2. Select Project/Options from Delphi's main menu.
3. In the resulting dialog box, select the Packages tab (Figure 4.1).
4. Select the Build with runtime packages check box. As soon as an edit box is enabled, enter the names of packages to be used in your application (Figure 4.2). Alternatively, you can use the Add button to search for the required package.

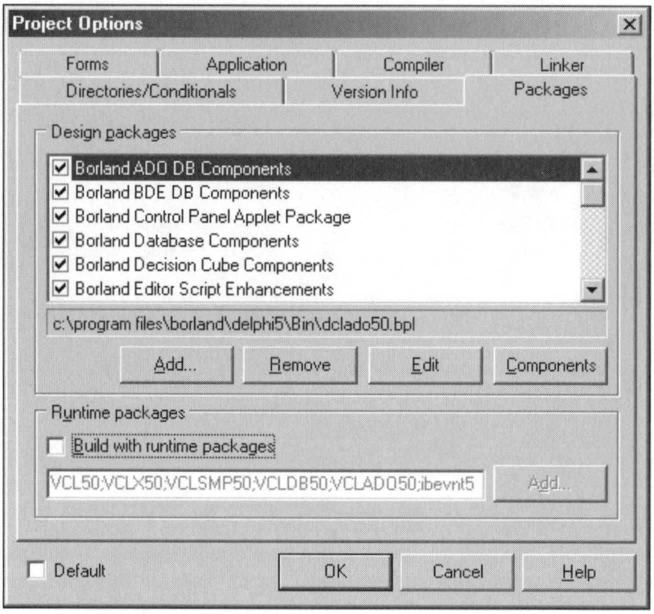

FIGURE 4.1 The **Packages** tab in the **Project Options** dialog box.

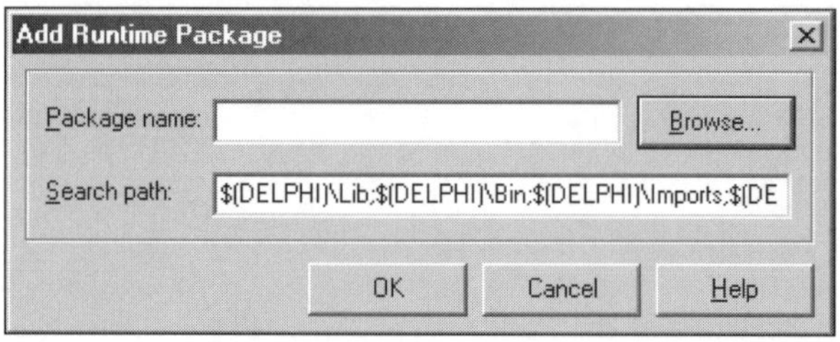

FIGURE 4.2 The dialog box for adding a package to a project.

NOTE

*By changing the **Search path** entry in the dialog box for adding a package (Figure 4.2), you thereby modify the global path mapping, which enables Delphi to find libraries.*

If you enter the name of your package manually, without using the Add button, you needn't add the extension of the package. Notice that the names of packages are delimited by semicolons:

```
VCL50;VCLX50;VCLSMP50;VCLDB50;VCLADO50
```

In the process of compilation, all the packages listed in the edit box will be automatically linked to your application. If no package name has been entered,

Delphi will reset the option and not build with runtime packages. If any package name is repeatedly entered in the edit field, all the redundant records will be ignored.

NOTE *All information concerning packages is saved only in the given application. In order to ensure that these settings will be valid for other applications as well, select the **Defaults** check box in the bottom part of the **Project Options** dialog box.*

It is important to remember that even if you utilize packages in your application, you must include the individual Delphi units in the `uses` clause:

```
unit Unit1;

interface

uses

Windows, Messages, SysUtils, Classes, Graphics, Controls, Forms, Dialogs;
```

In spite of the fact that all the units in this code are contained in the same VCL50.BPL package, the compiler will return an error if you remove their declarations from the `uses` clause.

DYNAMIC PACKAGE LOADING

If you need to load a package dynamically at runtime, use the `LoadPackage` function. The function in question is declared in the Delphi `SysUtils` unit as follows:

```
function LoadPackage(const Name: string): HMODULE;
```

This function uses a package file name of the `string` type as its parameter. Calling this function is a fairly easy operation:

```
LoadPackage('A package file name');
```

For dynamic package unloading, utilize the `UnloadPackage` procedure. This procedure is included into the `SysUtils` unit, and its declaration looks like this:

```
procedure UnloadPackage(Module: HMODULE);
```

Take care to destroy the class instances declared in the `UnloadPackage` before calling the package.

The Delphi environment is supplied to its users with a number of native component packages containing the basic components necessary for developing standard Windows applications. Most standard Delphi components are contained in the VCL50.BPL package that we mentioned earlier. However, this package doesn't include many important components, such as data access components, Windows 3.1 components, etc. These components are supplied with other Delphi packages (for instance, the data access components are provided with the VCLDB50.BPL package). Nevertheless, in order to work with databases, you will need both VCL50.BPL and VCLDB50.BPL. Table 4.2 lists the runtime packages provided with Delphi 5.0, along with the units included in these packages.

TABLE 4.2 The Standard Runtime Delphi Packages

Package file name	*Package units*
VCL50.BPL	Ax, Buttons, Classes, Clipbrd, Comctrls, Commctrl, Commdlg, Comobj, Comstrs, Consts, Controls, Ddeml, Dialogs, Dlgs, Dsgnintf, Dsgnwnds, Editintf, Exptintf, Extctrls, Extdlgs, Fileintf, Forms, Graphics, Grids, Imm, IniFiles, Isapi, Isapi2, Istreams, Libhelp, Libintf, Lzexpand, Mapi, Mask, Math, Menu, Messages, Mmsystem, Nsapi, Ole2I, Oleconst, Olectnrs, Olectrls, Oledlg, Penwin, Printers, Proxies, Registry, Regstr, Richedit, Shellapi, Shlobj, Stdctrls, Stdvcl, Sysutils, Tlhelp32, Toolintf, Toolwin, Typinfo, Vclcom, Virtintf, Windows, Wininet, Winsock, Winspool, Winsvc
VCLX50.BPL	Checklst, Colorgrd, Ddeman, Filectrl, Mplayer, Outline, Tabnotbk, Tabs
VCLDB50.BPL	Bde, Bdeconst, Bdeprov, Db, Dbcgrids, Dbclient, Dbcommon, Dbconsts, Dbctrls, Dbgrids, Dbinpreq, Dblogdlg, Dbpwdlg, Dbtables, Dsintf, Provider, SMintf
VCLDBX50.BPL	Dblookup, Report
DSS50.BPL	Mxarrays, Mxbutton, Mxcommon, Mxconsts, Mxdb, Mxdcube, Mxdssqry, Mxgraph, Mxgrid, Mxpivsrc, Mxqedcom, Mxqparse, Mxqryedt, Mxstore, Mxtables, Mxqvb
QRPT50.BPL	Qr2const, Qrabout, Qralias, Qrctrls, Qrdatasu, Qrexpbld, Qrextra, Qrprev, Qrprgres, Qrprntr, Qrqred32, Quickrpt
TEE50.BPL	Arrowcha, Bubblech, Chart, Ganttch, Series, Teeconst, Teefunci, Teengine, Teeprocs, Teeshape
TEEDB50.BPL	Dbchart, Qrtee
TEEUI50.BPL	Areaedit, Arrowedi, Axisincr, Axmaxmin, Baredit, Brushdlg, Bubbledi, Custedit, Dbeditch, Editchar, Flineedi, Ganttedi, Ieditcha, Pendlg, Pieedit, Shapeedi, Teeabout, Teegally, Teelisb, Teeprevi, Te-export
VCLSMP50.BPL	Sampreg, Smpconst

Let's now take a look at the list of design packages supplied with Delphi 5.0 (Table 4.3). As you probably remember, all these packages are used by the Delphi IDE to add components to the Component palette, set the component properties, and perform a whole host of other tasks.

TABLE 4.3 The Standard Design Time Delphi Components

Package file name	*Component palette tab*
DCLSTD50.BPL	**Standard, Additional, System, Win32, Dialogs**
DCLTEE50.BPL	**Additional** (the `TChart` component)
DCLDB50.BPL	**Data Access, Data Controls**
DCLMID50.BPL	**Midas**
DCL31W50.BPL	**Win 3.1**
DCLNET50.BPL, DCLIE50.BPL	**Internet**
DCLSMP50.BPL	**Samples**
DCLOCX50.BPL	**ActiveX**
DCLQRT50.BPL	**QReport**
DCLDSS50.BPL	**Decision Cube**
IBEVNT50.BPL	**Samples** (the `IBEventAlerter` component)
DCLINT50.BPL	Multilanguage support wizard
RCEXPERT.BPL	Resource expert
DBWEBXPRT.BPL	Web expert

While operating, all of the packages in Table 4.3 reference runtime packages. For example, the DCLSTD50.BPL package calls the VCL50.BPL package. The latter contains the code which enables access to many components of the Component palette, which in turn is contained in the former.

In addition to all the aforementioned packages, you can enrich the Delphi IDE by installing your custom packages and third-party packages. The Delphi DCLUSR50.BPL package is a standard container for new components.

INSTALLING COMPONENT PACKAGES

In order to install your own packages or third-party packages, do the following:

1. If you intend to install a new package, copy its files to the Delphi library directory. Make sure that you've copied all the necessary package files (those with the BPL, DCP, and DCU extensions). If you install a DCP (Delphi Package Collection) package file, then you needn't copy any other files, since a DCP file contains all the package files.
2. Select **Component/Install Packages** from the main menu, or use the **Packages** tab in the dialog for setting project options. This window can be called via the main menu by selecting **Project/Options** (Figure 4.3).
3. In the dialog, you'll see a list of all available packages. In order to install any of them, just select the check box next to the chosen package. If you later decide to remove this package from your project, simply clear the appropriate check box. To view the set of components of a given package, click the package name and then the **Components** button. Figure 4.3 shows the components included in the Borland ADO DB Components package.
4. If you choose to add a new component to this list, press the **Add** button and select the necessary package file. When a DPC file is selected, a dialog window appears for you to retrieve package files from the DPC file.
5. If you've decided to exclude any package from the list, select it and press **Remove**.

Package components are added to various tabs of the Delphi Component palette.

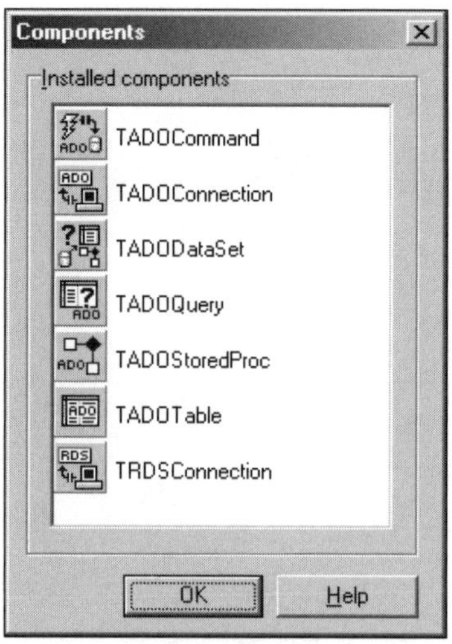

FIGURE 4.3 The window for viewing the components found in a given package.

CREATING AND EDITING PACKAGES

The process of package development involves the following stages:

- Specifying the name of a given package.
- Defining all the packages which are in any way linked to the package or required for its proper functioning.
- Listing all the unit files contained in or linked to the package. In fact, any package serves as a container for those files which are stored in it.

NOTE

For a better understanding of the following guidelines, you need to learn the basics of package architecture. This will be covered in the next section.

In order to build a new package, perform the following steps:

1. Select **File/New** from Delphi's main menu, and then click the **Package** icon (Figure 4.4).
   You'll see the generated package in the package editor window (Figure 4.5).
   This window has two sections: **Contains** and **Requires**.
2. To add a new unit to the **Contains** section, select this section and click **Add**. The **Add** window will pop-up (Figure 4.6).
   Enter the name of the PAS file that you want to include into your new package into the Unit file name field, located in the **Add Unit** tab of the **Add** dialog window. Or, alternatively, use the **Browse** button to find the required file. As a result, the chosen unit file will be added to the `Contains` section of your package.
   You can add as many units to your new package as you need by repeating these steps.
3. To add packages to the Requires section, select the section by clicking it, and then click the **Add** button.
   As soon as the dialog appears (Figure 4.7), enter the name of the DCP package file (**Package Name**) that you need for your package to function. You can also use the **Browse** button and directly specify the desired package file. Repeat this step for each package file you need to include in the `Requires` section of your package.

4. In order to determine the type for the package under design (runtime or design-time), select **Options** in the package editor window. The **Project Options** dialog will be displayed (Figure 4.8).
5. Specify the necessary type for your package by using the toggle in the **Usage Options** section.
6. Finally, compile your new package by clicking the **Compile** button in the package editor window.

An existing file can be edited in a number of ways. You can:

- Select **File/Open** from the Delphi main menu and find the file to be edited.
- Select **Component/Install Component** from the Delphi main menu, then choose the required package from the package list and click the **Edit** button.
- Find the required package in the **Requires** section in the package editor window, right-click it, and select **Open** from the pop-up menu.

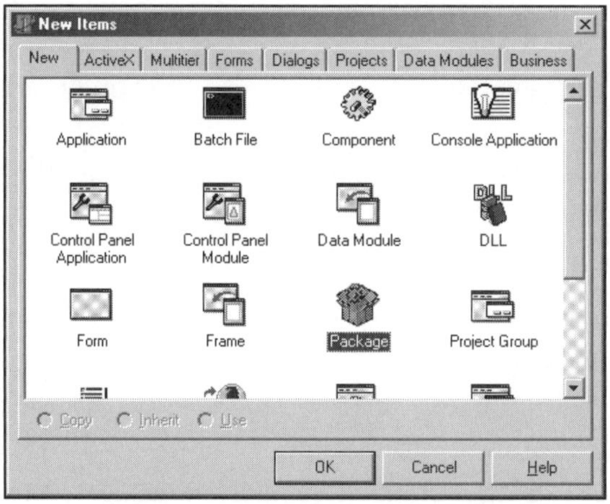

FIGURE 4.4 Click the **Package** icon in order to create a new package.

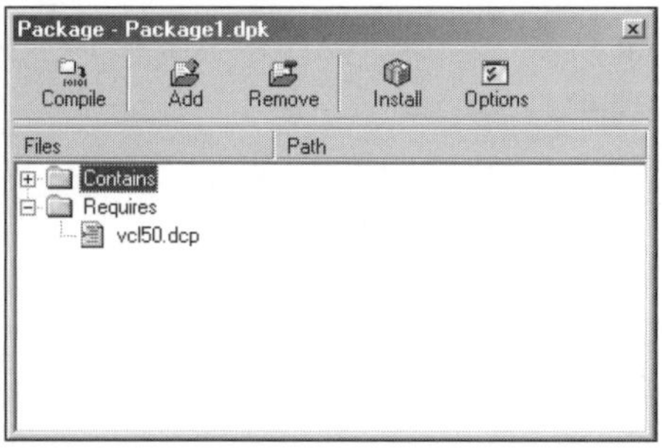

FIGURE 4.5 A sample package editor window.

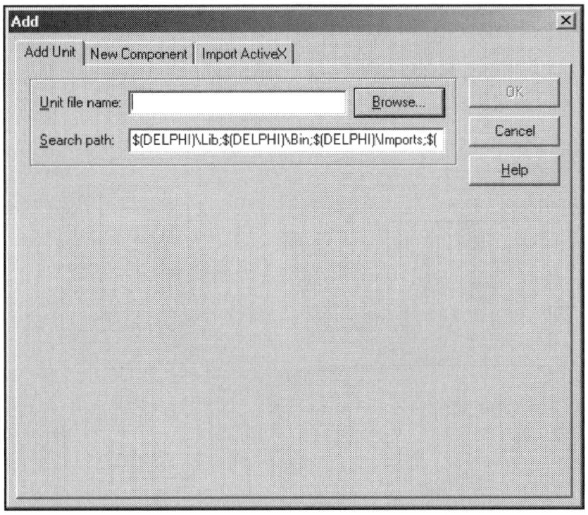

FIGURE 4.6 The dialog for adding a new unit to the **Contains** section of a package.

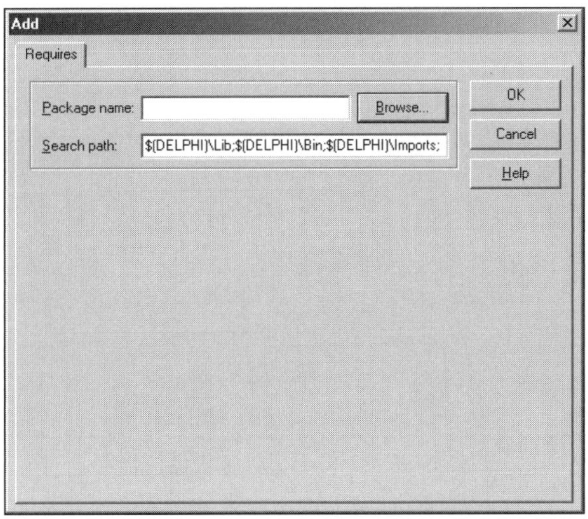

FIGURE. 4.7 A dialog for adding a new unit to the **Requires** section of a package.

You can also edit a DPK package file the same way as you do a DPR project file—that is to say, manually, as you would a text file. A package file contains three sections:

- A package name (in the `Package` section)
- The `Requires` section, which lists the files used by a given package
- The `Contains` section, which contains the names of the files that constitute a given package

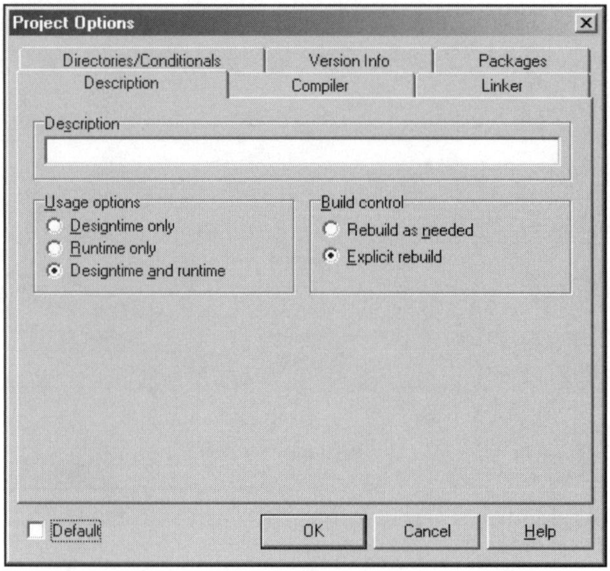

FIGURE 4.8 The **Project Options** dialog box.

For an example, let's look at the content of the VCLDB50.DPK package file:

```
package VCLDB50;

requires VCL50;

contains Db, Dbcgrids, Dbctrls, Dbgrids, Dbinpreq, Dblogdlg,
        Dbpwdlg, Dbtables, mycomponent in 'C:\components\mycomponent.pas';

end.
```

THE FUNDAMENTALS OF PACKAGE ARCHITECTURE

Now it's time to remember what you already know about packages, which will help you better understand their inner structure.

Any package consists of a name and two sections, `Requires` and `Contains`.

```
package the package name;

requires package files used by the package in its work;

contains unit files which constitute the package;

end.
```

A package name must be unique in the framework of a given project. For instance, you've named your package MyPack. The package editor creates a corresponding resource file with the MyPack.dpk name. And in the process of compilation, two more files with the MyPack.blp and MyPack.dcp names are generated.

The MyPack.bpl file is an executable file (analog to DLL), and the MyPack.dcp file is a binary file (similar to DCU).

A package name is necessary for calling it from your application or for including it into the `Requires` section of another package.

As you probably remember, the `Requires` section contains the names of those package files used by a given package. It should be noted that packages must not contain circular references—in other words, the following rules must be observed:

- A package must not reference itself.
- If `Package1` contains `Package2` in the `Requires` section, then `Package2` must not include `Package1` in its `Requires` section.
- If `Package1` needs `Package2`, and `Package2` needs `Package3`, then `Package3` must not contain `Package1` in its `Requires` section.

The `Contains` section includes the PAS or DCU unit files of a given project.

COMPILING A PACKAGE

You already know how to compile a package, but there are some details that remain to be considered.

To start, let's discuss the compiler directives that make up a package, which can be included with a DPK package file and the files of the units (Table 4.4).

TABLE 4.4 Package Compiler Directives

Directive	*Usage*
`{$IMPLICITBUILD OFF}`	Prevents package recompilation. It is used if few changes will be introduced to the package.
`{$G-}` or `{IMPORTEDDATA OFF}`	Prevents a unit placed inside a package from accessing global data in other packages. This directive is located within the unit in question. It is desirable for a given unit to be directly linked to a given application.

TABLE 4.4 Package Compiler Directives (*Continued*)

Directive	***Usage***
`{$WEAKPACKAGEUNIT ON}`	If a compiler finds this directive in a file of some unit, it doesn't include this unit in a given BPL file, but rather creates its local replica when necessary to be compiled into other applications or packages. A unit which contains such a directive is referred to as *weakly packaged.*
`{$DENYPACKAGEUNIT ON}`	Prevents unit with the directive from being placed in a package.
`{$DESIGNONLY ON}`	Compiles a package as a design time package.
`{$RUNONLY ON}`	Compiles a package as a runtime package.

NOTE

Notice that when you supply the compiled application together with all the necessary packages to your users, you have to make sure that both the application and packages have been designed using the same version of Delphi. In other words, a package designed with Delphi 6 will fail to work with an application that was developed in Delphi 5.

5 Win32 API

In order to develop increasingly powerful and sophisticated software, any programmer who designs applications to run under Windows must have a fairly good idea about the processes that take place within the operating system's framework. Understanding these processes will help him find the most appropriate and effective solutions to all the problems that inevitably arise when one develops applications closely linked to an operating system. In previous chapters you were introduced to the concepts of threads and multithreading. These concepts are intimately related to the operating system processes.

This chapter will provide you with the definitions of a kernel and an operating system kernel process. Then we will discuss the GDI and User objects. Also, you will learn how Windows manages memory and handles errors.

THE WINDOWS KERNEL OBJECTS AND PROCESSES

It should be noted that all the information provided in this chapter is pertinent only to such Windows versions as Windows 9x/2000/Me/NT, and XP; that is to say, to those versions that support 32-bit applications.

NOTE

Microsoft has developed the special Win32s package for Windows 3.1, in order to implement (with certain limitations) support of Win32 applications.

The *Windows kernel* is a part of an operating system that manages low-level functions that are essential for running applications. For example, any time an application needs additional memory, it calls on the Windows kernel.

All the aforementioned operating systems differ in a number of aspects as far as support of 32-bit applications is concerned. Table 5.1 lists some of these differences.

TABLE 5.1 Differences among some Windows Versions in their Win32 API Support

Feature	***Windows NT***	***Windows 95***	***Windows 3.1 supporting Win32***
32-bit coordinate system	Available	Not available	Not available
Asynchronous, packet-based I/O	Available	Not available	Not available
Asynchronous input	Available	Available	Not available
API multimedia	Available	Available	On the Windows 3.1 level
Multiprocessing motherboard support	Available	Not available	Not available
Dynamic Data Exchange (DDE)	Available	Available	Not available
Support of CPUs produced by other companies (i.e., not Intel)	Available	Not available	Not available
Preemptive multitasking	Available	Available	Not available
Security subsystem (C2)	Available	Not available	Not available
Shareable address space	Available	Available	Not available
TAPI (Telephone API) support	Available	Available	Not available
Threading	Available	Available	Not available
User and GDI system resources	Almost unlimited	Extended	Limited

So let's start exploring *Win32 API* (Application Programming Interface), the interface for developing 32-bit Windows applications.

Multitasking

The concept of *multitasking* refers to the capability of an operating system to process a number of concurrent applications.

> **NOTE** *Multitasking does not technically mean simultaneous processing of processes, something that none of these versions of Windows can actually do. What is really going on is switching between the processing of different tasks. But the high frequency of this switching is transparent to the user, so from the user's perspective, tasks appear to run simultaneously.*

16-bit versions of Windows and other 16-bit operating systems supported so-called *cooperative multitasking*. This type of multitasking implies that a running application "decides" whether it should pass the control to the operating system or go on with its work, monopolizing the CPU time. Other applications, which had started along with the first one, were suspended and idle. This type of multitasking too often resulted in operating systems and all the launched applications freezing if the application that monopolized all CPU resources froze.

Eventually, cooperative multitasking gave the way to preemptive multitasking. The latter became feasible only with the appearance of 32-bit operating systems. This type of multitasking means that it is the operating system that manages all of the executing of applications. The operating system allocates every application its quantum of the CPU time, depending on the priority level of a given application (*see Chapter 3*).

Windows Kernel Objects

This section deals with the objects on which Windows operates.

It is important to draw a line between Win32 objects and Delphi objects: Win32 objects fall into the following categories: Kernel, GDI, and User objects.

Processes and Threads

By the word *process*, we mean any executing Windows application. Due to its support of multitasking, Windows allows for the performance of multiple concurrent processes. Every process is allocated the appropriate address space (up to 4GB). This portion of address space contains the code of a given application, its data, and all the DLLs that it links to.

The processes themselves do not perform any tasks. Each process is made up of a number of threads which execute the code of a given application. (For a more in-depth discussion on the subject of threads, refer to *Chapter 3*.) Every process contains a *primary* or *main thread*. A process can have several threads, but only one of them will be the main thread.

A *thread* is an operating system object represented essentially by a block of code within a given process.

When an operating system creates a process, it creates the main thread of this process, which in turn can generate other threads. Win32 API manipulates processes by using special built-in functions, which are listed in Table 5.2.

TABLE 5.2 Win32 API Functions for Managing Processes

Win32 API function	***Usage***
`CreateProcess`	Creates a new process and its main thread. This function is used instead of the Windows 3.1 `WinExec` function. You can start your applications with this function.
`ExitProcess`	Terminates the process, along with all its threads.
`GetCurrentProcess`	Returns a pseudo-handle to the executing process. You can obtain the actual handle by using the `DuplicateHandle` function.
`DuplicateHandle`	Duplicates the handle of a process.
`GetCurrentProcessID`	Returns the ID of an executing process. This ID is unique to each process of an operating system.
`GetExitCodeProcess`	Obtains the exit status for a given process.
`GetPriorityClass`	Returns the priority class of a specified process.
`GetStartupInfo`	Returns the content of the `TStartupInfo` construct that is built when a process is being created.
`OpenProcess`	Returns the handle to a process based on its ID.
`SetPriorityClass`	Sets the priority level for a specified process.
`TerminateProcess`	Terminates a given process and all the threads associated with it.
`WaitForInputIdle`	Sets a given process to idle mode until an input occurs or a time-out period has ended.

Kernel Objects

By *kernel objects*, we mean all processes, threads, events, semaphores, mutexes—in short, all the objects on which the Windows kernel performs operations.

As soon as an object is created, it is allocated a portion of the address space of a given process; its handle is available to the process that opened this object. The handle in question (some sources call it a *descriptor*) is unique to this process and cannot be used by other applications to get access to a resource. But certain Win32 API functions provide a solution: they allow a process to obtain its own handle (which is different from the handle of the process that generated a given object) for this object.

Consider an example: one process creates a named or unnamed mutex and returns its handle using the `CreateMutex` command. For another process to use the same mutex, this second process needs to use the `OpenMutex` function, which returns the handle of an existing mutex.

Additionally, managing Windows kernel objects involves reference counting. When a kernel object is created and used by applications, the value of its reference counter increases. As soon as it is no longer being used, the value begins decreasing. When the reference count value reaches zero, this kernel object is destroyed.

GDI and User Objects

Windows 3.1 didn't support kernel objects. Every object of the operating system could be accessed using handles. All the objects were then subdivided into two groups: those objects that were located in the local memory of the GDI and User units, and those that were stored in the global memory.

Graphical Device Interface (GDI) is the part of Windows 3.1 that manages fonts, printer tools, and other Windows graphics subsystems. When an application displays anything on the screen, it uses GDI's services.

The *GDI object group* includes various palettes, images, fonts, etc.—in other words, all the objects that belong to the GDI domain of management.

User interface tools (User) is the part of Windows that is responsible for all windows that are created by applications.

The *User object group* is composed primarily of windows and menus.

The 16-bit Windows version provided a direct relationship between an object and its handle. Thus, that version included a table where descriptors of all the objects of the operating system were listed. This table was available to every Windows application or DLL. It was referred to as the *Local Descriptor Table*, and enabled every application (or DLL) to get access to an object used by some other application.

As for the 32-bit versions of this operating system, all the objects are stored in their own portions of the process's address space, and every process has its own local descriptor table. This means that every process in this version works with its own object handles.

All GDI and User object descriptors are managed by the corresponding Win32 API subsystems. For GDI it is GDI.EXE, and for User it is USER.EXE. These subsystems perform the functions of creating, releasing, and validating the work of all object handles.

MANAGING MEMORY IN WIN32

This section includes the details concerning managing memory in Win32 that we have not yet covered.

Virtual Memory Architecture in Windows

As stated earlier, Win32 is a 32-bit operating system. This means that every application started in Win32 can take up a portion of the address space, up to 4 GB. Every application (or operating system process) is allocated its own individual address space, which does not overlap the address space of other applications.

The process of allocating memory in Windows involves a sequence of two stages:

- Allocation of a memory segment (virtual address space) of the required size to a given application and its data: At this stage, the operating system does not allot a physical memory portion to a given application. In other words, even if you issue a command to the operating system to allocate 300 MB of address space to your application, it will still not use any system resources. You can directly specify the required addresses to the operating system, or you can rely on the OS to do it itself.

NOTE *Win32 address space allocation is implemented in 64 KB blocks. Consequently, whatever amount of memory you ask for, in reality, when it creates an address map, the operating system will grant you the first 64 KB segment of the address space. This pattern of address space mapping serves to accelerate the performance of the operating system kernel.*

- Division of the physical memory among the executing applications on the basis of the previously created virtual address space map: At this stage, the operating system provides the application with its share of physical memory, which also consists of small blocks.

NOTE *The minimum memory block that the operating system can work with is referred to as a memory page. Its size varies depending on the type of operating system. For instance, in Windows NT, a page is 8 KB; in Windows 95/98, a page is 4 KB.*

Due to the fact that the capacity of the main memory is comparatively small (in contemporary computers it is about 128–1024 MB), an operating system is forced at times, if some applications experience a shortage of memory, to use a so-called *swap file*, which is also referred to as *virtual memory*. The pattern is as follows: suppose that several applications are running simultaneously, and memory is lacking. Windows simply unloads those pages that have not been referenced for a long period of time to disk. If an application happens to need that unloaded page, Windows will release the page by again unloading another one that has not been linked to for a long time, and will load the required page from a disk in its place. After that, Windows will pass control over to the application.

All the above operations are absolutely hidden from the application. The application needn't worry about unloading/loading pages; all these tasks are performed by the operating system.

Heaps and Heap Managers

Nowadays, most sophisticated and efficient applications increasingly use the mechanisms of memory allocation and release. Commercial applications utilize a huge variety of such elements as dynamic arrays, strings, objects, etc. The point is, such elements are created very often, but are usually rather short-lived, and their size is comparatively small.

The work that is involved in allocating and releasing memory as far as small elements are concerned is apparently ineffective. First, this results in performance loss, because address space mapping and allocation of memory pages is conducted on the level of the operating system kernel. Second, large memory capacities are lost. For example, an application requires 256 B for a string and the operating system allocates one memory page (that is, 4 or 8 KB, depending on the operating system).

In order to get around the problem of allocating memory to small application elements, a new pattern was implemented whose basic underlying principle is that of a *heap*. A *heap* is a rather large, continuous memory segment in which small areas can be allotted for accommodating small elements. In order to ensure the heap's effective functioning, a so-called *heap manager* has been introduced in the operating system framework. A heap manager is essentially a mechanism that provides smoothly allocating and releasing memory segments. By default, Windows builds a heap for every newly created process. All such heaps are thread safe. Therefore, a programmer is able to reference the same heap from different threads simultaneously. You can use the following functions to work with Win32 API heap managers (Table 5.3).

TABLE 5.3 Win32 API Functions for Working with a Heap

Function	*Usage*
`HeapCreate`	Creates a heap by allocating to it a continuous segment of memory in the virtual address space of a process

TABLE 5.3 Win32 API Functions for Working with a Heap (*Continued*)

Function	*Usage*
HeapAlloc	Allocates an immovable block of memory within a given heap
HeapReAlloc	Modifies the size of the memory block that was allocated by the HeapAlloc function
HeapFree	Frees the memory block that was allocated by the HeapAlloc function
HeapDestroy	Destroys the heap created by the HeapCreate function
VirtualAlloc	Allocates pages in the virtual memory of a process
VirtualFree	Frees pages in the virtual memory of a process
VirtualLock	Protects (locks) virtual memory loaded into RAM from being swapped to disk
VirtualUnlock	Revokes the lock set by the VirtualLock function
VirtualQuery	Returns data about the range of pages in the virtual memory of the process that calls a given function
VirtualQueryEx	The same as VirtualQuery, but for a specified process
VirtualProtect	Modifies the access rights for a specified memory range in the address space of the process that calls a given function
VirtualProtectEx	The same as VirtualProtect, but for a specified process

In addition to the functions listed in Table 5.3, there are also such functions as LocalAlloc (GlobalAlloc) and LocalFree (GlobalFree). You can use any function notation, since there is no division between local and global heaps in Win32. These functions are used primarily for working with the Windows exchange buffer. These functions are out-of-date though, and so it isn't a good idea to use them.

Besides the standard Microsoft heap manager, the Delphi team has introduced a version of this utility which is supplied with Delphi. A Delphi heap manager allocates 1MB segments of virtual memory. Physical memory in Delphi is allocated in 16 KB segments. When working with a Delphi heap manager, you can use the following functions:

- **New, Dispose**: Used for allocating and releasing memory for dynamic work with application elements
- **GetMem, FreeMem**: Used for allocating and releasing memory for dynamic work with small binary memory segments (buffers, blocks, etc.)

And lastly, a programmer is always free to create his own heap manager.

Dynamic Storages

As often as not, you face the problem of accumulating incoming data. This can happen, for instance, when you perform data loading, sound recording, etc. There is no problem if you know in advance the amount of data you need to accumulate; then you just need to get a memory segment of the specified capacity ready to receive the input data. But the situation is quite different if you have no idea as to the actual amount of data you will accumulate. It is for just this purpose that *dynamic* (or *thread*) *storage* is used. This dynamic storage is implemented in Delphi in the form of dynamic arrays, the `TMemoryStream` object, and dynamic memory reallocation. The principle underlying the work of all of these types of storage is simple enough: a memory segment is allocated to receive the incoming data, and when it is full, the boundaries of the segment are moved and its size is increased.

You should remember, however, that such manipulations of the size of a memory segment within a heap are rather ineffective, in particular if the segment in question is large enough. The process of changing the size of a memory segment is system resource consuming.

HANDLING ERRORS IN WIN32

Many functions return either the `true` or the `false` value. The value indicates whether or not the function was executed successfully.

Handling Errors Using the *GetLastError* Function

If a given function has failed to execute, it returns `false`. In order to get the error code, use the `GetLastError` Win32 API function. This function is parameterless.

NOTE

Unfortunately, the `GetLastError` function does not always return the code of the error if the `false` value is returned by a function. This means that when you call the `GetLastError` function you cannot be absolutely sure that result will be useful.

Note that the error code reflects the thread where this error has occurred. For errors that took place in different threads, the `GetLastError` function will return their unique codes. This implies that you should call a given function in the same thread in which an error has occurred.

NOTE

The error codes are provided by Win32 Programmer's Reference, which is supplied with Delphi.

Take a look at the following example of utilizing the `GetLastError` function:

```
If not CreateProcess (CommandLine, nil, nil, nil, False,
        NORMAL_PRIORITY_CLASS, nil, nil, StartupInfo, ProcessInfo) then
        Raise Exception.Create ('The process creation error: ' +
                IntToStr (GetLastError));
```

This code is trying to create a process. If an error takes place, the exception will be generated that will display the error code obtained by using the `GetLastError` function.

Handling Errors Using the *SetErrorMode* Function

Some kinds of errors, such as "The device is not ready" (which occurs when you make an attempt to write to a write-protected diskette) call Windows message windows in order to inform the user that an error has occurred. Applications can specify how Windows will treat such errors by using the `SetErrorMode` function:

```
SetErrorMode (uMode);
```

You can set the `uMode` parameter of a given function to any value among those listed in Table 5.4.

TABLE 5.4 The Values of the `uMode` Parameter of the `SetErrorMode` Function

Parameter Value	*Operation*
SEM_FAILCRITICALERRORS	When this value is specified, the operating system doesn't display error messages. Instead, the OS returns the error to the process that generated it.
SEM_NOALIGNMENTFAULTEXCEPT	The value is not used by x86CPUs.
SEM_NOGPFAULTERRORBOX	This value is used during application debugging sessions. When this value is set, the operating system doesn't display general protection faults.
SEM_NOOPENFILEERRORBOX	When this value is specified, the operating system doesn't display error messages when a file to be opened isn't found. Every error is returned to the process that generated it.

Abnormal Termination of an Application

In order to ensure the termination of your application in case of emergency, use the `FatalAppExit` Win32 API function. This function displays a fatal error message and, as soon as a user has closed the window in question, the application is terminated.

NOTE

This function must be used only in case of grave emergency, when no other measures can help you correct the error. This function is dangerous because it doesn't release the system resources and memory used by the application.

PART II

Using VCL and Creating Your Own Delphi Components

6 Basic VCL Elements

This chapter will further cover Delphi components, their types and architecture, with particular emphasis on the hierarchy of Delphi visual components. The principles of the runtime type information (RTTI) model will also be briefly outlined.

COMPONENTS

Delphi components constitute an important part of the Delphi class hierarchy, which is referred to as a Visual Component Library (VCL). In spite of its name, VCL contains both visual (those that are visible at runtime) and non-visual (visible only at design time) components. For instance, such components as `TButton`, `TEdit`, and `TLabel` belong to the group of visual components, and `TTimer`, `TTable`, and `TQuery` provide examples of non-visual ones.

A *component* is a class on which you can perform various operations in the Delphi IDE. Components can be thought of as tiny "bricks" that you use to build a "house"—that is, an application.

You can organize your components in a separate tab of the Component palette, which is very convenient since you'll thus be able to get quick access to any component and place it on your form if need be.

All components vary significantly in their degree of complexity. Both simple (such as `Tlabel` and `TEdit`) and rather complex (such as a component that incorporates the capabilities of a text processor) can be successfully used for developing applications.

Efficient handling of Delphi components implies a fairly good understanding of the differences among their fundamental types, as well as of their inner structure and hierarchy. All these issues are covered in this part of the book.

COMPONENT TYPES

This book divides components into four basic types. You can use components of any of these types when you develop your applications. Moreover, you are free to create your own components of these types.

The first type are *standard components.*

Standard components contain various Windows controls. Such components as `TListView`, `TRichEdit`, `TImageList`, etc. belong to this category. All these components are located in the Win32 tab of the Delphi CComponent palette. Every one of these components is a so-called wrapper for a standard Windows control. These components enable you to easily employ Windows controls in your routines.

The second type are *custom components.*

This is the conventional name for all components that are not contained in the Delphi standard component library. Custom components are your own contribution to the existing component set. They are either created by you, or by other programmers.

NOTE

For more information on the subject of creating your own components, refer to Chapter 7.

The third type of components are *graphic components.*

Graphic components help you design visual controls that cannot be brought into input focus. Usually, components of this type are used for displaying some kind of information (both textual and graphic). Such components as `TShape`, `TLabel`, and `TImage` belong to this group.

The last type are *non-visual components.*

Non-visual components are hidden from the user at runtime. However, they also possess such characteristics as properties, methods, and events. One of the most illustrative instances of this type is represented by the `TTimer` component.

COMPONENT ARCHITECTURE

NOTE

Like other classes, components encapsulate properties, methods, events, and fields.

Let's discuss these in more detail.

Properties

The *properties* of a component enable a user to access the fields located inside this component. Properties allow you to modify component attributes by assigning to them, among other things, calculated values. A property declaration must contain the name and type of a given property, along with at least one attribute which specifies the method of accessing this property. Generally, the syntax of a property declaration looks like the following:

```
property name: type specifiers;
```

- **`name`**: Must be unique
- **`type`**: Determines what type of values can be assigned to a given property
- **`specifiers`**: Declares ways of accessing this property

As mentioned earlier, every component property must have at least one declaration of a method of accessing this property. Such specifiers are usually represented by one of the two following values: `read` or `write`. In addition, Delphi provides such optional attributes as `stored`, `default` (`nodefault`), `implements`.

Let's now take a closer look at specifiers.

The syntax of the required specifiers, `read` and `write`, looks like the following:

`read` *`field`* or *`method`*

`write` *`field`* or *`method`*

where *`field`* or *`method`* is the field from which you read (or to which you write) this property value, or the method that returns or assigns this property value, respectively.

It is quite obvious that the `read` declaration implies a readable field or a read-only method, and the `write` declaration describes a writable field or a write-only method of the property of a given component.

There are also optional specifiers that specify the methods of access, among them: `stored`, `default`, and `nodefault`.

These are referred to as stored specifiers. They don't influence the execution of any routine, but are responsible only for methods of variable storage in Delphi.

The stored specifier can assume one of two values: true or false. This specifier is used when Delphi saves the current state of a given component. Prior to saving, Delphi checks the component properties; if the property value differs from its default value while the stored specifier is set to true, then a new value of this property is saved. Otherwise (when the stored specifier is set to false) a new value is not set for this property.

Use the default specifier to set a default value for a given property.

Consider the following example of declaring a component property:

```
property MaxLength: Integer read FMaxLength write SetMaxLength default 0;
```

This example presents the declaration of a property of some component; the property has the MaxLength name, the Integer type, and is assigned the FMaxLength field value. In order to write to the FMaxLength field, you need to utilize the SetMaxLength methods. The default value is 0.

And finally, the implements specifier ensures that this property will support the interface. For instance,

```
property MyInterface: IMyInterface read FMyInterface implements
      IMyInterface;
```

The implements specifier must be the last attribute in a declaration. This specifier can contain several interfaces separated by commas. A property that has the implements specifier:

- Must be either a class or an interface
- Must not be an array
- Must have the read specifier

Property Types

It should be noted that all the Object Pascal rules for declaring types are equally applicable to properties. You should know property types of a given component primarily for displaying and editing the component in question in the Object Inspector window. The basic property types of Delphi components are listed in Table 6.1.

TABLE 6.1 Property Types

Property type	*Display of the property in the Object Inspector window*
Simple	Numerical, character, and string properties are represented as numbers, characters, and strings, respectively. A developer can edit the values of such properties directly in the **Object Inspector** window.

TABLE 6.1 Property Types (*Continued*)

Property type	***Display of the property in the Object Inspector window***
`Enumerated`	Enumerated properties (including Boolean) are represented in the **Object Inspector** window as editable strings. Besides directly entering property values, a developer can toggle the available values by double-clicking the value fields in the **Object Inspector** window, or by selecting any admissible value from the drop-down list.
`Set`	The properties of the `Set` type are represented as sets in the **Object Inspector** window. By double-clicking a property value, a developer can extend a given set and assign a Boolean value to each set element (`true` if a given element belongs to this set).
`Object`	Properties of this type often have a property editor of their own. Such properties must descend from the `TPersistent` class.
`Array`	Properties of the `Array` type must have their own property editor. Delphi's **Object Inspector** does not support editing such properties. While registering a component, a developer must also specify the property editor.

STANDARD PROPERTIES OF DELPHI COMPONENTS

This section covers the most common properties used in Delphi components.

The `Action` property specifies operations for a given control (a menu, a button, etc.). A value for such a property is set at design time by selecting the permitted actions from a drop-down list. The list in question is compiled on a form of the `TActionList` component, where its properties are also specified.

You also can set this property directly, for instance:

```
Table1.Active := true;
```

Or by calling either the `Open` (which sets the `Active` property to `true`) or the `Close` (which sets the `Active` property to `false`) method:

```
Table1.Open;
```

The `Align` property specifies the ways to be used in order to align a given component within its container component. The possible values for this property are as follows:

- **`alNone`**: The component stays at the location where it was originally placed at design time. This is the default value for the `Align` property.

- **alTop**: The component takes up the entire top part of the container component. At runtime, the width of the component is determined by the width of the container component. The height of the component is unchanged.
- **alBottom**: Similar to the `alTop` value, except that the component takes up the entire bottom part of its container component.
- **alLeft**: The component takes up the entire left part of the container component. At runtime, the height of the component depends on the height of its container component. Any changes you make to the width of the container component do not affect the width of the component; it remains constant.
- **alRight**: Like the `alLeft` value, except that the component takes up the entire right part of its container component.
- **alClient**: The component takes up the entire client part of the container component. Any changes to the width and height of the container component result in corresponding changes to the width and height of the given component. If there are other components in the client part of the container component, then the given component takes up the entire vacant part of the container component.

NOTE

The `alTop` and `alBottom` values have a higher priority level than the `alLeft` and `alRight` values. This means that if you placed two components on a form and set the `Align` property of the first component to `alTop`, and the same property of the second one to `alRight`, then the first component will supplant the top part of the second one (Figure 6.1).

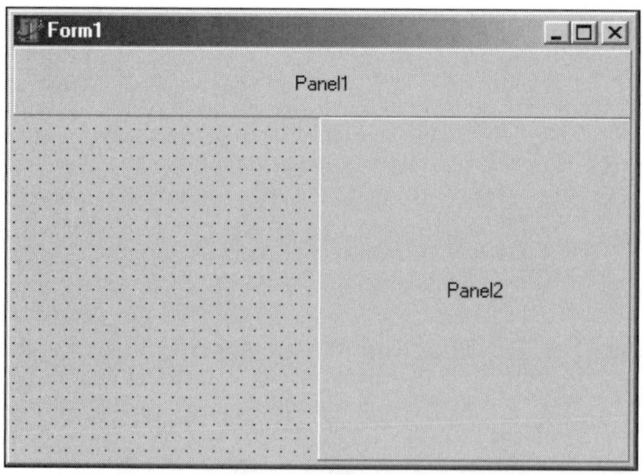

FIGURE 6.1 Using the `Align` property.

The `Anchors` property specifies the relationship between a component and its parent component when the parent component changes its size. This property was initially introduced in Delphi 4. The `Anchors` property belongs to the `Set` type; this set can contain the following elements:

- **akTop**: The component is connected to the top boundary of its parent component.
- **akLeft**: The component is connected to the left boundary of its parent component.
- **akBottom**: The component is connected to the bottom boundary of its parent component.
- **akRight**: The component is connected to the right boundary of its parent component.

If a given component is connected to opposite boundaries of its parent component, then any changes to the size of the latter will result in compression or extension of the child component respectively, up to its disappearance. Thus, this property in fact specifies the fixed distance between the component and the boundaries of its parent component.

The `AutoCalcFields` property sets the mode for automatic generation of the `OnCalcFields` event. The default value of this property is `true`. In this case, the `OnCalcField` event, which is associated with recalculating the calculated fields in data tables, is generated under the following conditions:

- When a data set is opened
- When a data set assumes the `dsEdit` state
- When the focus moves around components that contain data, or navigates along columns of the table related to data
- When any kind of record is being searched for

In order to reduce the time necessary for recalculating fields, you can set the `AutoCalcField` property to `false`.

The `AutoEnable` property allows for automatic indication of the media player buttons available in a given mode. If this property is set to `true`, then the value that was specified by the `EnabledButtons` property is ignored. Otherwise, the available buttons are defined by the `EnabledButtons` property (which will be described later in this section).

The `AutoMerge` property lets you join menus of secondary forms with the main form menu. In order to enable such an operation, set this property to `true` for all secondary forms.

> **NOTE**
>
> *The* `AutoMerge` *property is optional for an MDI application, since the menus of all forms are joined automatically in these applications.*

The `AutoOpen` property enables the automatic starting of the media player at runtime. If this property is set to `true`, the media player will open the device specified by the `DeviceType` property (to be described later in the chapter) as soon as a form has been created. If an error occurs when the device is being opened, the application generates the `EMCIDeviceError` exception. If the value of the `AutoOpen` property is `false`, use the `Open` method to open the device in question.

The `AutoSelect` property determines whether or not the text in the component is highlighted when the component is focused. Multiline editors (such as `Memo`, `RichEdit`, etc.) do not support this property. If the property is set to `true`, then the text contained in a single-string editor will be highlighted as soon as the component is focused. The `AutoSelect` property can be very handy if you are more likely to enter a new value in an edit field than edit the old one.

The `AutoSize` property enables your application to automatically set the height of an edit field depending on the font being used. If the value of this property is `true`, then the edit field automatically changes its size when you switch from one font type to another.

The `BoundsRect` property simultaneously returns the coordinates of all four vertices of a given component.

> **NOTE**
>
> *You can get these coordinates through the following component properties:* `Left` *(the leftmost boundary of a component),* `Top` *(the uppermost boundary),* `Width` *(horizontal size) and* `Height` *(vertical size). These properties will be discussed later.*

We assume that the origin of coordinates in this frame of reference coincides with the top left corner of the window containing the component.

The `Brush` property is used for reading the current color and window style values. Note that this is a read-only property. However, you can change its value by modifying the `Color` and `Style` properties.

Use the `Canvas` property for creating and modifying drawings, and handling images in many other ways. This property is supported by all the components provided with drawing surfaces.

The `Capacity` property lets you define a number of components that can be stored in a component of the `TList` class. At times, when the exceedingly big value of this property provokes a shortage of the main memory, the `EOutOfMemory` exception is generated. The `Capacity` property is very similar to the `Count` property, except for the fact that the former stores the value that indicates the number of elements that can be contained in a `TList` class instance, and the latter indicates the actual number of elements in a given component. Therefore, the value of the `Capacity` property is always greater than or equal to the value of the `Count` property. Consequently, if you need to increment the value of the `Count` property, bear in mind that the value of the `Capacity` property will also grow. This property helps you prevent memory reallocation from happening too frequently. If you force conditions where the value of the `Capacity` property is less than the value of the `Count` property, your application will generate the `EListError` exception.

The `Caption` property associates with the component a certain text string explaining this component's purpose. This string is usually the caption of the component (a button caption, a label caption, a menu item caption, etc.). The default value of this property coincides with the component name (the `Name` property). By using this property, you can create shortcuts for various menu items and buttons. In order to do this, just place an ampersand (&) before the character in the caption of a given button. For example, if you've decided to build a shortcut to the File item, you can put the & before the F character in the `Caption` property (`&File`). Note that the F character in the menu item will be underlined. Now if you need to call this item, simply press <Alt>+<F>.

The `Charset` property specifies the character set of a font you use. Every font supports one or more character sets. Table 6.2 shows some of the constants that are used by the `Charset` property.

TABLE 6.2 The Constants of Character Sets

Constant	*Numerical value*	*Character set*
ANSI_CHARSET	0	ANSI characters.
DEFAULT_CHARSET	1	A default character set. Font is selected only by name and size.
SYMBOL_CHARSET	2	A standard character set.
MAC_CHARSET	77	Macintosh characters.
GREEK_CHARSET	161	Greek characters.
RUSSIAN_CHARSET	204	Cyrillic characters.
EASTEUROPE_CHARSET	238	The set of additional characters for Eastern-European languages.
OEM_CHARSET	255	Operating system characters.

The `ClientHeight` property is used for setting or reading the height of the client area of a component. You can modify this property to change the size of a component that contains a number of other components. By doing so, you are simultaneously changing the components that constitute the container component.

Use the `ClientOrigin` property to obtain the top left screen coordinates (`x` and `y`) of the client area of a given component. The top left corner of the screen is taken for the origin of the coordinates. The coordinates are returned as a construct of the `TPoint` type. This is a read-only property.

The `ClientRect` property returns the coordinates of the corners of the component client area. This is also a read-only property. The coordinates are returned as a construct of the `TRect` type.

The `ClientWidth` property is used for setting or reading the horizontal size of the component client area.

The `ClipRect` property determines the area that allows drawing. That is, you cannot draw outside the borders of the area specified by `ClipRect`. Using this property saves time if you need to update the drawing in question.

The `Color` property specifies the background color for a given component. This property value can be expressed either numerically according to the intensity of the three primary colors (red, green and blue), or by a constant declared in Delphi (Table 6.3).

TABLE 6.3 Color Constants

Constant	***Color***
`clBlack`	Black
`clMaroon`	Maroon
`clGreen`	Green
`clOlive`	Olive
`clNavy`	Navy
`clPurple`	Purple
`clTeal`	Teal
`clGray`	Gray
`clDkGray`	Dark Gray
`clLtGray`	Light Gray
`clSilver`	Silver

TABLE 6.3 Color Constants (*Continued*)

Constant	***Color***
`clRed`	Red
`clLime`	Lime
`clBlue`	Blue
`clYellow`	Yellow
`clFuchsia`	Fuchsia
`clAqua`	Aqua
`clWhite`	White
`clBackground`	The background desktop color in Windows
`clScrollBar`	The color of scrollbars
`clActiveCaption`	The background color for the title bar in the active window
`clInactiveCaption`	The background color for the title bar in an inactive window
`clMenu`	The background color for the menu
`clWindow`	The background color for the window
`clWindowFrame`	The color of the window frame
`clMenuText`	The color of the text in a menu
`clWindowText`	The color of the text in a window
`clCaptionText`	The title bar text color in an active window
`clActiveBorder`	The border color in an active window
`clInactiveBorder`	The border color in an inactive window
`clAppWorkSpace`	The color of the application work area
`clHighlight`	The background color for highlighted text
`clHighlightText`	The color of highlighted text
`clBtnFace`	The color of a button face
`clBtnShadow`	The color of a button shadow

TABLE 6.3 Color Constants (*Continued*)

Constant	***Color***
`clGrayText`	The color of unavailable elements of a window
`clBtnText`	The color of the text of a button
`clInactiveCaptionText`	The color of the title bar text in an inactive window
`clBtnHighlight`	The color of a highlighted button
`cl3DDkShadow`	The color of the dark shadows of 3D elements in a window
`cl3DLight`	The light color that fringes 3D elements in a window
`clInfoText`	The color of information text in tooltips
`clInfoBk`	The background color for information text in tooltips

Starting with `clBackground`, the constants in Table 6.3 are determined according to the active Windows color scheme on the computer. The Windows team recommends using these colors if you develop commercial applications or an application which you intend to submit to any form of public repository.

The `CommonAVI` property specifies a standard Windows clip from the Shell32.dll file-library, for example, file copying, file searching, deleting (moving them to a trash), etc.

The `ComponentCount` property defines the number of components contained in a given container component. This is a read-only property.

The `ComponentIndex` property specifies the index (the ordinal number) of a component located in a container component.

The `Components` property stores the component array owned by a component. The `Index` parameter of this property enables you to select any component from this array using the `ComponentIndex` property of the component. The indexes are numbered beginning from zero. The number of components which constitute the array can be found by using the `ComponentCount` property.

We'll illustrate using these properties with an example. Suppose you have several components on your form, and your task is to shift all of them, except for the `Button1` component, 10 places to the right. In order to do this, you can use the following code:

```
for i := 0 to ComponentCount—1 do
if (Components[i].Name <> 'Button1') then
(Components[i] as TControl).Left:=(Components[i] as TControl).Left + 10;
```

The `ControlCount` property defines the number of child controls of a given window element. By *child* controls, we mean those controls which are located in the client area of an element and have that element declared in their `Parent` property. The `ControlCount` property is a read-only property.

The `Controls` property is an array that contains all the child components of a given element. The `Index` parameter defines the index of the corresponding component. Indexes are numbered from zero. This is a read-only property.

The `ControlState` property specifies the various conditions affecting the state of the given component instance. An example is double-clicking, or the necessity of aligning this component.

The `ControlStyle` property sets various attributes of a given component. For example, it determines if a given component can be dragged-and-dropped by a mouse, have a fixed size, etc. This property pertains not to an individual class instance, but to a whole class.

The `CopyMode` property specifies the mode of image copying when you either use the `CopyRect` method or draw an object of the `TBitmap` type. This property enables you to achieve various effects for merging images. Table 6.4 lists possible options for the `CopyMode` property.

TABLE 6.4 The Optional Values of the `CopyMode` Property

Property value	***Operations performed during copying***
`CmBlackness`	Blackens the target area to which an image is being copied. The image that was originally located in the copy target area is removed along with the source image.
`CmDstInvert`	Inverts the image that was originally located in the target area to which an image is being copied (native image). The source image being copied is not inverted and can be of any kind.
`CmMergeCopy`	Merges the source image being copied with the image that was originally located in the target area to which the copying is being done, by using the Boolean `AND` operation.
`CmMergePaint`	Merges the image that was originally located in the target area to which the copying is being done, with the inverted source image which is being copied, by using the Boolean `OR` operation.
`CmNotSrcCopy`	Places the inverted source image being copied in the target area to which the copying is being done; the image that was originally located in the target area is ignored.
`CmNotSrcErase`	Merges the source image being copied with the image that was originally located in the target area to which the copying is being done, by using the Boolean `OR` operation. The result is then inverted.

TABLE 6.4 The Optional Values of the `CopyMode` Property (*Contiuned*)

Property value	*Operations performed during copying*
`CmPatCopy`	Copies the source image template to the target area; the image that was originally located in the target area is ignored.
`CmPatInvert`	Merges the native image of the target area with the source image template using the Boolean `XOR` operation.
`CmPatPaint`	First merges the inverted source image with its template by using the Boolean `OR` operation, and after that merges the result with the native image of the target area by using the Boolean `OR` operation.
`CmSrcAnd`	Merges the native image of the target area with the source image by using the Boolean `AND` operation.
`CmSrcCopy`	Copies the source image to the target area. The native image of the target area is ignored. This is the default mode.
`CmSrcErase`	Inverts the native image of the target area to which the copying is being made with the source image, by using the Boolean `AND` operation.
`CmSrcInvert`	Merges the source image with the native image of the target area using the Boolean `XOR` operation. Repeated copying restores the original image in the target area.
`CmSrcPaint`	Merges the native image of the target area with the source image by using the Boolean `OR` operation.
`CmWhiteness`	Whitens the target area; both the native image and the source image are ignored.

Let's consider an example of using copy modes. Suppose you need first to copy some image to an area which contains its own native image, and then want to remove the copied image and restore the image that was originally in the target area. To do this, you can use the following code:

```
Image1.Canvas.CopyMode := cmSrcInvert;
Image1.Canvas.CopyRect (Rect (0,0,200,200), Image2.Canvas,
                        Rect (0,0,200,200));
Image1.Canvas.CopyRect (Rect (0,0,200,200), Image2.Canvas,
                        Rect (0,0,200,200));
```

The `Count` property is used for storing the value that indicates the number of items in a component of the `TList` class. When you add or delete items (by using the `Add` and `Delete` methods), the `Count` property value is automatically updated.

If you increment this value manually, the corresponding number of empty elements will be added to this component. You can remove empty items by invoking the `Pack` method. If you decrement the `Count` property value, the last items contained in the component are deleted.

The `Ctl3D` property determines the appearance of the component. If this property is set to `true`, the component will be displayed as three-dimensional; if the property is set to `false`, the component will be displayed as two-dimensional.

The `Cursor` property specifies the appearance of the mouse cursor when it is placed over a component. Another property, `DragCursor`, determines the appearance of the mouse cursor while dragging one component over another. Delphi has a number of built-in mouse pointers. Developers can also add their own custom pointers to the built-in ones. Table 6.5 lists the standard built-in mouse pointers.

TABLE 6.5 The Built-In Mouse Pointers

Value of the cursor property	*Mouse pointer appearance*
`crDefault`	The default pointer, often `crArrow`
`crNone`	No pointer
`crArrow`	An arrow-like pointer
`crCross`	A cross-like pointer
`crIBeam`	A pointer that looks like an uppercase 'I'
`crSizeAll`	A pointer that indicates changes in the size of a window
`crSizeNESW`	A pointer that indicates changes in the size of a window that occur in the top right or in the bottom left corner of the window
`crSizeNS`	A pointer that indicates changes in the vertical size of a window
`crSizeNWSE`	A pointer that indicates changes in the size of a window that occur in the top left or in the bottom right corner of a given window
`crSizeWE`	A pointer that indicates changes in the horizontal size of a window
`crUpArrow`	An up-arrow pointer
`crHourGlass`	An hourglass-like pointer
`crDrag`	A pointer that indicates dragging a component
`crNoDrop`	A pointer that indicates that dragging a component to a specified area is forbidden

TABLE 6.5 The Built-In Mouse Pointers (*Continued*)

Value of the cursor property	***Mouse pointer appearance***
`crHSplit`	A horizontal splitter
`crVSplit`	A vertical splitter
`crMultiDrag`	A pointer that indicates dragging multiple components
`crSQLWait`	A pointer that indicates waiting for an SQL query to be processed
`crNo`	A pointer that indicates that a specified action is forbidden
`crAppStart`	A pointer that indicates waiting for a given application to start (an arrow with hourglass)
`crHelp`	An arrow-and-question mark pointer
`crHandPoint`	A hand-like pointer

The `DesktopFont` property determines if a given component uses the current Windows font for displaying text. If the `DesktopFont` property is set to `True`, then the component uses the current Windows font for the `Font` property. The font in question is specified by the `IconFont` property of the Screen global variable. Therefore, every time you change the Windows font you are using, the `Font` property of the component will automatically change and assume a new value.

The `DeviceType` property sets the type of the multimedia device opened by the media player. The default value is `dtAutoSelect`, which means that the device type will be determined by the extension of the file indicated by the `FileName` property.

The `Display` property defines the component in a given window to be used by a multimedia device for outputting its information. This component can be a form or a panel. By default, this property is set to `nil`, which means that this device creates its own output window. For example, if you want the image to be output to `Panel1`, you can use the following code:

```
MediaPlayer1.Display := Panel1;
```

The `DragMode` property determines the behavior of the component while it is being dragged by a mouse. This property can assume one of two values: `dmAutomatic` and `dmManual`. If the first value is used, the developer is not required to process the event. He simply needs to click a given component and begin dragging. If the second value is set, dragging cannot begin until the `BeginDrag` method is called by the application.

The DrawingStyle property sets the style for a given image. This property can assume the following values:

- **dsFocused**: The image is mixed with the color specified in the BlendColor property by 25%. Setting this value influences only those images which contain masks.
- **dsSelected**: The same as dsFocused, but in this case the image is mixed by 50%
- **dsNormal**: The image is created in the color specified by the BkColor property. If BkColor is set to clNone, then the image is transparent and created using a mask.
- **dsTransparent**: The image is created by using a mask, regardless of the value of the BkColor property.

The Enabled property determines whether or not a given component will be available to a user at runtime. An unavailable component (Enabled = False) is grayed. Such a component ignores keyboard, mouse, and timer events. Use this property when you need to temporarily limit the user access to components. For example, if you want to make a button temporarily unavailable, set the Enabled property of a given button to False:

```
Button1.Enabled := False;
```

The Font property sets the font along with its attributes (size, style, color, etc.).

The GroupIndex property is used to specify the technique of merging menus.

The Handle property enables you to provide access to the handle of a window when you call Win32 API functions that require the handle in question. This is a read-only property.

NOTE

When you invoke the Handle property, your application creates the handle if it has not been created before. This means that you shouldn't call this property when you are developing a component or reading a component from a thread.

The Height property specifies the height of a given component.

The HelpContext property defines the number that is used in a pop-up menu. That is to say, you set the number of the page containing the help information that you need to display to a user when he presses <F1>.

The Hint property is used for specifying the appropriate text for a pop-up hint. It usually consists of two parts that are divided by a pipe character (|). For example:

```
Button1.Hint := "Open|Select and open an image file";
```

In this example, as soon as you place your cursor on the `Button1` button, the first part of the hint will pop up: "Open"; the second part will be displayed in the area specially used for allocating such hints, for instance, the Status bar. A developer can use only the first part of a hint, omitting the pipe character (|). Also, in order to enable this type of service, you need to first set the `ShowHint` property to `True`.

The `ImageIndex` property enables you to display image indexes shown to the left of the caption of a given menu item. The indexes are numbered starting with zero.

The `IsControl` property sets the technique of saving a given form. If this property is `True`, then only those properties that pertain to the controls are saved. If `IsControl` is set to `False`, then all the properties of a given form are saved.

The `Left` property specifies the horizontal coordinate of the top left corner of a given component. Typically, the origin coordinate for all components is the top left corner of the client area of their parent components. With forms, the origin coordinate is assumed to be the top left corner of the screen.

The `List` property provides access to the index array of an object of the `TList` type. This is a read-only property.

The `LockCount` property indicates how many times the component area for outputting images has been locked in order to prevent the overlapping which can occur due to simultaneous usage of multiple threads in a multithreaded application. This is a read-only property.

The `Mode` property specifies the mode of data transfer for importing data from one table to another. Table 6.6 shows the optional values which this property can assume.

TABLE 6.6 The Optional Values for the Mode Property

Value	*The mode of data transfer*
`batAppend`	Records are transferred from a data source to a receiver without changing the data contained in the receiver. A receiver table must exist before the transfer begins.
`batUpdate`	When records are transferred from a data source to a receiver, they replace the records in the receiver table. This means that the data that have been transferred are not appended to the existing data in the receiver, and that records in the receiver table are simply updated. A receiver table must exist before the transfer begins.
`batAppendUpdate`	As soon as data are transferred from a data source to a receiver, they update existing and add new records. A receiver table must exist and be indexed before the transfer begins.

TABLE 6.6 The Optional Values for the Mode Property (*Continued*)

Value	*The mode of data transfer*
`batDelete`	The records in a receiver table that correspond to records in a source table are deleted from the receiver. A receiver table must exist and be indexed before the transfer begins.
`batCopy`	A new copy of a source table is created. If the receiver table existed before the copying, its content is completely replaced by the content of the source table.

The `Name` property specifies the name that is to be used by other components in order to call this one; this name is also used by the developer. The name in question is set at design time and must not be changed at runtime. Although Delphi assigns default names to new components, for example: `Button1`, `Button2`, `Label1`, etc., it is recommended that you replace these default names with ones that reflect the purpose of the component.

The `Parent` property specifies the parent component of a container type that contains the given component (a parent component is not a parent object).

NOTE

It is important to recognize the crucial difference between two properties that seem to have much in common. The `Parent` property specifies the parent component in which a given component is located. The `Owner` property defines the owner of a given component—in other words, the component set as a parameter of a given component constructor and that owns a given component. For example, a form owns all the components placed on it (and is also the parent of all those components).

The `ParentCtl3D` property determines whether a given component will inherit the value of the `Ctl3D` property from its parent component.

The `ParentFont` property defines whether a given component uses the font which is used by the parent container component. For example, if a form contains a button, and the `ParentFont` property of the button is set to `true`, then the same font that is specified in the `Font` property of the form will be used in the button caption.

The `ParentShowHint` property determines whether to turn the parent `ShowHint` property on or off. This property is used for enabling or forbidding all pop-up hints within a certain form or a container component.

The `Pen` property sets the attributes for a pen that is used for drawing lines. This property belongs to the `TPen` type. The `Pen` property specifies such attributes as the width, color, and style of lines, and the mode of working with the pen.

The `PenPos` property sets the location of a pen within the drawing area. You can modify this property value by calling the `MoveTo` method and others. You can directly set a required value for this property, which is tantamount to invoking the `MoveTo` method.

The `Pitch` property sets the width value for characters of a given font. The fonts supported by Windows fall into two groups:

- Fonts with a fixed width for all characters. That is, every character has the same fixed width as all other characters.
- Fonts with a different width for different characters.

The `Pitch` property can be set to the following values:

- **`fpDefault`**: The width for a given font is set by default.
- **`fpFixed`**: The same width for all characters.
- **`fpVariable`**: A varying width for different characters.

The `Pixels` property allows you to obtain the color value for the point with coordinates `X` and `Y`, which is located within the borders of the area specified by the `ClipRect` property. If you try to perform the same operation for a point located outside the area defined by the `ClipRect` property, the `Pixels` property will return a value of `-1`.

The `ShortCut` property specifies hot key combinations employed by the user in order to accelerate access to necessary menu items.

The `ShowHint` property turns on/off the display of hints when the user places the cursor over a component. Textual contents of hints are set by using the `Hint` property.

The `Showing` property determines whether the component is currently visible to a user. The fact that the component can be hidden from view by other components is not taken into account. This is a read-only property. The `Showing` property is related to the `Visible` property. If the `Visible` property for a component and for all its parents is set to `true`, then `Showing` is also `true`. However, if the `Visible` property of the component or any one of its parents is `false`, then the value of the `Showing` property is `false`.

The `TabOrder` property is used to set the sequence of moves when navigating around the components on a form by employing the <Tab> key. The moves are numbered beginning with zero. If you give a value of `-1` to the `TabOrder` property, you will not be able to bring this component into focus by using the <Tab> key. Consider an example. Suppose you have three buttons on your form: `Button1`, `Button2` and `Button3`. In order to focus these buttons in the following order:

the Button2 button is active first, then Button1, and Button3, you have to set TabOrder for Button1 to 1, for Button2 to 0, and for Button3 to 2.

The TabStop property is used for enabling the user to focus a given component by using the <Tab> key. If the value of this property is true, then you can use the <Tab> key for focusing the component in accordance with the rotation order specified by the TabOrder property. Otherwise, if the value of the TabStop property is false, then regardless of the TabOrder property, you will be unable to perform this operation.

The Tag property's functions are defined by the programmer himself. This property is a Longint. A developer can use the Tag property as he so desires by programmatically modifying its content.

The Text property enables you to read or specify a text sting connected to a given component. This property is used for TEdit components and component lists.

The TextFlags property specifies the mode for outputting text when you use the TextOut and TextRect methods for this purpose. You can set the mode by utilizing the following constants:

- **ETO_CLIPPED**: Outputs the text located within the specified clip
- **ETO_OPAQUE**: Outputs the text with an opaque background
- **ETO_RTLREADING**: Outputs the text from right to left (only in those Windows versions which are intended for certain countries)
- **ETO_GLYPH_INDEX**: Outputs the text directly to Windows GDI. Can be used only for TrueType fonts

The Top property is used for setting or reading the value of the vertical coordinate of the top left corner of a component.

The Visible property determines whether the component is visible at runtime. If this property is set to true, the component is visible; otherwise it is invisible.

The Width property is used for setting the horizontal size of the component and for reading the current value of the component's width.

Methods

By methods we mean those procedures and functions that are encapsulated by a given object. Methods determine the behavior of a given object. In order to invoke a certain method, you need first to write the name of the object with which this method is associated, and then the name of the method itself; these names are delimited by a period. For example, the following code:

```
Button1.Click
```

calls on the Click method for Button1.

In order to create a method, you first need to declare it in a special clause in the declaration of the class or the component which owns the method in question. For instance:

```
type
  TMyComponent = class(TObject)
    ...
    procedure DoSomething;
    ...
  end;
```

In the above declaration of a new component, the `DoSomething` method is declared by using the `procedure` keyword. As soon as a new method is declared, you need to create the body of this method. You can place this procedure wherever you choose within the unit in which the component is declared. For instance:

```
procedure TMyComponent.DoSomething;
begin
     // Place the commands and statements that must execute when the
     // DoSomething method is invoked here
end;
```

Note that when you define the `DoSomething` procedure, you must specify its full name, together with the name of the component or class (`procedure TMyComponent.DoSomething;`).

Let's examine the most essential Delphi methods.

The `Add` method adds a new element to a list of components such as `TList`, `TStringList`, or `TStrings`. If the list has not been sorted, then a new element will be appended to the end of the list. If the list is sorted, then a new element will be positioned in the list according to the requirements imposed by the sorting. By calling this method, you automatically increment the value of the `Count` property of the list. At times—if the list has been sorted—the string being added is already contained in this list, and the `Duplicates` property of the list is set to `dupError`. The `EListError` exception may occur during this method's execution.

The `Arc` method is used for drawing circle and ellipse arcs on a `TCanvas`. This method uses four parameters, the coordinates of four points. The first two (`X1, Y1`) and (`X2, Y2`), define a rectangle that circumscribes a given ellipse. The third point (`X3, Y3`) sets the initial point of the arc, which is located on the linear segment of the straight line which passes through the circle (ellipse) center and the point with the coordinates (`X3, Y3`). The point with coordinates (`X4, Y4`) specifies the terminal point of the arc, which is located on the linear segment

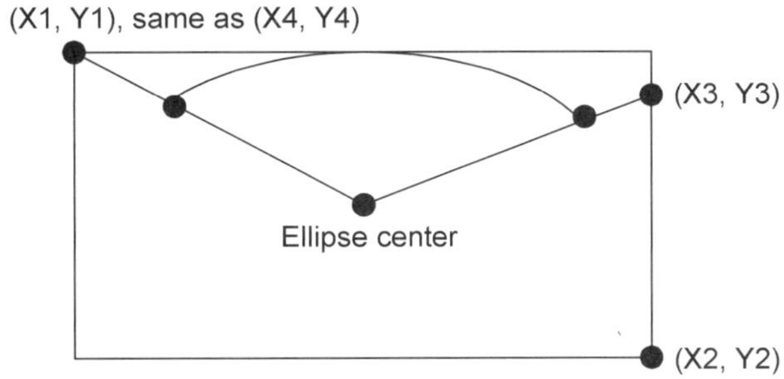

FIGURE 6.2 Setting the coordinates for points using the `Arc` method.

of the straight line that passes through the center of the circle or ellipse and the point (`X4, Y4`). An arc is drawn counterclockwise, beginning with the initial and finishing with the terminal point. Figure 6.2 shows an example of using the method.

Figure 6.2 can be illustrated by the following code where the `Arc` method is called:

```
Image1.Canvas.Arc (0,0, 200,100, 200,10, 0,0);
```

NOTE: *If you are developing an application that is to run in Windows 95, always make sure that the sum of* `X1+X2`, `Y1+Y2`, *and* `X1+X2+Y1+Y2` *do not exceed 32,768.*

The `Assign` method is used for copying data from one object to another. A distinction should be made between this method and a simple assignment—`object1 := object2`. The difference lies in the fact that when you change an assignment, the pointer to a `<target object>` begins to point to a `<source object>`. The `Assign` method, however, creates a new duplicate of the object. As soon as the `Assign` method has executed, you have two identical objects with identical properties. If these objects belong to different types, then when you call `D.Assign(S)`, the `D` type must "know" how to copy the `S` type to it (and the `S` type may know nothing about type conversion). If the `Assign` method cannot implement this type conversion, it calls on the protected `AssignTo` method, which is declared in the `TPersistent` class and reloaded to the classes that derive from `Tpersistent`. The call looks like this: `S.AssignTo(D)`. However, if the `AssignTo` method cannot implement the conversion—or if it has not been reloaded—then `AssignTo` of the `TPersistent` class is invoked and an exception is generated. The `Assign` method can be useful in various circumstances. A good example that illustrates the use of this method is copying an image from the clipboard to a graphic component, `TImage`:

```
Image1.Picture.Assign (Clipboard);
```

and back from the component to the clipboard:

```
Clipboard.Assign (Image1.Picture);
```

NOTE

If you intend on working with the clipboard, add `clipBrd` to the clause of the unit that works with `Clipboard`.

The `BeginDrag` method is called when you begin dragging a component. This method can be invoked only under the condition that the `DragMode` property of a given component is set to `dmManual`. If this property is assigned the `dmAutomatic` value, dragging is implemented automatically. The code for calling the `BeginDrag` method is usually inserted in the `OnMouseDown` event handler. The `Immediate` parameter of the `BeginDrag` method determines whether the cursor's appearance will change in the way indicated by the `DragCursor` property, and if the dragging will begin as soon as you click the component. If the `Immediate` parameter is set to `False`, dragging won't begin until a user moves the cursor the number of pixels specified in the threshold parameter after clicking a component. This is convenient if you need to process a click before starting to drag a component.

The `BringToFront` method is used for bringing components to the front, according to the so-called *Z-order*. Z-order determines the hierarchical order in which components are arranged in the `Controls` property of the parent window component (for more information, refer to the "Hierarchy of Visual Components" section in this chapter). In the case of partial or complete overlapping of components, a higher-level component (according to the Z-order) will be visible. This means that the `BringToFront` method enables you to bring to the front those components that have been hidden from view by other components. This method applies both to non-window and window components. However, according to Z-order, all the non-window components are lower than window ones, and this implies that if a non-window component is hidden from view by a window component (for instance, if an image is hidden by a component of the `TMemo` type), then invoking the `BringToFront` method for this button will produce no result.

The `BrushCopy` method is invoked in order to copy a part of a bitmap image to the output area and to replace the specified color of the image with the value assigned to the brush. This method is from previous Delphi versions, and is used only to provide compatibility with them.

The `CanFocus` method is used for determining if a given component can be brought to focus. This method returns `true` if the component and all its parents have the `Visible` and `Enabled` properties set to `true`.

The `ChangeScale` method modifies the scale of the component and its child elements. Such component properties as `Top`, `Left`, `Width`, and `Height` can be scaled by using this method. The `ChangeScale` method has two parameters that specify the scaling multiplier (m) and divider (d), respectively. Take a look at the following example. Suppose you need to double the size of the `Form1` form, and then set the scaling multiplier to 2 and the divider to 1:

```
Form1.ChangeScale (2,1);
```

Once the `ChangeScale` method has executed, the size of `Form1` will be doubled.

Conversely, in order to achieve, let's say, a threefold reduction in the size of a component, set the scaling multiplier to one and the divider to three:

```
Form1.ChangeScale (1,3);
```

The `Chord` method is used for drawing closed figures with sides of a circle/ellipse arc and a chord. The parameters of this method are identical to those of the `Arc` method. The resulting figures could look like the figures shown in Figure 6.3.

The `ClassName` method returns the name of a given component type.

The `Clear` method deletes all the elements from a list and clears all the textual content of the component.

Consider the following examples:

```
ListBox1.Clear;
```

```
Memo1.Clear;
```

The `Clear` method can also be used for the `Clipboard` object. When you call the `Clear` method for the clipboard, the method in question removes all its content.

The `Click` method calls the `OnClick` event handler for the component. This method simulates left-clicking a given object. For instance, in order to invoke the `OnClick` event handler for the `Button1` button, act as follows:

```
Button1.Click;
```

The `ClientToScreen` method converts coordinates of the client area of a given component to screen coordinates. The origin coordinate of the client area is the top left corner of this area. The origin coordinate of the screen is the top left corner of the screen. Back conversion can be done using the `ScreenToClient` method.

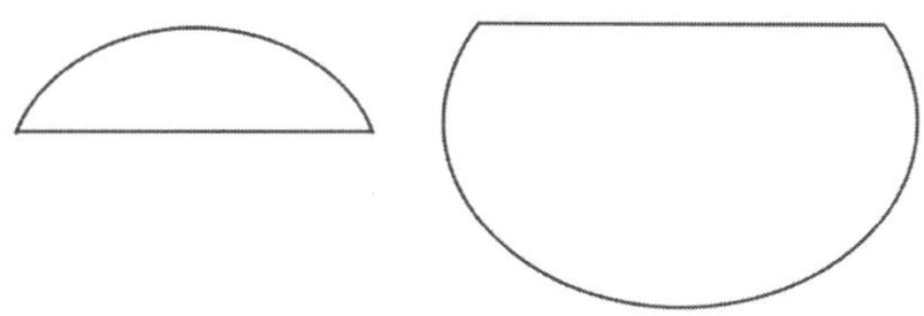

FIGURE 6.3 Using the Chord method for creating closed figures.

The `ContainsControl` method identifies whether a given component is a direct or indirect descendant of another window component. If a given component is a direct descendant, then this method returns `True`; otherwise it returns `False`.

The `ControlAtPos` method operates on window components. It is used in order to identify the child component located at the point with the coordinates specified by the `Pos` parameter. If there is no a child component at the specified position, the `ControlAtPos` method returns `nil`. The second parameter, `AllowDisabled`, determines whether the currently disabled components must be also taken into account when this method is called (property `Disabled = True`).

The `CopyRect` method is used for copying the defined rectangular area of a given image to some other area. The copying is implemented in the same mode that is set by the `CopyMode` property.

The `Delete` method is used for such components as `TList`, `TStringList`, `Tstrings`, and `TMenuItem`. This method is invoked in order to delete an element from a given list. `Delete` has a parameter that indicates the index of the item which is to be deleted. All elements are numbered beginning with zero. When you delete a menu item that contains a submenu, the submenu in question is also deleted.

> **NOTE** *Notice that as soon as you remove an element from a list, the list is immediately rearranged. That is to say, if you delete the third element, the fourth element will be put into the vacated place. Thanks to this feature, there are no gaps in lists.*

The `Destroy` method calls the appropriate destructor for a given object. In other words, by invoking this method, you destroy the object and release the memory that was allocated to this object.

> **NOTE** *Avoid overusing the `Destroy` method if you need to delete objects. It makes more sense to use the `Free` method for this purpose, which prior to calling the `Destroy` method checks whether the memory allocated to the object has already been freed. Moreover, the `Free` method generates a more compact code. In order to destroy forms, use the `Release` method.*

The `DisableAlign` method temporarily disables aligning the child components of a window component. The reverse operation can be performed by using the `EnableAlign` method.

The `Dormant` method creates a bitmap in the main memory in order to release the map descriptor. This method ensures more effective use of the GDI resources utilized by an application. Consider an example (Listing 6.1).

LISTING 6.1

```
// Load the image to Bitmap1
Bitmap1.LoadFromFile ('mypicture.bmp');
// Copy to Bitmap2 from Bitmap1
Bitmap2.Assign (Bitmap1);
// Invoke the Dormant method and release GDI resources
Bitmap2.Dormant;
```

The `Draw` method is used for drawing an image stored in an object characterized by the `Graphic` parameter in the area specified by the `X` and `Y` coordinates. The picture can be represented either in the form of a bitmap, an icon, or a metafile. For example:

```
Image1.Canvas.Draw (10, 10, Image2.Picture.Bitmap);
```

Now you have copied the picture stored in `Image2` to the canvas of `Image1`, which is specified by the coordinates `10`, `10`.

The `DrawFocusRect` method draws rectangles using the Boolean `XOR` operation. This means that when you repeatedly try to draw the same rectangle in the same area, the former rectangle will be deleted. For example:

```
Image1.Canvas.DrawFocusRect (Rect (0,0,30,30);
```

The `Ellipse` method helps you draw a circle or ellipse. Its parameters, (`X1`, `Y1`) and (`X2`, `Y2`), specify the rectangle that circumscribes a given ellipse.

The `Error` method raises an exception when you work with an object of the `TList` type. This method is more efficient than the `Raise` command. The following code illustrates how you can use `Error`:

```
List.Error ('An error in the %u element of List', I);
```

Once this code is processed, a message will be generated informing you that an error has occurred in one of the list elements.

The `Exchange` method switches the places of two list elements. The positions of these elements are defined by the `Index1` and `Index2` parameters respectively.

NOTE

Never use the `Exchange` method for files that have been sorted. By doing so, you could break the ordering in these lists.

The `Expand` method serves to enlarge the capacity of a list of the `TList` type. Calling this method provides the additional memory allocation necessary for appending new items to a given list. If the list in question is not full at the moment of this method's invocation, the capacity is not changed; otherwise, it increases.

The `FillRect` method fills the specified canvas rectangle with the color indicated by the value of the `Brush` property. For example, execution of the following code will result in filling the whole `Image1` canvas with the background color defined by the `Brush` property:

```
with Image1.Canvas do
 FillRect (Rect (0, 0, Width, Height));
```

The `FindNextControl` method is used in order to determine the child window component that immediately follows the component specified by the `CurControl` parameter, in accordance with the tabulation order. If the parameter is not a child element of the given window component, then the method returns the element which comes first in the tabulation order. The second parameter, `GoForward`, indicates the search direction. If this parameter is set to `true`, the next component is searched for; otherwise, the previous component is returned. Another parameter, `CheckTabStop`, indicates whether the components that have their `TabStop` property set to `false` will also be taken into account in the process of searching. If this parameter is set to `true`, then such components are ignored. If not, they are also included in the search. Finally, the last parameter, `CheckParent`, determines whether only those components which directly descend from a given window component are to be searched for. If this parameter is set to `false`, then all elements are considered indiscriminately; otherwise, only direct descendants are included in the search.

The `First` method returns the first element of a list of the `TList` class.

The `FloodFill` method is used for flood filling an arbitrarily formed, closed area of a canvas with the current `Brush`. This method uses parameters which set the initial point for flood filling, the color, and the filling style. The initial (`X`, `Y`) point must be located within the borders of the area that is to be flood filled. The rest of the parameters specify the borders of this area. The `Color` parameter sets the color which serves as the boundary of the area to be filled. The `FillStyle` parameter can assume one of two values. If it is set to `fsSurface`, then only the area colored with the `Color` color is flood filled, and the rest will not be filled. If the `FillStyle` parameter is set to `fsBorder`, then the area that is able to contain color is filled with any color except for the one indicated by `Color`, which is used only for the border of the area.

The `Focused` method lets you learn whether a given window component is currently activated. This method returns `True` if the window component is currently focused; otherwise the method returns `False`.

The `FrameRect` method draws a rectangular frame on a canvas. This method uses the current `Brush` settings. The frame is one pixel thick. The area within this frame is left colorless. By way of example, let's consider a codc that draws a rcd rectangular frame on the canvas of the `Image1` component:

```
with Image1.Canvas do begin
  Brush.Color := clRed;
  FrameRect ( Rect (10,10,150,100));
end;
```

The `Free` method invokes the destructor for a given object. This method also checks whether the memory allocated to a given object has already been freed, after which it calls the `Destroy` method.

The `GetTabOrderList` method builds a `TList` list of child window components arranged in tabulation order. The `TabStop` property value is ignored. This list includes both direct and indirect child components.

The `HandleAllocated` method shows whether the component has a handle, and if so, the `HandleAllocated` method returns `True`. This method is very handy if you need to know if a component has a handle. Directly checking the `Handle` property results in creating a window handle.

The `HandleNeeded` method creates a window handle for a component that hasn't had one before. When it is invoked, the method begins by calling the `CreateHandle` method for a parent component, and after that proceeds with creating a handle for a given component.

The `Hide` method makes the component invisible. Using this method is tantamount to the executing the command

```
Component.Visible := false;
```

If this component is a window component and contains other components, then all the components contained in it also become invisible.

NOTE

Although a component is invisible, its properties and methods remain available to the user.

The `IndexOf` method indicates the index of the first occurrence of a given element in a `TList` component. If no such element has been found in the list, the method returns `-1`.

The `Insert` method inserts a new list element into the position specified by the only parameter of this method: `Index`. As soon as a new element has been inserted, the rest of the elements in the list are rearranged (their indexes are increased by one). If an attempt is made to insert a new element into a list that has already been sorted, the `EListError` exception is generated. In this case, it is preferable to use the `Add` method.

The `Invalidate` method allows you to completely update or redraw a component if visual changes have occurred in it.

The `Last` method returns the value of the last index of a `TList` list that is equal to a `-1` value for the `Count` property.

The `LineTo` method is used for drawing a straight line on the canvas of a given object. The initial point of such a line coincides with the current pen position (`PenPos`), and the terminal point is specified by the (`X,Y`) parameter.

The `Lock` method is used for locking the canvas of a given component and for preventing all other threads of a multithreaded application from drawing on this canvas. The reverse operation is implemented through the `Unlock` method. Multiple use of the `Lock` method results in increasing the `LockCount` property's value, which records the number of locks. As far as other threads are concerned, the canvas will become unavailable until locking is completely revoked. If you don't want to implement multiple locking, use the `TryLock` method. Locking the canvas may produce the side effect of an overall performance loss.

The `Move` method moves a list element from the position set by the `CurIndex` parameter to the position specified by the `NewIndex` parameter.

The `MoveTo` method moves the pen from its the current position (`PenPos`) to the position specified by the (`X, Y`) parameters. This operation does not produce any drawing. This method is analogous to setting the pen coordinates through the `PenPos` property.

The `OpenBit` method returns the index of the first element of a `TBits` array that has the `false` value.

The `Pack` method deletes all the elements with the `nil` value from a `TList` list. Once the deletion is completed, all the rest of the elements in the list are assigned new indexes.

The `Pie` method draws a closed segment of a circle or ellipse. The parameters used by this method are similar to those of the `Arc` method. The result of using the `Pie` method may look like the figures shown in Figure 6.4.

The `Polygon` method creates a polygon by using the point set specified by the `Points` array as the basis; the first point of this array is linked to the last one, after which the whole polygon is filled with the color determined by `Brush`. For example:

```
Image1.Canvas.Polygon ( [ Point (10, 10), Point (30,10),
                          Point (130, 30), Point (240, 120) ]);
```

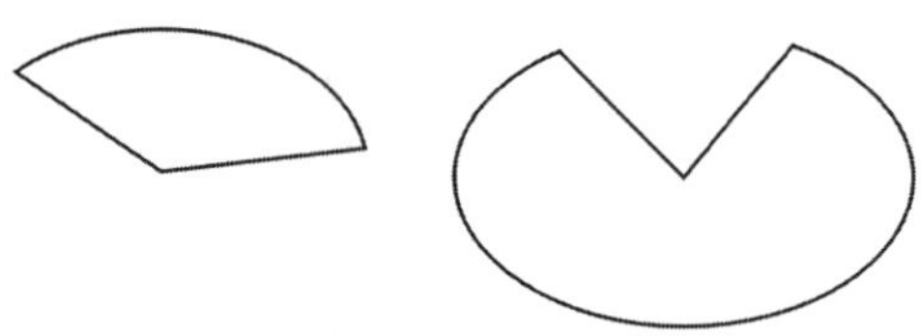

FIGURE 6.4 Using the `Pie` method for drawing figures.

This code draws a filled rectangle with the directly specified coordinates on the canvas of the Image1 component.

The PolyLine method draws an open polygon (that is to say, a polygon line). The fundamental difference between this method and Polygon is that PolyLine does not connect the first and the last points of the Points array.

The Rectangle method draws a rectangle in compliance with the specified coordinates of the top left and bottom right corner. The rectangle is created using the current Pen, and is filled with the color determined by the Brush property.

NOTE: *Use the FillRect method if you need to create a frameless rectangle; in order to draw a rectangle with rounded corners, utilize the RoundRect method. Finally, you also can invoke the FrameRect method if you wish to get an unfilled rectangle.*

The Refresh method implements an immediate update of a given image. This method calls on the Repaint method.

The Remove method removes the element whose value is equal to the value of the Item parameter from a TList list. You will find this method useful when you don't know the index of the element which you intend to delete, but know this element's value. Otherwise, you can invoke the Delete method.

The Repaint method repaints an image of a given component. This method can be used as an alternative to the Refresh method. The Repaint method calls the Invalidate method first, and then the Update method.

The RoundRect method creates rectangles with rounded corners. Such a rectangle is filled with the color set by the Brush property. Two parameters, (X1, Y1) and (X2, Y2), specify the coordinates of this rectangle's corners (just as we saw in the Rectangle method). Two more parameters, X3 and Y3, define the major and minor axial diameters of a given ellipse. The corners of this rectangle are rounded using this ellipse.

The SaveToClipboardFormat method copies an image with the Windows Clipboard format and places the copy on the Windows clipboard. However, there is an easier way to place an image on the clipboard: use the Assign method.

The ScreenToClient method converts screen coordinates into coordinates of the client area of a given component.

The ScrollBy method enables scrolling of the content of a given window component (including all its child components). Two parameters, DeltaX and DeltaY, specify the horizontal and vertical shift, respectively. Positive values indicate right and downward scrolling, and negative values show left and upward scrolling. For instance, the following code shifts the content of Form1 10 pixels to the left:

```
Form1.ScrollBy (-10, 0);
```

The `SelectFirst` method brings focus to the component first in the tabulation order. For example, the code

```
Form1.SelectFirst;
```

will select for `Form1` the first component in the tabulation order.

The `SelectNext` method brings focus to the component that immediately follows in the tabulation order the component specified by the `CurControl` parameter. The second parameter, `GoForward`, sets the direction of the search. If it has a value of `True`, a forward search is implemented; otherwise, the search is backward. The last parameter, `CheckTabStop`, determines whether the `TabStop` property of the next component should be set to `True`.

The `SendCancelMode` method cancels the modal state of a given component. The *modal state* is the state of a component when it is waiting for the user's action—and until this action occurs, no other application component is available. The `SendCancelMode` method revokes this state of waiting for the user's action.

The `SendToBack` method places the specified component at the bottom of the Z-order. This implies that this component can become invisible because it may be hidden by other components. If this component has been focused before, it will lose it as soon as you invoke this method.

The `SetBounds` method enables you to simultaneously modify four properties of a given component: `Left`, `Top`, `Width`, and `Height`. The corresponding parameters are as follows: `ALeft`, `ATop`, `AWidth` and `AHeight`. Using this method helps you make the code in your application more compact. In addition, this method involves only one refreshing of an image as opposed to four such operations that would be necessary should you change every property separately.

The `SetChildOrder` method is used to change the position of the component defined by the `Child` parameter in the list of child components of a given window component. The component is assigned a new index indicated by the `Order` parameter. For example:

```
Form1.SetChildOrder (Button1, 5);
```

This code places `Button1` at the sixth position (beginning with zero) in the list of child components of `Form1`.

The `SetFocus` method brings focus to a given component, for example:

```
Memo1.SetFocus;
```

The `SetZOrder` method positions a given component at the top or bottom of the Z-order. If its `TopMost` parameter is set to `True`, the component is moved to the top of the Z-order; otherwise it is put on the bottom.

The `Show` method makes an invisible component visible. This means that this method is similar to setting the `Visible` property to `True`.

The `Sort` method provides a QuickSort for elements of a `TList` list.

The `StretchDraw` method is used for drawing an image contained in the component specified by the `Graphic` parameter within the rectangular area on a canvas—which is in turn set by the `Rect` parameter—by stretching or compressing the image, depending on the size of a given rectangle. For example, the following code reduces the image contained in the `Image2` component and with a size of more than 20 × 20 pixels, to the required size of 20 × 20 pixels, and places it into the `Image1`component:

```
Image1.Canvas.StretchDraw ( Rect (0,0,19,19), Image2.Picture.Bitmap);
```

The `TextExtent` method allows you to determine the width and height of the `Text` that you intend to output to the canvas of a given component by using the current font. Values that are returned by this method have the `TSize` type.

The `TextHeight` method returns the value of the length of the `Text` that you intend to output to the canvas of a given component by using the current font.

The `TextOut` method outputs a text string indicated by the `Text` parameter to a canvas at the position with the (`X, Y`) coordinates. For instance:

```
Image1.Canvas.TextOut (10, 100, 'I like Delphi');
```

This code will output the "I like Delphi" string to the canvas of the component, beginning with the point (10, 100).

The `TextRect` method is similar to `TextOut`, except that text that goes beyond the borders of the specified rectangular area is cut off.

The `TextWidth` method returns the width of `Text` (which is to be output to a component canvas by using the current font) in pixels.

The `TryLock` method locks the canvas of a given component and forbids all other threads to use this canvas for drawing. This method returns `True` and sets the `LockCount` property to `1` if the canvas has not been locked before. Otherwise, if it has, the method returns `False` and the `LockCount` value is not incremented.

The `Unlock` method unlocks the canvas of a given component. Every time you call this method, the value of the `LockCount` property decrements by one.

The `Update` method provides immediate updating of a component without waiting for other processes to be completed.

Fields

The data contained in a component (or class) is represented in the form of *fields*. A field can be thought of as a variable that is declared inside a component or class. For instance:

```
type
  TMyComponent = class
  private
```

```
        FMyField1: char;
        FMyField2: real;
        FMyField3: string;
        FMyField4: boolean;
    end;
```

In this code, four fields are being declared inside the `TmyComponent` declaration: `FMyField1`, `FMyField2`, `FMyField3`, and `FMyField4`, and each of these fields has a different type. Fields can belong to the same type as normal variables.

NOTE

All descendants of a given component (class) inherit all the fields of their ancestor class. In the preceding example, the `TMyComponent` component will contain all the fields of its ancestor: the basic `TObject` class, and, in addition to them, four new fields that were discussed earlier. Keep in mind that you cannot delete or redeclare fields inherited from an ancestor class. This means that the more ancestors a given component has, the more fields it contains.

Events

It is safe to say that every single aspect of Windows programming in one way or another deals with events. Examples of events are numerous: moving a mouse, pressing a key, clicking, closing a window, etc. A programmer needs simply to capture these events and create methods that will execute when a particular event takes place.

An event is a mechanism that links an occurrence with a particular piece of code referred to as an *event handler.*

Let's consider a simple case of an occurrence: clicking a button on a form. From the programmer's point of view, an event is just a name associated with the occurrence—in this example it is `OnClick`–which in turn is related to the event handler. For example, `Button1` owns the `OnClick` method. By default, Delphi generates the event handler—the `Button1Click` method associated with the `OnClick` event. The programmer has to add the code that should execute as soon as you press `Button1` inside the `Button1Click` method.

Let's now consider a rather simple schematic diagram that illustrates the stages of processing events (Figure 6.5).

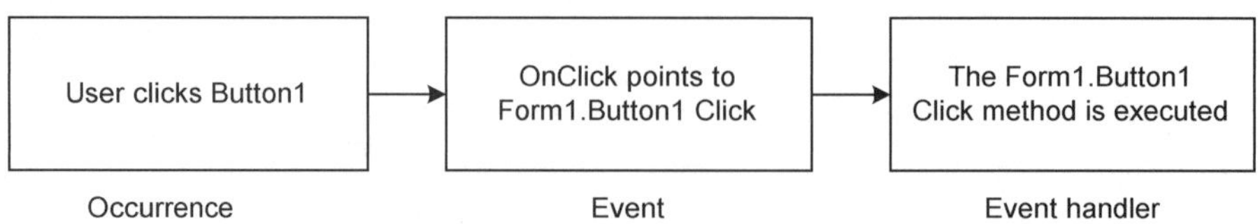

FIGURE 6.5 The stages of processing events.

Standard Events

This section covers the standard events processed by a Delphi compiler. First, take a look at the list of standard events:

- OnChange
- OnClick
- OnDblClick
- OnDragDrop
- OnDragOver
- OnEndDrag
- OnEnter
- OnExit
- OnKeyDown
- OnKeyPress
- OnKeyUp
- OnMouseDown
- OnMouseMove
- OnMouseUp
- OnPaint
- OnProgress
- OnStartDrag

Now we'll discuss all of these events in more detail.

The `OnChange` event occurs after any graphic object has been modified. Create the handler for such an event, which performs certain operations as soon as changes have been introduced to a graphic object.

The `OnClick` event occurs if a user left-clicks a component and lets the mouse button go while the mouse cursor is still pointing to this component. Besides this, the `OnClick` event is also generated in a number of cases:

- When a user selects an element from a grid, tree, list or drop-down list using the cursor control keys.
- If a user presses the spacebar or the <Enter> key at the moment a component (for example, a button) is focused (`Button1.Focused = True`).
- If a user presses the <Enter> key and a given form has the default button.
- If a user presses the <Esc> key and a given form has a cancel button.
- If a user presses any of the shortcut keys (hot keys) in order to access a button or a menu item. For example, say the `Caption` property of a button is set to the `&Start` value, and the caption on the button itself looks like this: Start. This means that as soon as a user presses the <Alt>+<S> combination, the `OnClick` event occurs.
- When the `Checked` property of `RadioButton` is set to `true`.
- When the `Checked` property of `CheckBox` is changed by an application.
- When the `Click` method of a menu element is invoked.

With forms, the `OnClick` event is generated when a user clicks any free space (a space not occupied by components) within a given form.

The `OnDblClick` event is generated when a user double-clicks a component and lets the mouse button go after the second click.

NOTE

Remember that you should not write both event handlers—`OnClick` *and* `OnDblClick`*—for the same component, because the* `OnClick` *event handler always "catches" the first click. The* `OnDblClick` *event handler will also be called, but seldom will there be a need for the two event handlers when the user was trying to do one thing.*

The `OnStartDrag` event occurs when a user begins dragging a component; that is, when he presses the mouse button and, while holding it down, begins moving the mouse cursor. This event has the `Sender` parameter, which specifies the name of the component to be dragged or, if the component in question belongs to a container type, the one that contains the object that must be dragged.

The `OnDragDrop` event takes place when a user drops an object that has been dragged over another component. The event handler for `OnDragDrop` must contain the code that determines the operations that are to be performed as soon as the object being dragged has been dropped. The `Source` parameter indicates the object being dragged, and the `Sender` parameter specifies the component over which the first object will be dropped. Two more parameters, `X` and `Y`, allow you to store the coordinates of the mouse cursor when it is located over a given component. It is assumed that the frame of reference corresponds to the frame of reference of the client part of a component.

The `OnDragOver` event occurs when the object being dragged crosses the boundary of a given component and is positioned over it. This means that this event is generated throughout the time a user is moving an object over the receiver component. As soon as the user drops the object (releases the left mouse button), the `OnDragDrop` event that we discussed earlier occurs. Use the `Accept` parameter to specify which types of objects that can be accepted by a particular component. If the component can accept any kind of components, then the `OnDragOver` event handler can be left empty, but must be present in any case. Consider an example:

```
procedure TForm1.ListBox2DragOver(Sender, Source: TObject; X, Y: Integer;
  State: TDragState; var Accept: Boolean);
begin
// This comment is included so that the compiler doesn't remove
// this empty handler
end;
```

When you are dragging a component, the appearance of the mouse cursor can change. This ability is provided by the `DragCursor` property of the component to which the other component will be dragged.

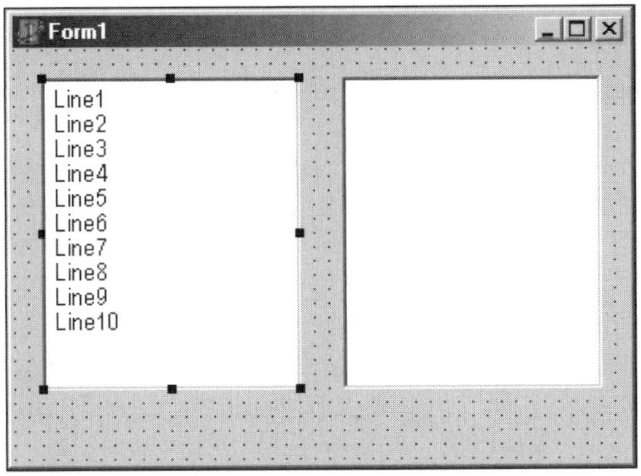

FIGURE 6.6 Using the `OnDragDrop` and `OnDragOver` events.

The following is a simple example of using the `OnDragDrop` and `OnDragOver` events.

In order to visually illustrate how the `OnDragDrop` event is used, let's create an application that allows for dragging items from one list to another. To start, place two listboxes on a form: `ListBox1` and `ListBox2`. Add ten items to `ListBox1` by editing its `Items` property, and name these items `Item 1...Item 10` (Figure 6.6).

Let's now proceed with dragging the items from `ListBox1` to `ListBox2`. First, change the value of the `DragMode` property of `ListBox1` to `dmAutomatic` in order to enable dragging to start automatically. Then, write the `OnDragOver` event handler for `ListBox2` (Listing 6.2).

LISTING 6.2

```
procedure TForm1.ListBox2DragOver(Sender, Source: TObject; X, Y: Integer;
  State: TDragState; var Accept: Boolean);
begin
   Accept := Source is TListBox;
end;
```

The code of this event handler indicates that `TListBox` components can be dragged onto the `ListBox2` component. Now write the following code in the `OnDragDrop` event handler:

LISTING 6.3

```
procedure TForm1.ListBox2DragDrop(Sender, Source: TObject; X, Y: Integer);
begin
   ListBox2.Items.Add(ListBox1.Items[ListBox1.ItemIndex]);
end;
```

By performing the operations in Listing 6.3, you are inserting the selected item of the `ListBox1` component into the `ListBox2` component.

That's it! Now you can start your application and test your code by trying to drag any item from the first list to the second.

The last event that should be mentioned in relation to processing the dragging of one component onto another is the `OnEndDrag` event. This event occurs every time the process of dragging is finished regardless of whether the process was successful or not (when a component is dropped over a form or component that is unable to accept it). This event is generated for the component that is being dragged. The `OnEndDrag` event can be used when you need to provide a response from your application concerning the result of dragging (such messages as "Successfully performed" or "Failed"). This event handler has two parameters: `Sender` (indicates the object being dragged) and `Target` (can assume either the value of the receiver component, if the dragging was successfully completed, or `nil` if the dragging failed). Consider the following example (Listing 6.4).

LISTING 6.4

```
procedure TForm1.Component1EndDrag(Sender,
                              Target: TObject; X, Y: Integer);
begin
 If Target = Nil
  then ShowMessage('Moving the '+
                  (Sender as TControl).Name +
                  ' object was unsuccessful')
  else
     ShowMessage((Sender as TControl).Name +
                 ' has been moved to '
                 + (Target as TControl).Name);
end;
```

Let's insert the code from Listing 6.3 in the above application. This code should be appended to the `OnEndDrag` event handler for `ListBox1`. Now your resulting code ensures that the message window shown in Figure 6.7 will appear every time dragging an item from the first list to the second is successful. Otherwise, if the dragging has failed, the message window shown in Figure 6.8 will be displayed.

The `OnEnter` event occurs when a given component is focused. This event is not generated when you switch from one form of an application to another, or from one application to another. When you toggle from one container component (a component that can contain other components) to another, the `OnEnter` event occurs first for the container component, and after that is generated for a component stored in this container component.

`OnExit` is the event that is the opposite of the `OnEnter` event. It occurs when a component loses its focus; that is, when another component is focused. Like `OnEnter`, this event is not generated when a user switches between forms or applications. But the difference between these events is that `OnExit` occurs first for a component stored in a container component, and only after that is it generated for the container component itself.

Let's discuss an example of handling the `OnEnter` and `OnExit` events. Let's begin by placing `Button1` and a group of radio buttons, `RadioGroup1`, in a form (Figure 6.9). After that, we'll add several items to `RadioGroup1` (by editing its `Items` property).

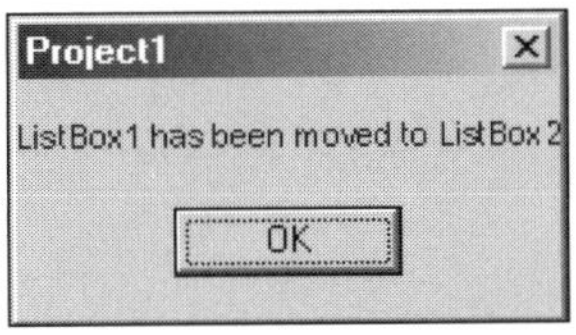

FIGURE 6.7 The message window displayed if dragging an item from `ListBox1` to `ListBox2` was successfully completed.

FIGURE 6.8 The message window displayed if dragging an item from `ListBox1` to `ListBox2` failed.

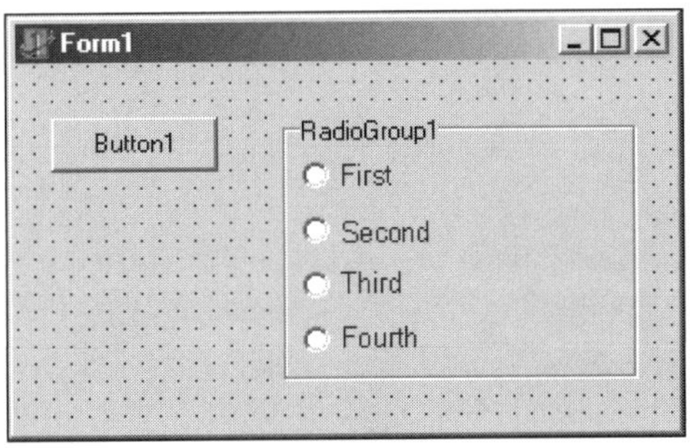

FIGURE 6.9 Handling of the `OnEnter` and `OnExit` events.

The next step is to start the application. At startup, the component placed first on a given form (in this example it is `Button1`) will be brought into focus. If you now select any radio button from `RadioGroup1` by clicking it, the result will be as follows:

- The `OnExit` event will occur for `Button1`.
- The `OnEnter` event will occur for `RadioGroup1`.
- Finally, the `OnEnter` event will occur for the selected radio button.

If you now select `Button1` by clicking it, the sequence of events will be as presented here:

- The `OnExit` event will occur for the active radio button.
- The `OnExit` event will occur for `RadioGroup1`.
- The `OnEnter` event will occur for `Button1`.

The `OnKeyDown` event is generated when a user presses any key. This event pertains to the component that is focused at the moment of pressing the key. By using this event, you can process all keys, including such special keys as <Shift>, <Alt>, and <Ctrl>. The `OnKeyDown` event handler, in addition to the `Sender` parameter, must contain such parameters as `Key` and `Shift`. The `Key` parameter indicates the key that is being pressed. If the key in question is not a character/number key, then the virtual code of a given key is assigned to this parameter. The table of key codes is given in Table 6.6.

TABLE 6.6 Key Codes

Key	*Decimal number*	*Hexadecimal number*	*Symbolic name*
<F1>	112	70	VK_F1
<F2>	113	71	VK_F2
<F3>	114	72	VK_F3
<F4>	115	73	VK_F4
<F5>	116	74	VK_F5
<F6>	117	75	VK_F6
<F7>	118	76	VK_F7
<F8>	119	77	VK_F8
<F9>	120	78	VK_F9

TABLE 6.6 Key Codes (*Continued*)

Key	*Decimal number*	*Hexadecimal number*	*Symbolic name*
<F10>	121	79	VK_F10
<Space>	32	20	VK_SPACE
<Backspace>	8	8	VK_BACK
<Tab>	9	9	VK_TAB
<Enter>	13	0D	VK_RETURN
<Shift>	16	10	VK_SHIFT
<Ctrl>	17	11	VK_CONTROL
<Alt>	18	12	VK_MENU
<CapsLock>	20	14	VK_CAPITAL
<Esc>	27	1B	VK_ESCAPE
<Insert>	45	2D	VK_INSERT
<PageUp>	33	21	VK_PRIOR
<PageDown>	34	22	VK_NEXT
<End>	35	23	VK_END
<Home>	36	24	VK_HOME
<LeftArrow >	37	25	VK_LEFT
<UpArrow >	38	26	VK_UP
<RightArrow >	39	27	VK_RIGHT
<DownArrow >	40	28	VK_DOWN
<Delete>	46	2E	VK_DELETE
<PrintScreen>	44	2C	VK_SNAPSHOT
<ScrollLock>	145	91	VK_SCROLL
<Pause>	19	13	VK_PAUSE
<NumLock>	144	90	VK_NUMLOCK
On a Numeric Keypad When the NumLock Mode Is Inactive			
<0>	96	60	VK_NUMPAD0
<1>	97	61	VK_NUMPAD1
<2>	98	62	VK_NUMPAD2

TABLE 6.6 Key Codes (*Continued*)

Key	*Decimal number*	*Hexadecimal number*	*Symbolic name*
<3>	99	63	VK_NUMPAD3
<4>	100	64	VK_NUMPAD4
<5>	101	65	VK_NUMPAD5
<6>	102	66	VK_NUMPAD6
<7>	103	67	VK_NUMPAD7
<8>	104	68	VK_NUMPAD8
<9>	105	69	VK_NUMPAD9
<*>	106	6A	VK_MULTIPLY
<+>	107	6B	VK_ADD
<->	109	6D	VK_SUBTRACT
<.>	110	6E	VK_DECIMAL
</>	111	6F	VK_DIVIDE

These codes are case insensitive, and are also insensitive to the keyboard layout pattern. The parameter can either be empty or contain the following elements:

- **`ssShift`**: When the <Shift> key is held down
- **`ssAlt`**: When the <Alt> key is held down
- **`ssCtrl`**: When the <Ctrl> key is held down

Let's consider an example of using the `OnKeyDown` event. Suppose you need to detect when a user will press the <Ctrl>+<Shift>+<L> shortcut key. Write the following code in the `OnKeyDown` event handler:

```
if ((Key = ord ('L')) and (ssShift in Shift) and (ssCtrl in Shift))
   then ShowMessage ('The key combination <Ctrl>+<Shift>+<L> has been pressed');
```

In this example, we used the `ord ()` function, which enables you to obtain the key code through the key character (in the preceding example, this operation was performed with the <L> key). From this point on, every time the component associated with a given event handler is focused, and a user presses <Ctrl>+<Shift>+<L>, the following window will be displayed (Figure 6.10).

FIGURE 6.10 The window that appears when the `OnKeyDown` event is being processed.

The `OnKeyPress` event is generated when a user presses a character key. This event has the `Key` parameter of the `Char` type, which contains the character of a given key. Keep in mind that there are uppercase and lowercase characters, as well as different keyboard layout patterns.

The `OnKeyUp` event is generated when a user releases any key that has been held down. This event enables you to process all keys (in a manner similar to the one used by the `OnKeyDown` event). Its parameters and behavior are also analogous to those of the `OnKeyDown` event.

The `OnMouseDown` event occurs if a user clicks a mouse button at the moment when the mouse cursor is pointing to a component. This event has four parameters: `Button`, `Shift`, `X`, and `Y`. The `Button` parameter defines which mouse button is being pressed:

- **`mbLeft`**: The left button
- **`mbMiddle`**: The middle button
- **`mbRight`**: The right button

The `Shift` parameter is analogous to the `Shift` parameter of the events associated with handling a keyboard. This implies that you are able to process both the clicking of any mouse button at the same time as pressing the <Shift>, <Ctrl>, or <Alt> key.

The `X` and `Y` parameters contain the coordinates of the mouse pointer within the component area.

The `OnMouseUp` event occurs when a user releases any mouse button over a component. The parameters and functionality of this event are similar to those of the `OnMouseDown` event.

The `OnMouseMove` event is generated when a mouse pointer is moving over a component, regardless of whether or not a mouse button is being pressed.

NOTE

The `OnMouseMove` event is not generated if the left mouse button is pressed before moving over the component. The reason for this is that when you press the left button and then move over a control you would be processing the `OnDragOver` event. This peculiarity for some reason is not mentioned in the documentation on the subject.

The parameters of this event, `Shift`, `X`, and `Y`, are analogous to the parameters of other events discussed earlier.

The `OnPaint` event occurs when an application receives a Windows message about the necessity of repainting a damaged image. An image can be damaged as a consequence of overlapping windows of one or several different applications. A programmer must include the procedure that provides image repainting into the `OnPaint` event handler. For example, if an image stored in the `BitMap` component is placed on a form, you can use the following `OnPaint` event handler to repaint this image:

```
Canvas.Draw (0, 0, BitMap);
```

The `OnProgress` event is generated when slow and lengthy processes that somehow affect a given image take place. This event enables you to create indicators which will inform you as to how a given process is progressing. The `OnProgress` event has the following parameters: `Stage`, `PercentDone`, `RedrawNow`, `R`, and `Msg`. The `Stage` parameter specifies the current stage of a given process (starting, running, ending) and can assume the `psStarting`, `psRunning` and `psEnding` values, respectively. The `PercentDone` parameter indicates the percentage of work done. The `RedrawNow` parameter determines whether a given image can currently be successfully displayed on a screen. The `R` parameter specifies the area that has been changed and needs repainting. And finally, the `Msg` parameter is responsible for displaying messages that reflect the progress of a given process. This parameter has a string type, and can be left empty.

HIERARCHY OF VISUAL COMPONENTS

This section covers the hierarchical structure of Delphi classes, of which VCL forms a part (Figure 6.11).

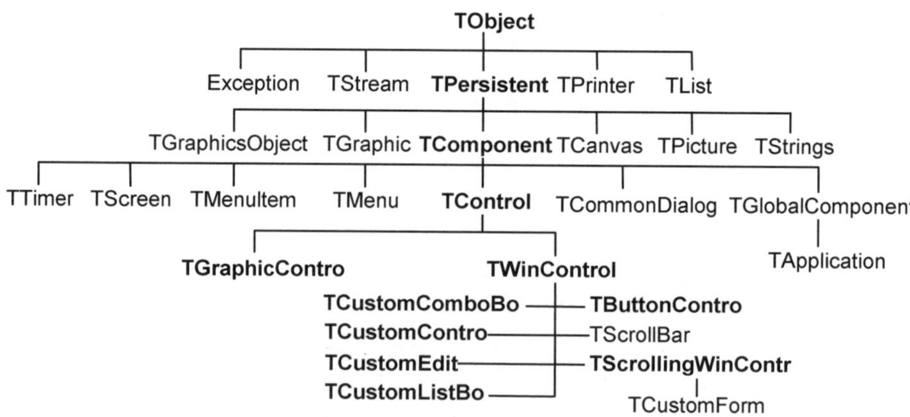

FIGURE 6.11 The hierarchy of Delphi classes.

As you probably remember, all classes and components are either direct or indirect descendants of the `TObject` class. The class encapsulates a rather compact set of the methods common to all classes:

- The capability to create, support, and destroy class instances, and accompany these processes by allocating, initializing, and releasing main memory for a given class instance
- The capability to provide information on a class instance and on a runtime type (RTTI)
- Support of message processing
- Support of interfaces that implement a class instance

The next base class, which descends directly from `TObject`, is the `TPersistent` class. This class is the ancestor for all classes designed for handling threads. The `TPersistent` class inherits all the properties and methods of its ancestor, the `TObject` class, and in addition, it can read data from a thread and write it to a thread. The `TPersistent` class provides:

- Specifying procedures for loading and placing data into a thread
- Setting the properties of a given class instance
- Tools for passing the content of one class instance to another

The `TPersistent` class is the ancestor of the `TComponent` class, which is the base class for all Delphi VCL components. All descendants of the `TComponent` class take after their ancestor as far as the following capabilities are concerned:

- They can be placed in the Delphi Component palette and on a form.
- They can own and manage other components.
- They can be converted to ActiveX controls or COM objects by using the appropriate wizard.

The next class, a descendant of the `TComponent` class, is `TControl`. This class is the base class for all *visual components*, which means that this class's descendants will be visible and available to the user at runtime. All classes that descend from the `TControl` class have the properties, methods, and events inherent to this class and that determine the behavior of all its instances: how a component is positioned on a screen, its size, etc.

We now have just two more classes to discuss—those which descend from `TControl`.

The first of them, the `TGraphicControl` class, is used for creating those visual components that are not windows, which implies that such components cannot contain other components or get input focus. The main purpose of this class is to display graphics or text on a component. Among the descendants of `TGraphicControl` are such components as `TBevel`, `TImage`, `TSpeedButton`, etc. They inherit the `Canvas` property from the `TGraphicControl` class, which allows for accessing the canvas of a given component in order to draw or write on it. Additionally, all descendants of the `TGraphicControl` class inherit the `Paint` method from it. Due to the fact that a graphic component that descends from the `TGraphicControl` class doesn't need a Windows window handle, it doesn't require many resources, and working with a graphic component is far less time consuming than performing the same operations using a window component.

The second class, `TWinControl`, is the base class for all *visual components of a window type.* A visual window component is a component that:

- Can get input focus while the application is running.
- Can contain other components. A component that contains other components is referred to as a *parent* component. A component that is contained inside another component is called a *child* component.
- Has a *Windows window handle.* Every window component is processed directly by the operating system, and therefore requires a unique handle.

Among this type of component we can include those like `TButtonControl`, `TCustomEdit`, etc.

RUNTIME TYPE INFORMATION (RTTI)

Runtime type information (RTTI) is the Delphi functionality that provides applications with necessary information on objects at runtime. Due to the fact that all Delphi objects are descendants of the same `TObject` class, each of them contains a pointer to type information, as well as the methods for handling this information. Several such methods are listed in Table 6.7.

TABLE 6.7 Methods for Handling RTTI

Method name	*Type of the returned result*	*Result*
`ClassInfo`	`Pointer`	A pointer to information on the type of a given object
`ClassName`	`String`	The name of an object class
`ClassParent`	`Tclass`	The class of an ancestor object
`ClassType`	`Tclass`	An object type

TABLE 6.7 Methods for Handling RTTI (*Continued*)

Method name	*Type of the returned result*	*Result*
`InheritsFrom`	`Boolean`	Does the object descend from a given class
`InstanceSize`	`Word`	The size of the object as a class instance, in bytes

Delphi processes type information using two basic statements: `is` and `as`. The former is utilized when you need to compare types, and the latter allows for converting runtime types.

Runtime type information enables Delphi to determine the type of an object which is presently being handled by a given application. Let's see how RTTI can be put to use. First, let's place a number of various components on a new form. Suppose that you need to ensure that at some specific moment during runtime, all the buttons on a given form must be deactivated. This problem can be solved by moving through a list of all the components on the form, learning their types, and if a component has the `TButton` type, set its `Enabled` property to `false`. The code for this is given in Listing 6.5.

LISTING 6.5

```
for i:=0 to ComponentCount-1 do
  if Components[i] is TButton then
     TButton(Components[i]).Enabled:=false;
```

In Listing 6.5, the `is` operator was used to specify the type of the component. Now let's take a look how the `as` operator can be utilized. The code presented in Listing 6.6 deactivates all the components that descend from a common ancestor: `TControl`.

LISTING 6.6

```
for i:=0 to ComponentCount-1 do
  (if Components[i] is TButton then (Components[i] as
     TButton).Enabled:=false;
```

7 Introduction to Component Building

This chapter introduces you to the creative process of designing your own components. Various techniques that can be employed for creating new components will be discussed. Specifically, this chapter focuses on building non-visual components.

FUNDAMENTALS OF COMPONENT BUILDING

Now it's time to begin creating your own visual and non-visual components. If you intend to design a component of your own, you obviously need to have an idea of Delphi's VCL and of the component hierarchy. Both these issues have been discussed earlier in this book. You might want to know why we need to create new components. New components are a way to reuse code for a variety of different purposes, including the following:

- To develop a new user interface for subsequent use in other applications
- To create a radically new class which neither Delphi VCL nor the ActiveX control set contains
- To simplify the code in our applications

- To share our components with fellow programmers
- To master Delphi, and also to gain insight into the elusive subtleties of the art of programming

You will undoubtedly be able to add many of your own reasons to the list. The process of creating components is by no means more difficult than the process of developing new applications. Certainly, it all depends on the degree of complexity of your future component. If you have already resolved to build a new component, you should perform the following tasks:

- Determine the operations that must be performed by your component.
- Produce a brief algorithm of your component's future performance.
- Break the architecture of your component into several independent parts.
- Ensure that your new component will be an open system—that is, that it allows for further modifications and enhancement (it is very likely that you will want to create descendant components for it in the future).
- Write the code for your new component. This stage involves the following steps:
  - Select the ancestor for your component.
  - Create the shell (unit) for your component.
  - Develop the properties, methods, and events for your component.
  - Debug and test.
  - Register your new component in the Delphi environment.
  - Create a help file for your component.

These stages will be elaborated on in subsequent sections.

SELECTING THE ANCESTOR FOR YOUR COMPONENT

You have already familiarized yourself with the standard classes included in Delphi VCL. Also, you already have an idea about the base classes from which your new component can be derived (*see Chapter 6*). These base classes are listed in Table 7.1.

TABLE 7.1 Basic VCL Classes

Class	*Functionality*
`TObject`	The classes that have this class as their ancestor are not components. The `TObject` class is used for creating those objects which will become ancestors for other components.
`TComponent`	This class is used for building non-visual components.

TABLE 7.1 Basic VCL Classes (*Continued*)

Class	*Functionality*
`TGraphicControl`	This class is used for creating non-window-type components—that is, those components without window handles. Descendants of this class are placed in the client area of their parent components and do not need system resources.
`TWinControl`	This class is used for creating components with window handles. These components are of the window type and can contain other components.
`TCustomControl`	This class descends from the `TWinControl` class, and has features beyond those of `TWinControl` such as an output area (a canvas). `TCustomControl` also has a new method: Paint. This class is recommended for building components of a window type.
`TCustomClassName`	VCL includes a number of classes with properties that are not declared as `published`; that is, these properties are not available from other units. However, it is possible to build their descendant classes and declare the properties in question in these new classes. Therefore, a developer is able to create several identical classes on the basis of a single `ClassName` ancestor class and declare the necessary properties from the set of predefined ones.
`TComponentName`	This class allows for creating descendant components derived from the usual Delphi VCL components or classes. This means that if a developer needs to enhance the capabilities of any Delphi component, he can use this class.

Note that in order to correctly choose the ancestor class for your future component, you must be familiar with the potentialities of existing Delphi classes.

CREATING A SHELL FOR A NEW COMPONENT

Now that you've chosen the ancestor class for the component under design, you can set to work building the unit for your component. Building a unit can be begin by calling the Delphi component wizard dialog. You can call this window through the Component/New Component command of the Delphi main menu. Figure 7.1 depicts the dialog in question.

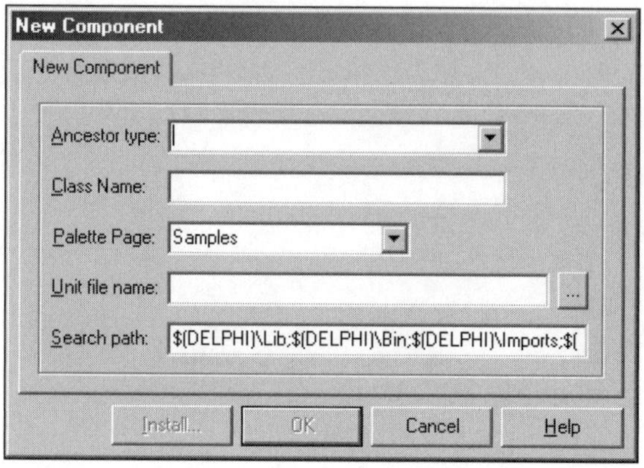

FIGURE 7.1 The Delphi component wizard dialog.

Let's take a closer look at the window in Figure 7.1. The **Ancestor type** field is used for entering the ancestor class from which a new component will be derived. This field contains all the registered VCL classes in its drop-down list. Suppose you need to create a component which descends from `TButton`. Select the `TButton` class from the drop-down list. The **Class Name** field is designed for entering the name of a new class. Let's make it the `TMyButton` class in this example. Note that, by default, Delphi fills this field with the name of the ancestor class and adds an ordering number to this name (in this example it will be `TButton1`). Another field, **Palette Page**, indicates the tab of the Component palette where this new component will be placed as soon as it is registered. Let's leave the `Samples` value provided by Delphi by default in this field. The next two fields, **Unit file name** and **Search path**, are filled by Delphi automatically, but the developer is free to change this data as he chooses. We will not do this in this example, so leave the records as they are. The resulting window should look something like Figure 7.2.

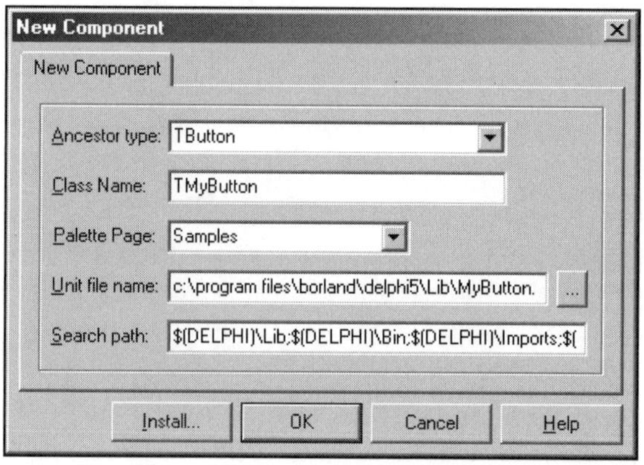

FIGURE 7.2 Filling in the fields in the component wizard dialog.

Once you've filled in all the fields, click OK, and Delphi will automatically create the "skeleton" which is eventually to become your new component unit. Your sample unit shell is represented in Listing 7.1.

LISTING 7.1

```
unit MyButton;
interface
uses
  Windows, Messages, SysUtils, Classes, Graphics, Controls, Forms, Dialogs,
  StdCtrls;
type
  TMyButton = class(TButton)
  private
    {Private declarations}
  protected
    {Protected declarations}
  public
    {Public declarations}
  published
    {Published declarations}
end;
procedure Register;
implementation
procedure Register;
begin
  RegisterComponents('Samples', [TMyButton]);
end;
end.
```

Now you have the shell for your new component ready. This shell contains no new properties, methods, or events for the component under design. It should be noted that this component already owns all the properties, methods, and events declared for the `TButton` class. The Object Oriented Programming section in *Chapter 1* provided you with a brief overview of the fundamental stages involved in creating a new class. That same section discussed the fundamental types of properties owned by a class. Next we will cover the fundamental types of component methods.

All methods fall into one of four major categories: *static methods*, *virtual methods*, *dynamic methods*, and *message methods*. By default, a method is assigned the static type.

STATIC METHODS

Static methods are, in fact, just ordinary Delphi functions and procedures. The address of any such method is known to Delphi at the compilation stage, so Delphi can call a static method at runtime. Static methods execute faster than all other types of methods, but they cannot be *overloaded.*

Overload of a method means that a given class or a component can contain several methods with the same name but with different lists of parameters.

A static method can be declared in the following way:

```
type
  TComponent = class
    procedure MyProcedure;
end;
```

In this example, the `MyProcedure` method is a static method. Here we omitted the name of the basic `TObject` class which must follow the `class` word. By default, a compiler creates the descendants of the `TObject` class.

VIRTUAL METHODS

As opposed to static methods, virtual methods support overload. That's why invoking such methods in the Delphi environment is a far more complicated task (because you don't know in advance the address of a given method). Delphi solves this problem by building a virtual method table. This allows a compiler to identify the address of a given method at runtime. This table includes the virtual methods of both a class (or component) and this class' (component's) ancestors. Quite naturally, storing such tables requires extra memory, but virtual methods can be accessed faster than dynamic methods.

A declaration of a virtual method may look like the following:

```
type
  TComponent = class
    procedure MyProcedure; virtual;
end;
```

In this case the `MyProcedure` method is a virtual method.

DYNAMIC METHODS

Similar to virtual methods, dynamic methods can also be overloaded. These types of methods vary in the technique best for calling them. As stated earlier, a virtual method table is built for virtual methods; every dynamic method is assigned its own unique numerical index. After that, this index, along with the method address, is placed in a dynamic method list. Another difference between virtual and dynamic methods is that a dynamic method list contains only the methods of a given component or class (and does not include its ancestors' methods). This feature certainly helps to save memory, but it also makes using dynamic methods far more time consuming, because you usually have to look through a number of dynamic method tables in order to find the required address.

A declaration of a dynamic method may look like the following:

```
type
  TComponent = class
procedure MyProcedure; dynamic;
end;
```

Message Methods

Unlike other methods, message methods are not called directly from a routine. This type of method is used to implement a certain operation in response to a Windows message. Look at the following sample declaration of a message method:

```
type
  TComponent = class
procedure MyProcedure(Var A: TMessage); message WM_MESSAGEWINDOWS;
end;
```

The `message` keyword is followed by a value that specifies the Windows message (in this case it is `WM_MESSAGEWINDOWS`), in response to which the `MyProcedure` method will be invoked.

Virtual and dynamic methods can be *overridden* or *abstract.*

OVERRIDDEN METHODS

The concept of *overriding* in relation to methods implies modification of the methods that have been inherited by a descendant component (or class) from its ancestor component (class). As mentioned before, only virtual and dynamic methods can be overridden. Consider the following example:

```
type
  TComponentChild = class (TComponentParent)
```

```
procedure MyProcVirtual; override;
procedure MyProcDynamic; override;
end;
```

By putting the `override` keyword immediately after the method name, you can replace the original method inherited from the ancestor component with the method of a descendant component. This override operation is implemented directly in the virtual method table (or the dynamic method list). By using the `virtual` or `dynamic` keywords in the place of the `override` keyword, you will simply create a new method instead of overriding the old one.

The override operation cannot be applied to static methods; if you try to override a static method with a new one, this ancestor method will simply be changed in the descendant component.

ABSTRACT METHODS

Virtual and dynamic methods can be abstract. By abstract methods we mean those methods which are declared in a class (or component) declaration, but do not contain any operations and can never be invoked. Such methods are used only in ancestor classes (components). A declaration of an abstract method looks like the following:

```
procedure MyProcedure; virtual; abstract;
```

NOTE

Never call abstract methods, because they do not contain any commands that can execute. If you invoke an abstract method, the `EAbstractError` *exception will be generated.*

For more information on creating properties, methods, and events for your new components, refer to *Chapter 8*.

8 Building Components

In this chapter, you will learn how to furnish the shell unit of your new component with various necessary features such as properties, methods, and events. You will see how to create a workable component and register it with Delphi. Also, we'll discuss the problem of adding a help section to your component, which may come in handy if you mean to distribute your components among fellow programmers. Lastly, you will learn to modify the components stored in Delphi VCL.

ADDING PROPERTIES TO A COMPONENT

Adding properties to a component is surprisingly easy. You need just to specify certain fields and properties and declare their types and attributes, such as how to access (read/write) them. Listing 8.1 presents an example of a simple code that sets the properties for a new component.

LISTING 8.1

```
TMyButton = class(TButton)
  private
    {Private declarations}
    FMyCount: Integer;
```

```
      FStringOfText: String;
    protected
      {Protected declarations}
    public
      {Public declarations}
    published
      {Published declarations}
      property MyCount: Integer read FMyCount write FMyCount;
      property StringOfText: String read FStringOfText write FStringOfText;
  end;
```

In the Listing 8.1, two new fields and two new properties are being added to the `TMyButton` component—one of the `Integer` type, and the other the `String` type. For the sake of simplicity, the values of these properties are read and written to fields with the same name. Setting these properties guarantees that you will be able to access them in the **Object Inspector** window (due to the declaration of these properties in the `published` section) without writing some additional methods for accessing the properties in question.

NOTE

By convention, the names of fields are prefixed with the letter `F`, and the names of components and objects begin with the letter `T` (type).

Adding Enumerated Properties to a Component

By enumerated properties, we mean the properties of a component which, once you begin to edit them in the **Object Inspector** window, call a drop-down list that contains a number of possible values for a given property. Among the enumerated properties are those such as `Align`, `BorderStyle`, `Color`, etc. If you've decided to add your own enumerated property to a component, you first need to specify the desired enumerated type, for example:

```
TMyEnumType = (eFirst, eSecond, eThird);
```

After that, define the field of the component that will contain a value of the enumerated type and then declare the property. The sample code in Listing 8.2 illustrates adding a new enumerated type to the `TMyButton` component.

LISTING 8.2

```
type
  TMyEnumType = (eFirst, eSecond, eThird);
  TMyButton = class(TButton)
  private
    {Private declarations}
    FMyEnum: TMyEnumType;
  protected
    {Protected declarations}
  public
    {Public declarations}
  published
    {Published declarations}
    property MyEnumProp: TMyEnumType read FMyEnum write FMyEnum;
  end;
```

Now as soon as you try to change the `MyEnumProp` property in the Object Inspector window, you'll get a drop-down list with three items in it: `eFirst`, `eSecond`, and `eThird` (Figure 8.1).

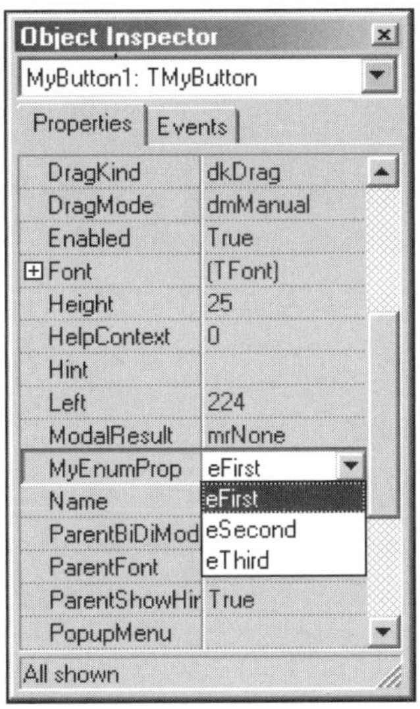

FIGURE 8.1 Adding the enumerated `MyEnumProp` property to the new `TMyButton` component.

Adding Set-Properties to a Component

Object Pascal often deals with the `Set` type, and a number of properties of Delphi components are of this type as well. When you handle a property of the `Set` type, remember that every element of a set represents an individual property that has its own logical type in the **Object Inspector** window.

To add a new set-property, begin by setting the desired type:

```
TMySetTypeFirst = (poFirst, poSecond, poThird);
TMySetType = set of TMySetTypeFirst;
```

The first string sets the enumerating `TMySetTypeFirst` type that specifies the range of the future set, and the second string defines the `TMySetType` set itself.

Let's consider an example of adding a set-property to a component, which is demonstrated by the code in Listing 8.3.

LISTING 8.3

```
type
  TMyEnumType = (eFirst, eSecond, eThird);
  TMySetTypeFirst = (poFirst, poSecond, poThird);
  TMySetType = set of TMySetTypeFirst;
type
  TMyButton = class(TButton)
  private
    {Private declarations}
    FMyEnum: TMyEnumType;
    FMyOptions: TMySetType;
  protected
    {Protected declarations}
  public
    {Public declarations}
  published
    {Published declarations}
    property MyEnumProp: TMyEnumType read FMyEnum write FMyEnum;
    property MyOptions: TMySetType read FMyOptions write FMyOptions;
  end;
```

For convenience' sake, the declaration of the enumeration is preserved in the `TMyButton` component.

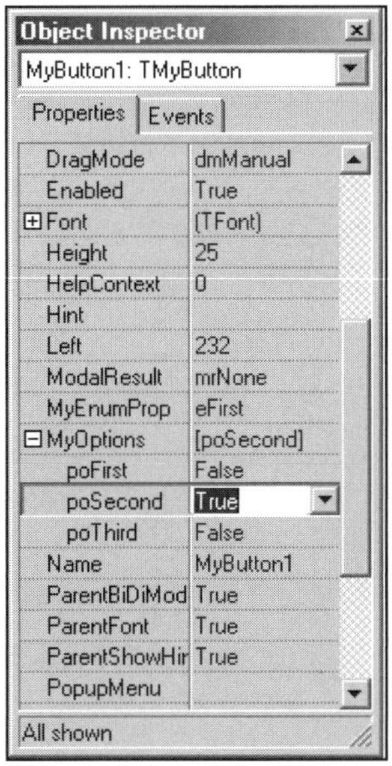

FIGURE 8.2 Adding the `MyOptions` set-property to the `TMyButton` component.

As a result, your new set-property will be displayed in the Object Inspector window as shown in Figure 8.2.

Adding Object-Properties to a Component

Any component can contain an object-property. Object-properties can be by any Delphi component or object. Additionally, object-properties of a new component can be new components or objects that you yourself have created. Make sure, however, that your custom objects meet the condition imposed on all object properties: they must descend from the `TPersistent` class. This is necessary in order that the properties of an object that in turn is acting as a property of a component can be displayed in the Object Inspector window. Let's take a look at an example of creating an object-property for your `TMyButton` component.

To begin, let's build a random new object that will be a direct descendant of the `TPersistent` class (Listing 8.4).

LISTING 8.4

```
type
  TMyObject = class (TPersistent)
  private
    {Private declarations}
    FProperty1: Real;
```

```
    FProperty2: Char;
  protected
    {Protected declarations}
  public
    {Public declarations}
    procedure Assign (Source: TPersistent); override;
  published
    {Published declarations}
    property Property1: Real read FProperty1 write FProperty1;
    property Property2: Char read FProperty2 write FProperty2;
end;
```

The `TPersistent` class and any of its descendants can act as an ancestor for a new class. In the Listing 8.4, a new class, `TmyObject`, is being created. This new class contains two simple properties, `Property1` and `Property2`. In addition, this new object contains a procedure used for providing correct access to the property of your future component, `TMyButton`. The code in Listing 8.5 adds this the new object-property to the `TMyButton` component.

LISTING 8.5

```
type
  TMyButton = class (TButton)
  private
    {Private declarations}
    FMyObject: TMyObject;
    procedure SetMyObject (Value: TMyObject);
  protected
    {Protected declarations}
  public
    {Public declarations}
    constructor Create (AOwner: TComponent); override;
    destructor Destroy; override;
  published
    {Published declarations}
    property MyObject: TMyObject read FMyObject write SetMyObject;
  end;
```

Note the newly-added `Create` and `Destroy` methods for the new object to the code of the component.

Now you have to write the constructor and destructor for the `TMyButton` component, which respectively creates and destroys the `TMyObject` object along with the `TMyButton` component. Also, you need to add the code of the `SetMyObject` method to assign each new value to the properties of the `TMyObject` object. Finally, write the code of the `Assign` method for the `TMyObject` object. The complete extended version that includes all the methods mentioned is given in Listing 8.6.

LISTING 8.6

```
type
  TMyObject = class (TPersistent)
   private
    {Private declarations}
    FProperty1: Real;
    FProperty2: Char;
   protected
    {Protected declarations}
   public
    {Public declarations}
    procedure Assign (Source: TPersistent); override;
   published
    {Published declarations}
    property Property1: Real read FProperty1 write FProperty1;
    property Property2: Char read FProperty2 write FProperty2;
  end;
type
  TMyButton = class (TButton)
   private
    {Private declarations}
    FMyObject: TMyObject;
    procedure SetMyObject (Value: TMyObject);
   protected
    {Protected declarations}
   public
```

```
    {Public declarations}
    constructor Create (AOwner: TComponent); override;
    destructor Destroy; override;
   published
    {Published declarations}
    property MyObject: TMyObject read FMyObject write SetMyObject;
  end;
procedure Register;
begin
  RegisterPropertyEditor (TypeInfo(String), TControl, 'Hint',
  THintProperty);
end;
implementation
procedure TMyButton.SetMyObject (Value: TMyObject);
begin
   if Assigned (Value) then FMyObject.Assign (Value);
end;
constructor TMyButton.Create (AOwner: TComponent);
begin
  inherited Create (AOwner);
  FMyObject:=TMyObject.Create;
end;
destructor TMybutton.Destroy;
begin
  FMyObject.Free;
  inherited Destroy;
end;
procedure TMyObject.Assign (Source: TPersistent);
  begin
  if Source is TMyObject then
    begin
      FProperty1:=TMyObject (Source).Property1;
      FProperty2:=TMyObject (Source).Property2;
      inherited Assign (Source);
    end;
  end;
```

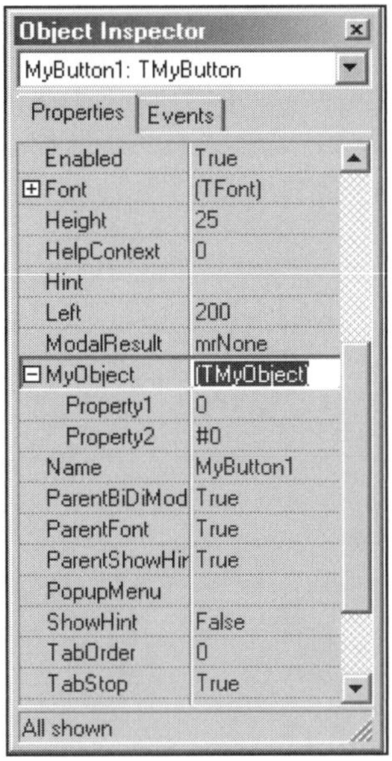

FIGURE 8.3 The `MyObject` object as one of the properties of the new `TMyButton` component.

Notice the way the `TMyObject.Assign` method is implemented. First, a check is run to make sure that an instance of the `TMyObject` object is being passed. If the instance is valid, then the values of the `Source` properties are transferred to the `FProperty1` and `FProperty2` fields of the `TMyButton` object. As soon as the above code executes, you will get your new `TMyButton` component containing the `TMyObject` object as its property. Figure 8.3 shows what this will look like in the Object Inspector window.

Adding Array Properties to a Component

In fact, properties of a component can be of any type, as long as this type is supported by Object Pascal. Some properties can be represented by arrays. The most illustrative examples of such properties are provided by `TMemo.Lines`, `TDBGrid.Columns`, etc. Such properties require their own editors. At this point, we will confine ourselves to creating a simple array property. (For information on how to build custom property editors, refer to the next section.) Let's create a new component, `TWeek`, that will contain two properties: `Month` and `Number`. The `Month` property will be represented by an array that will return the name of a month that corresponds to the passed argument: an integer from 1 to 12, inclusive. The `Number` property is also an array property that returns the number of the month that corresponds to the month's name.

So let's look at the code of the `TWeek` component given in Listing 8.7.

LISTING 8.7

```
unit Week;
interface
uses
  Windows, Messages, SysUtils, Classes, Graphics, Controls, Forms, Dialogs;
type
  TWeek = class(TComponent)
   private
    {Private declarations}
    function GetMonthName (const AIndex: Integer): String;
    function GetMonthNumber (const AMonthName: String): Integer;
   protected
    {Protected declarations}
   public
    {Public declarations}
    property MonthName[const AIndex: Integer]: String
        read GetMonthName; default;
    property MonthNumber[const AMonthName: String]: Integer
        read GetMonthNumber;
   published
    {Published declarations}
  end;
procedure Register;
implementation
const
MonthNames: array[1..12] of String[9]=
('January','February','March','April','May',
'June','July','August','September','October',
'November','December');
function TWeek.GetMonthName(const AIndex: Integer): String;
begin
  if (AIndex<=0) or (AIndex>12) then
```

```
    raise Exception.Create('The number of a month must be an
    integer from 1 through 12')
  else Result:= MonthNames[AIndex];
end;
function TWeek.GetMonthNumber(const AMonthName: String): Integer;
var
i:Integer;
begin
  Result:=0;
  for i:=1 to 12 do begin
    if UpperCase(AMonthName)=UpperCase(MonthNames[i]) then
    Result:=i;
  end;
end;
procedure Register;
begin
  RegisterComponents('Samples', [TWeek]);
end;
end.
```

Let's study the code in Listing 8.7 more thoroughly. As you can see, the properties of an `Array` type are declared together with indexes. The `AIndex` index is specified for the `MonthName` property, and the `AMonthName` index is set for the `MonthNumber` property. In order to access the properties of such a type, you need to use certain methods. There are no inner fields here. If a property of an `Array` type is multidimensional, then this array property is declared with a set of several indexes. When you call the access methods for such properties, you must pass your arguments in the same order as you specified them in the property.

The `GetMonthName` function returns a string that contains the name of a month that corresponds to an integer from 1 through 12 that was passed as this function argument. If a number that doesn't fall within the required range is passed, then an exception will be generated using the `raise` command (issuing exceptions is discussed in detail in *Chapter 2*).

Lastly, the `GetMonthNumber` function returns the integer from 1 through 12 that corresponds to the name of a month that has been set as this function's argument. If none of the month names passed are valid according to the names contained in the `MonthNames` array, this function returns 0.

Therefore, if you place an instance of the `Week1` component on a form, a window with the message May will be displayed as soon as the following code string executes:

```
ShowMessage (Week1.MonthName[5]);
```

Adding Custom Property Editors

Before showing you how to create your own editor to help you modify component properties, let's see what Delphi has to offer in terms of generic property editors. All these in-built editors can be seen in the **Object Inspector** window when you try to modify a property of a component. For example, when you change the `Color` property of any component, you can see the **Color Editor**. It is important to keep in mind that all the component properties—even those as simplistic as `Caption`, `Height`, and `Enabled`–have their exclusive editors. Components don't know what editors you use to change their properties. This implies that you are free to use your own property editor instead of a predefined one. For example, you can write an editor for the `Width` property that can limit it to some specific value.

Property editors have their own hierarchy. Let's discuss it here.

The base class in the hierarchy of property editors is called `TPropertyEditor`. The names of all classes are self-explanatory. For instance, the `TColorProperty` class is responsible for the color property of a component, the `TIntegerProperty` class is associated with the properties of an `Integer` type, etc. Listing 8.8 presents the code for declaring the `TPropertyEditor` base class.

LISTING 8.8

```
TPropertyEditor = class
 private
  FDesigner: TFormDesigner;
  FPropList: PInstPropList;
  FPropCount: Integer;
  function GetPrivateDirectory: string;
  procedure SetPropEntry(Index: Integer; AInstance: TComponent;
  APropInfo: PPropInfo);
 protected
  constructor Create(ADesigner: TFormDesigner; APropCount: Integer);
  function GetPropInfo: PPropInfo;
```

```
    function GetFloatValue: Extended;
    function GetFloatValueAt(Index: Integer): Extended;
    function GetMethodValue: TMethod;
    function GetMethodValueAt(Index: Integer): TMethod;
    function GetOrdValue: Longint;
    function GetOrdValueAt(Index: Integer): Longint;
    function GetStrValue: string;
    function GetStrValueAt(Index: Integer): string;
    procedure Modified;
    procedure SetFloatValue(Value: Extended);
    procedure SetMethodValue(const Value: TMethod);
    procedure SetOrdValue(Value: Longint);
    procedure SetStrValue(const Value: string);
  public
    destructor Destroy; override;
    procedure Activate; virtual;
    function AllEqual: Boolean; virtual;
    procedure Edit; virtual;
    function GetAttributes: TPropertyAttributes; virtual;
    function GetComponent(Index: Integer): TComponent;
    function GetEditLimit: Integer; virtual;
    function GetName: string; virtual;
    procedure GetProperties(Proc: TGetPropEditProc);virtual;
    function GetPropType: PTypeInfo;
    function GetValue: string; virtual;
    procedure GetValues(Proc: TGetStrProc); virtual;
    procedure Initialize; virtual;
    procedure SetValue(const Value: string); virtual;
    property Designer: TFormDesigner read FDesigner;
    property PrivateDirectory: string read GetPrivateDirectory;
    property PropCount: Integer read FPropCount;
    property Value: string read GetValue write SetValue;
end;
```

The methods of a given class, which are listed next, can be re-declared in order to modify the behavior of the property editor.

- The `Activate` method is called when a given property is selected in the Object Inspector window.
- The `AllEqual` method is called when more than one component is selected on a form.
- The `Edit` method is called when you either click the (...) button or double-click the property. This method can activate the dialog window for editing a given property, as we see when editing the `Font` property.
- The `GetAttributes` method returns a set of values of the `TProperyAttributes` type, which specify the way in which a given property will be displayed in the Object Inspector window.
- The `GetComponent` method is used to determine a component by its index (the `Index` parameter) in a case where a number of components are simultaneously selected on a form.
- The `GetEditLimit` method returns the maximum number of characters in a string that a user is allowed to enter when editing the property.
- The `GetName` method returns the name of the property. Using this method makes sense only if the name of the property differs from the name displayed in Object Inspector.
- The `GetPropType` method returns the type of the property.
- The `GetValue` method returns the value of the property in the form of a string.
- The `Initialize` method is called when you are initializing a property editor.
- The `SetValue` method is used for setting a value for the property.

In most cases it is not necessary to use the base `TPropertyEditor` class as an ancestor class in order to create a new editor. As often as not, developers simply inherit from existing editors by overriding some of their methods.

Let's take, for example, the `Hint` property, used for providing users with pop-up tips when they pause with the mouse pointer on a component. Typically, any hint has only one string. Let's try to make the `Hint` property multistringed. Listing 8.9 demonstrates how to build a new editor for the `THintProperty` property. Let's select the `TStringProperty` editor as the ancestor class for our new editor.

LISTING 8.9

```
THintProperty = class(TStringProperty)
 public
  function GetAttributes: TPropertyAttributes; override;
  function GetValue : String; override;
```

```
  procedure Edit; override;
end;
function THintProperty.GetAttributes: TPropertyAttributes;
begin
  Result := inherited GetAttributes + [paDialog, paReadOnly];
end;
uses
   Windows, SysUtils, Controls, Forms, Dsgnlntf, StrEdit;
function THintProperty.GetValue : String;
var
i : Byte;
begin
  Result:=inherited GetValue;
  for i:=1 to Length (Result) Byte(result[0]) do
  if Result[i]<#32 then Result[i]:='>';
end;
procedure THintProperty.Edit;
var
  HintEditDlg : TStrEditDlg;
  s : String;
begin
  HintEditDlg:=TStrEditDlg.Create(Application);
  with HintEditDlg do
    try
      Memo.MaxLength := 254;
      s:=GetStrValue+#0;
      Memo.Lines.SetText(@s[1]);
      UpdateStatus(nil);
      ActiveControl := Memo;
      If ShowModal = mrOk then begin
        s:=StrPas(Memo.Lines.GetText);
         if Length(s)>2 then Setlength (s, length(s)-2);
        SetStrValue(s);
      end;
```

```
    finally
      Free;
    end;
end;
```

Let's look at the methods of our new class:

- The `GetAttributes` function adds the `paDialog` attribute (this results in the (...) button appearing in the **Object Inspector** window) and the `paReadOnly` attribute (which is used to ensure that the property can be edited only through a dialog) to the inherited set of attributes.
- The `GetValue` function replaces the carriage return character (#10) and the line feed character (#13) by the greater than character (>).

Finally, the `Edit` procedure is called to display the dialog that will allow you to enter the strings of a hint.

In order to register your new editor, place a declaration of the `Register` procedure in the interface part of a given unit. Then write the procedure itself in the `implementation` section of the unit (Listing 8.10).

LISTING 8.10

```
procedure Register;
begin
  RegisterPropertyEditor (TypeInfo(String), TControl, 'Hint',
                          THintProperty);
end;
```

This procedure allows you to attach the same editor to properties, depending on their names and types. This operation is implemented by using the parameters assigned to the `RegisterPropertyEditor` procedure. The first parameter specifies the type of the property (in this example it is `String`), and the second parameter sets the class of the component. The third parameter enables you to specify the name for the property. And the last parameter defines the name of the property editor.

To install a new property editor in Delphi, do the following:

1. Select **Component/Install Components**.
2. Click the **Add** button.
3. Specify the name of the unit which is being installed.

As soon as the library is compiled, you can create a new form and place any component on it. Then set the `ShowHint` property of this component to `True`, and press the (...) button in the `Hint` property. As a result, your newly created multistring editor for the `Hint` property will be displayed on your screen.

The *Default* and *NoDefault* Commands

Now you know how to create properties of an arbitrary type for your components. Note that many properties can be assigned a particular value that will be the set by default. To do this, assign the desired value to a component field, for instance:

```
FMyProperty := 10;
```

From this point on, every time you place the component on a form, the `MyProperty` property will be set to `10`.

The `Default` and `NoDefault` commands are used to accelerate the process of loading a form at runtime. For example,

```
property MyCount: Integer read FMyCount write FmyCount Default 0;
```

This code *does not* set the `MyCount` property to `0`. Using the `Default 0` command in the above code means that if the `MyCount` property does not have the `0` value when you save a form that contains the given component, the actual current value will be saved to the form file. Otherwise, the value of the property will not be saved.

NOTE

Use the `Default` command whenever possible if you want to build fast, responsive applications.

The `NoDefault` command is used for disabling the `Default` command. The command annuls the `Default` command that is inherited from its ancestor components. For example:

```
TSecondComponent = class (TMyButton)

published

property MyCount NoDefault;
```

ADDING EVENTS TO A COMPONENT

We have already discussed standard events in the previous chapters. This section will provide you with the definitions of an *event* and an *event handler.*

By an *event*, we mean any operation that is performed by a user, an operating system, or a routine.

An event can be "caught" and processed by using the appropriate event handler. An event and its handler are linked by an *event-property*. Thus, when a component's event occurs the handler can process it. Prior to invoking the event handler for a given event, the event-property must check on the availability of the handler in question. If the necessary code is found, then it executes.

By way of example, let's discuss a common event: left-clicking, or the `OnClick` event. This event, like many others, has its so-called *event-dispatching methods.* These methods are required in order to determine whether the code that is to handle the event for a given component exists. These methods are declared using a protected keyword. In this particular example, `OnClick` has its own event-dispatching method: `Click` (Listing 8.11).

LISTING 8.11

```
TControl = class (TComponent)
private
  FOnClick: TNotifyEvent;
protected
  procedure Click; dynamic;
  property OnClick: TNotifyEvent read FOnClick write FOnClick stored
           IsOnClick Stored;
end;
implementation
procedure TControl.Click;
begin
  if Assigned (FOnClick) then FOnClick (Self);
end;
```

Note that the `OnClick` property belongs to the `TNotifyEvent` type, which is represented by a procedure with only one parameter, `Sender`, of the `TObject` type:

```
TNotifyEvent = procedure (Sender: TObject) of object;
```

When you call the `Click` method, a check is run to establish whether `FOnClick` is linked to some method, and if so, then this method is invoked.

The point of the above example is obvious: the process of creating events involves writing a code for the event itself, and then creating relevant event-dispatching methods and properties. Event handlers are built by the user.

When any event occurs, the operating system not only notifies the application of this event, but also provides it with some additional information. In the preceding example, when the left-clicking event is processed, the application receives information on the coordinates (in the client part of the component) of the point where this event has taken place. For example, the code presented in Listing 8.12 outputs the coordinates of the mouse cursor when the left-clicking event occurs.

LISTING 8.12

```
procedure TForm1.FormMouseDown(Sender: TObject; Button: TMouseButton;
  Shift: TShiftState; X, Y: Integer);
begin
  Canvas.TextOut(X, Y, '('+IntToStr(X)+', '+IntToStr(Y)+')');
end;
```

This code is included in the `OnMouseDown` event-handler of the `Form1` form. Now, if you run this program and left-click various places on the form, the coordinates of all the points of clicking will be output. Figure 8.4 illustrates the result of this program's execution.

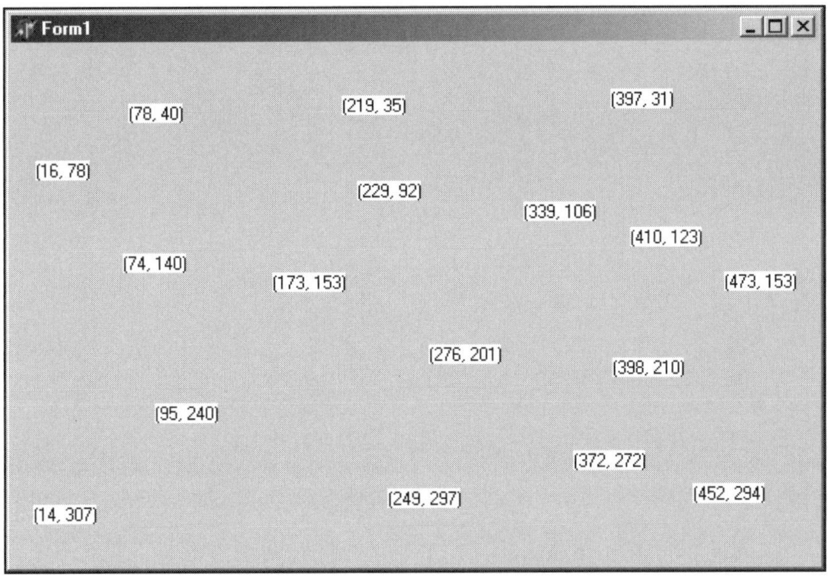

FIGURE 8.4 The result of processing the `OnMouseDown` event.

Creating an Event for a Component

It's time to try your hand at creating your own event. But first you should make sure that there is no such event in Delphi VCL. Suppose you need to develop an event that must occur every 30 seconds. You can by all means use the `Timer` component located in the System tab of the Delphi Component palette for this purpose. But let's assume that your component needs to have such an event for convenience' sake. The code that creates this event is given in Listing 8.13.

LISTING 8.13

```
unit halfmin;
interface
uses
  Windows, Messages, SysUtils, Classes,Graphics, Controls, Forms,
  Dialogs,
  ExtCtrls;
type
  TTimeEvent = procedure (Sender: TObject; TheTime: TDateTime) of object;
  THalfMinute = class (TComponent)
   private
    FTimer: TTimer;
    FOnHalfMinute: TTimeEvent;
    FOldSecond, FSecond: Word;
    procedure FTimerTimer (Sender: TObject);
   protected
    procedure DoHalfMinute (TheTime: TDateTime); dynamic;
   public
    constructor Create (AOwner: TComponent); override;
    destructor Destroy; override;
   published
    property OnHalfMinute: TTimeEvent read FOnHalfMinute write FOnHalfMinute;
  end;
implementation
constructor THalfMinute.Create (AOwner: TComponent);
begin
  inherited Create (AOwner);
  if not (csDesigning in ComponentState) then begin
```

```
    FTimer:=TTimer.Create(self);
    FTimer.Enabled:=True;
    FTimer.Interval:=500;
    FTimer.OnTimer:=FTimerTimer;
  end;
end;
destructor THalfMinute.Destroy;
begin
  FTimer.Free;
  inherited Destroy;
end;
procedure THalfMinute.FTimerTimer (Sender: TObject);
var
  DT: TDateTime;
  Temp: Word;
begin
  DT:=Now;
  FOldSecond:=FSecond;
  DecodeTime (DT,Temp,Temp,FSecond,Temp);
  if FSecond <> FOldSecond then
    if ((FSecond=30) or (FSecond=0)) then
      DoHalfMinute (DT);
end;
procedure THalfMinute.DoHalfMinute(TheTime: TDateTime);
begin
  if Assigned (FOnHalfMinute) then
    FOnHalfMinute (Self, TheTime);
end;
end.
```

In order to test if the code in Listing 8.13 works, you can add another procedure to register your new `ThalfMinute` component. But prior to this you have to insert the following string in the `interface` part of the program:

```
procedure Register;
```

Here is the code for registering the component:

```
procedure Register;
begin
  RegisterComponents('Samples', [THalfMinute]);
end;
```

Now you can test the code for its workability. Create a new form and place your new component on it. Then add the `TEdit` component to the form. Finally, add the `OnHalfMinute` event handler for the component (Listing 8.14).

LISTING 8.14

```
procedure TForm1.HalfMinute1HalfMinute(Sender: TObject;
  TheTime: TDateTime);
begin
  Edit1.Text:=('Time'+TimeToStr(TheTime));
  Edit1.Refresh;
end;
```

The execution of this routine will ensure that the current time will be output in the component every 30 seconds.

BUILDING METHODS FOR A COMPONENT

Adding methods to a new component is a very simple operation. Still, you need to keep in mind a couple of basic rules which will help you facilitate the work of those users who will be dealing with your component in the future.

First of all, the methods must not be interdependent; in other words, every method should be self-sufficient and complete. Second, a method must not lock a given component. And finally, the name of the method should match the operations it performs.

As you already know, methods are declared in the `private`, `public`, and `protected` sections of code. When you are creating a new method, you should have a very clear idea as to how it will be utilized in the future and whether a given component can become an ancestor for some other components. Taking all these factors into account, choose the section in which to place your methods. Table 8.1 provides you with some hints on this.

Table 8.1 Recommended Sections in Which to Place Various Component Methods

Section	*Recommended methods to be included in the section*
`Private`	This section is most suitable for placing methods that cannot be changed in descendant components. Such methods are unavailable outside a given component.
`Protected`	This section is good for placing methods which you mean to leave open to changes in descendant components.
`Public`	This section is designated to include those methods that are available to any user of a given component. The access is unlimited at runtime, but restricted at design time, because these methods are not available in the **Object Inspector** window.
`Published`	This section is used for placing those component properties which are available at design time in the **Object Inspector** window.

REGISTERING COMPONENTS WITH DELPHI

You need to register a component in order to place it in the Component palette.

If you use the component wizard to register your component, Delphi takes care of creating the registration procedure in the shell unit of your component. In this case, you need to perform the following steps:

1. Select Component/Install Components.
2. Click the Add button.
3. Specify the name of the unit that you are installing (it goes without saying that the component unit must have been previously saved).

As soon as compilation is completed, your new component will appear in the chosen tab of the Component palette.

However, if you do not use the component wizard to build your component, you must complete the registration procedure manually. To do this, write the following code string in the `interface` section of the component unit:

```
procedure Register;
```

and add the registration procedure to the `implementation` section, for example:

```
procedure Register;
begin
  RegisterComponent ('Samples', [TMyComponent]);
end;
```

As a result, your new component, named `TMyComponent`, will be placed on the `Samples` tab in the Component palette.

Note that the icon that represents your component can be replaced by another image. If you want to create your own icon, you should probably use **Image Editor**, a very helpful tool that is provided together with the other standard Delphi tools. But you can certainly use any available bitmap image editor for this purpose as well.

Create an image for your component with a size of 24 × 24 pixels and save it in a DCR file. By convention, the name of this file is the name of your component, with all the characters as capital letters. For example, the name of the file that stores the image of the `TMyButton` component will be TMYBUTTON.DCR. The image will be named the same as the component. The file will be named the same as the unit. Place this image file in the folder in which you store the file that contains the component unit. Recompile the unit, and your component will then be represented in the Component palette by the new image.

PART

III Application Developing Based on COM and ActiveX Technologies

9 COM Basics

One of the primary benefits of Delphi is its support of technologies such as COM and ActiveX. This chapter provides an overview of COM and discusses the relationship between COM, ActiveX, and OLE.

Let's start with COM. COM is an acronym that stands for Component Object Model. COM is the basis for both ActiveX and OLE. The OLE and ActiveX technologies are simply built on top of COM. The role of COM in relation to OLE and ActiveX is somewhat like the role of the `TObject` base object in the Delphi VCL architecture, where all classes are derived from the object in question. Similarly, COM is the foundation for OLE and ActiveX.

COM is used for building the API and binary standard in order to implement interprocess communication between objects created using various programming languages and in different programming environments. COM is concerned with providing interaction between components and applications within a network.

The COM technology uses so-called COM objects. COM objects are similar to all the other objects that constitute Delphi VCL, but unlike Delphi VCL objects, COM objects are characterized by properties, methods, and interfaces.

An ordinary COM object contains at least one interface. Every interface of a COM object has an individual pointer by which it can be referenced.

The COM technology has two essential and obvious advantages:

- COM object creation is language-independent. This means that COM objects can be written in different programming languages.

- COM objects can be used in any existing Windows programming environment: Delphi, Visual C++, C++ Builder, Visual Basic, and many others.

NOTE

COM is not perfect, and among its major drawbacks is its dependence on the platform. This means that COM is exclusively tied to the Windows operating system and the Intel platform.

COM objects are usually contained in either a DLL or an OCX file. Such a file can contain one or several COM objects.

A key aspect of COM is its ability to enable connection and interoperability between components and applications, and to implement client-server systems via interfaces.

COM is implemented using COM libraries (including such operating system files as OLE32.DLL and OLEAut32.DLL). COM libraries contain a set of standard interfaces that provide for the COM object's functioning, and a number of API functions responsible for creating and managing COM objects.

Delphi implementation and support of COM is referred to as the *Delphi ActiveX framework*, or DAX. The DAX implementation code is contained in the `AxCtrls` unit.

COM BACKGROUND

While upgrading and promoting the Windows operating system, Microsoft has always seen the task of providing effective interoperability for the variety of programs that run under Windows as an issue of top priority.

In their attempt to resolve this problem, developers came up with a number of various solutions. The very first of them included shareable files, exchange buffers, and the *Dynamic Data Exchange* technology (DDE).

Later, the Object Linking and Embedding technology (OLE) was developed; its first version, OLE 1, was aimed at creating compound documents. This version had several significant drawbacks to it, and was soon replaced by the second version, OLE 2. This new version enabled various programs to use shareable functions. OLE 2 had been the dominant technology in this field until 1996, when another competing technology, ActiveX, stepped in. ActiveX provides automation (OLE automation), containers, controls, Web technology, etc.

COM TERMINOLOGY

Every newly introduced technology brings new terms with it, and COM is no exception.

COM Objects

A COM object is a chunk of binary code that performs some function and may have one or more interfaces.

A COM object possesses its own methods to allow an application to use this COM object. These methods are made available thanks to COM interfaces. A client needs only to know a few base COM object interfaces in order to get the most comprehensive information on the properties and methods of a given COM object. A COM object may have only one interface, but it may also have several. From a programmer's point of view, a COM object operates like an Object Pascal class.

COM Interfaces

A *COM interface* is used for integrating all the methods of a given COM object. A COM interface enables the user to correctly access the COM object and ensures that this COM object in turn provides a valid and appropriate response to the user. By convention, all names of COM interfaces should begin with the letter `I`. A client need not necessarily know what interfaces a COM object has. In order to get a full list of interfaces, the base `IUnknown` interface (which every COM object must contain) can be used.

COM Object Users

By a *COM object user* we mean an application or a part of an application that uses a COM object and its interfaces for its own purposes. As a rule, a COM object is located elsewhere inside another application.

COM Classes

The classes that contain at least one COM interface are referred to as *COM Coclasses.* You can avoid directly calling a COM interface by using the appropriate `CoClass` to access the desired interface. `CoClasses` are identified by their CLSID.

Type Libraries

COM objects often use type libraries. A *type library* is a special file which contains information on a given COM object: a list of properties, methods, interfaces, structures, and other COM object elements. In addition, a type library stores information about the data types of each property and the data types of the structures that are returned by COM object methods.

Type library files have the TLB extension.

DCOM

Distributed COM (DCOM) is used for providing access to COM objects across networks (including the Internet).

The Windows NT 4 and Windows 98 operating systems have built-in DCOM support.

Reference Counts

Every COM object is supplied with a reference count. This reference count contains the number of processes that are currently using a given COM object. Here, by process we mean any application or DLL that uses a COM object—in other words, COM object users.

Reference counts are necessary because they perform such vital functions as freeing CPU time and memory when a COM object is no longer being used by its clients.

After a COM object is created, its reference count is incremented by 1 every time a new application accesses it. When a process detaches from a COM object, its reference count decreases by 1. When a reference count goes to zero, the memory used by the COM object is freed.

OLE Objects

A part of data that can be shared (used collectively) between several applications is called an *OLE object.* Those applications that can contain OLE objects are referred to as *OLE containers.* And, finally, the term *OLE servers* pertains to applications that can store their data in OLE containers.

Compound Documents

A document that contains one OLE object or several OLE objects is called a *compound document.* An application that can be contained within another document is referred to as an *ActiveX document.*

Other COM terms will be explained later in this book.

COM APPLICATION ARCHITECTURE

Every COM application must necessarily include the following parts:

- A COM interface

- A COM server
- A COM client

Let's discuss each of the above constituent parts of a COM application in more detail.

COM Interfaces

Clients access COM objects by means of interfaces. An *interface* incorporates semantically or logically grouped procedures that enable connection between a server and its client.

NOTE

By convention (UML), the interfaces of a COM object are indicated by circles to the right or left of the COM object. The base `IUnknown` *interface is indicated by a circle on top of the COM object.*

For example, every COM object necessarily supports the base `IUnknown` interface that is responsible for providing clients with the information about all the interfaces implemented by an object.

As mentioned earlier, a COM object can support several interfaces, each one performing its own specific function.

Key aspects of COM interfaces are as follows:

- Once they are declared, interfaces cannot be changed. You can therefore delegate a certain set of functions to an individual interface. Extra functionality can be implemented by creating additional interfaces.
- By convention, names of all interfaces begin with `I`, for example: `IPersist`, `IMalloc`.
- Every interface must have its own *Globally Unique Identifier*, or GUID, which is also sometimes called an *Interface Identifier*, or IID. Such identifiers serve to prevent all kinds of conflicts over names of different versions of the same application or different applications.
- Interfaces are language-independent. You can implement a COM interface using any programming language. The programming language is required only to support the pointer structure and to be able to call a function using a pointer, either directly or indirectly.
- Interfaces are not self-sufficient independent objects; they are only the means by which a user can access a COM object. This implies that a user cannot directly call a COM object, but must use the system of interface pointers.
- All interfaces are descendants of the `IUnknown` base interface.

The COM *Iunknown* Base Interface

Chapter 2 covered the `IUnknown` base interface. The only essential feature of this interface that has been left unmentioned is the `IUnknown` interface's support of reference counting (COM object reference count). When you pass the pointer to this interface, its `IUnknown AddRef` method is implemented. As soon as work with the interface is finished, client applications call the `Release` method that decrements the reference count.

When the `QueryInterface` method of the `IUnknown` interface is called, it receives the `IID` parameter, which belongs to the `TGUID` type (that is, the `ID` interface). The `Out` parameter returns either a pointer to the requested interface or a value of `Nil`. This method can return one of the values listed in Table 9.1.

TABLE 9.1 The Values That Can Be Returned by the `QueryInterface` Method

Value	*Interpretation*
`S_OK`	The interface is supported.
`E_NOINTERFACE`	The interface is not supported.
`E_UNEXPECTED`	An unknown error.

The Pointer to a COM Interface

The *pointer to a COM interface* is a 32-bit pointer to an object instance, which in turn points to the functions that implement methods of the interface. These methods can be implemented using the array of pointers to these methods, called `vtable`. The technique of using the `vtable` array is similar to the Object Pascal mechanism that supports virtual functions.

COM Servers

A *COM server* is an application or library that provides its services to a client application/library. A COM server contains at least one COM object, which acts as a set of properties, methods, and interfaces.

The whole logic of the COM object's functioning is completely hidden from clients. The client can access the functionality of such an object via COM interfaces. Moreover, a client application doesn't need to know the exact address of the COM object it deals with. The COM technology ensures transparent bridging regardless of the COM object's location.

When a client sends a request to a COM object, it uses a CLSID (a Global Unique Identifier for a class) to access this COM object. Once a CLSID is passed, the COM object must get its *class factory* (for more information on class factories, refer to the next section) to create the required COM object instances.

Typically, a COM server performs the following tasks:

- Registers the data with the Windows registry in order to uniquely identify a given server unit by its CLSID
- Provides a class factory that creates COM object instances
- Ensures that those COM servers that are not required at a given moment are freed from the memory

NOTE

Delphi has a special wizard that substantially simplifies the process of creating COM objects and COM servers. This Delphi feature will be covered in Chapter 10.

Class Factories

All COM objects are `CoClass` instances. As you may know, `CoClass` is a class that supports one or more interfaces. COM objects can provide only those services that are specified in `CoClass` interfaces. The creation of `CoClass` instances is handled by a special COM object type, a class factory.

A *class factory* is a special COM object type that supports the `IClassFactory` interface and is responsible for creating instances of the class associated with it.

The `IClassFactory` interface is declared in the Delphi ActiveX unit in the following way:

```
type
  IClassFactory = interface (IUnknown)
    ['{00000001-0000-0000-C000-000000000046}']
    function CreateInstance (const unkOuter: IUnknown; const iid:
                             TIID out obj): HResult; stdcall;
    function LockServer (fLock: BOOL): HResult; stdcall;
  end;
```

As you can see from the preceding code, this interface has two methods: `CreateInstance` and `LockServer`.

The `CreateInstance` method is the function of a class factory responsible for producing an instance of the requested COM object.

The `LockServer` method is used for storing a COM server in memory. If the `fLock` parameter of this method is set to `true`, the reference count is increased; otherwise it is decreased. When a reference count goes to zero, the memory used by the server is freed up.

Every time a COM object is requested by a client, the class factory creates the object instance for this particular user and registers this instance with the system. If the same COM object is requested by another client, the class factory produces a second instance of this object to provide services to the second user.

`CoClass` must have its class factory and CLSID. The `CoClass` mechanism of using CLSID implies that all CLSIDs can be updated when new interfaces are introduced to a class. Thus, unlike DLLs, new interfaces can change their existing methods and add new ones without influencing old versions.

The Delphi wizard that creates COM objects takes care of building class factories.

Local and Remote Servers

A COM client doesn't need to worry about knowing the address of a desired COM object; it just calls the object interface. The COM technology provides all the necessary steps for implementing these calls. The steps can vary depending on the exact location of the object. An object can be located in the same process as its client, in another process on the same machine, or on a remote machine. You use one of the following server types depending on where exactly a given object is located:

- An in-process server
- A local server (an out-of-process server)
- A remote server

An *in-process server* is a DLL that is running in the same process as its client. For example, an ActiveX control embedded into a Web page and viewed using Internet Explorer or Netscape Navigator is an in-process server. In this instance, this ActiveX control is loaded on its client machine and shares a single process with the Web browser. A client application connects an in-process server by directly calling a COM interface. Figure 9.1 illustrates the pattern of interaction between an in-process server and its client.

An in-process COM server must export four functions:

```
function DllRegisterServer: HResult; stdcall;

function DllUnregisterServer: HResult; stdcall;

function DllGetClassObject (const CLSID, IID: TGUID; var Obj): HResult; stdcall;

function DllCanUnloadNow: HResult; stdcall;
```

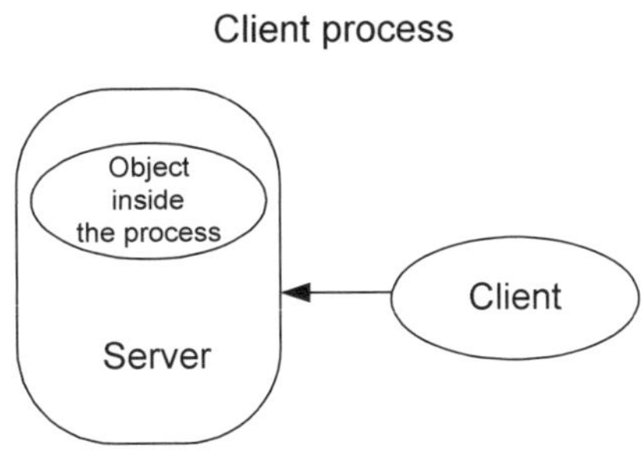

FIGURE 9.1 The interaction between an in-process server and its client.

All of the above functions are already implemented in the `ComServ` unit; you just need to add them to the `exports` clause of your project.

Let's discuss these functions in more detail:

- **`DllRegisterServer`**: This function is used to register a COM DLL server with the Windows registry. When a COM class is registered, a special string of numbers is added to the `HKEY_CLASSES_ROOT\CLSID` registry key: `HKEY_CLASSES_ROOT\CLSID\{xxxxxxxx-xxxx-xxxx-xxxx-xxxxxxxx}`, where the number in question represents the class ID (CLSID) of a given COM class. An additional section, `InProcServer32`, is created for the in-process server, which includes the DLL address of a given in-process server (Figure 9.2).
- **`DllUnregisterServer`**: This function is used to remove all sections, subsections, and parameters that were created in the registry by the `DllRegisterServer` function when the COM DLL server was registered.
- **`DllGetClassObject`**: This function returns the class factory for a particular COM class.
- **`DllCanUnloadNow`**: This function is used to determine whether a given COM DLL server can currently free up the memory it's using. This function checks if pointers to any COM objects of a given DLL are available, and if they are it returns `S_FALSE`, which means that the DLL cannot free memory. If no COM object of a given DLL is currently being used, the function returns `S_OK`.

A local server is an application that runs in another process but on the same machine as its client. It can be, for example, a Microsoft Excel spreadsheet that is linked to a Microsoft Word document. Both applications in this case run on the same computer. Local servers use COM to connect to their clients.

When a server and its client are located in different applications or on different computers, COM uses an *in-process proxy* to implement a remote call. An in-process proxy shares the same process with the client; that's why, from the client's point of view, the pattern of calling interfaces in this case is similar to the one used

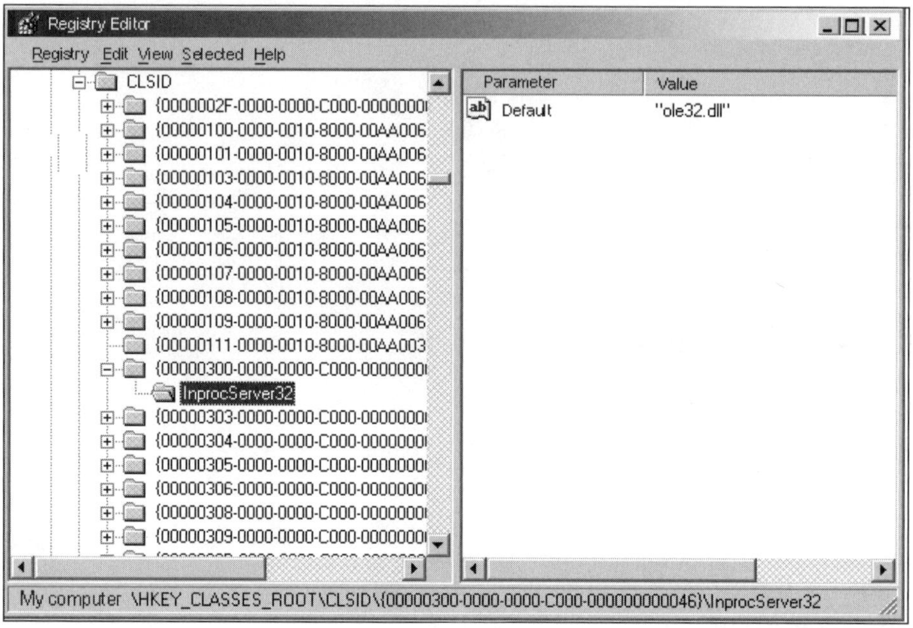

FIGURE 9.2 A path to a local COM server as shown in the Registry Editor window.

when a server and its client are inside the same process. The in-process proxy picks up a client call and directs it to the server, wherever it is. This mechanism that enables a client to access remote objects (those located in another address space or on another machine) is called *marshaling*.

Marshaling is used to:

- Receive interface pointers from server processes and make the corresponding proxy pointer available inside client processes
- Transmit arguments of interface calls as if they were issued by clients, and place these arguments within the processes of remote objects

In order to call any interface, a client places its arguments to a stack, then invokes the necessary COM object function via the pointer to this interface. If a call is made somewhere outside the process, then this call is marshaled through a proxy. The proxy server packages the arguments into *marshaling packets*, and further marshals the resulting data structures to the remote object. The so-called stub of this object unpacks the received marshaling packet, recovers the arguments from the stack, and invokes the necessary COM object function.

In other words, marshaling is the process of packaging data into packets for transmission, and unmarshaling is the process of recovering data.

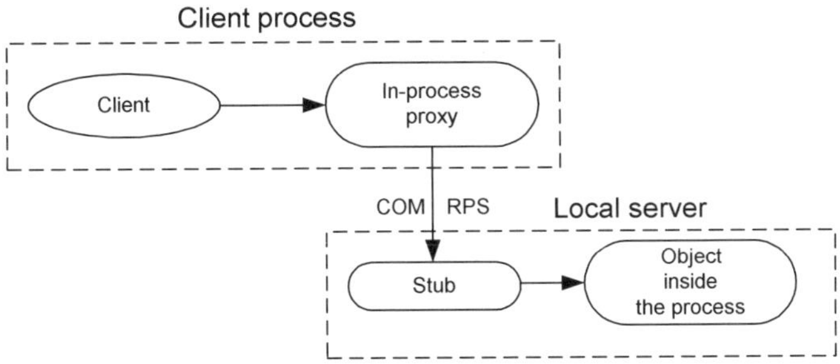

FIGURE 9.3 Client–server interaction when the applications run on the same computer but in different processes.

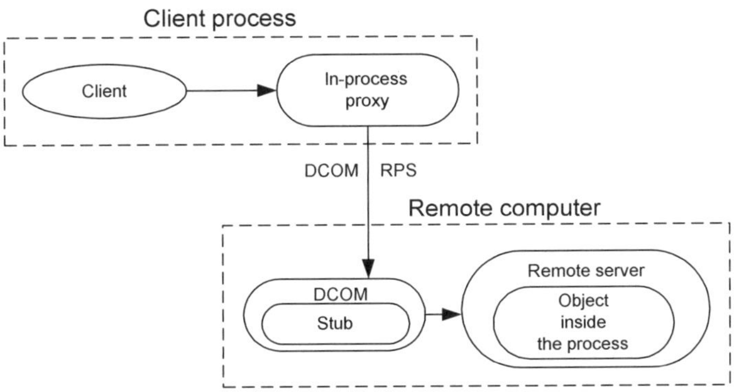

FIGURE 9.4 The interaction between a client and a remote server.

The type of marshaling depends on the type of remote COM object. COM objects can use the standard marshaling mechanism provided by the `IDispatch` interface. The technique of *standard marshaling* enables you to establish a connection by utilizing the *Remote Procedure Call (RPC)* standard.

Figure 9.3 presents a schematic diagram that illustrates the technique of interaction between a client and a server in cases where the applications run on the same computer but in different processes.

You must register a local server with the Windows registry in the same manner as you register an in-process COM server.

A *remote server* is a DLL or other application that runs on another computer. In other words, the client and server work on different machines. For example, a database application that was developed with Delphi connects to a server located somewhere on another computer in the net. Remote servers use *distributed COM interfaces* (DCOM) in order to establish links to their clients.

A remote server also uses a proxy in its work. The key difference between the functioning of a local server and that of a remote server lies in the type of interprocess mechanism: local servers use COM, and remote servers use DCOM. A schematic diagram of the interaction between a client and a remote server is given in Figure 9.4.

COM Clients

One of the most important aspects of developing COM applications is the creation of applications to call COM interfaces and obtain information on the services that can be provided by a particular COM object. These applications are called COM clients.

A typical COM client is represented by an automation controller. An *automation controller* is the part of an application that "knows" what kind of information the application requires from various server objects, so that it can generate appropriate queries when necessary.

COM Extensions

Originally, COM technology was developed to serve as the kernel for implementing cross-platform interprocess communication among various programs. At the very first stage of developing this technology, the COM team worked on the assumption that the architecture of COM would allow various extensions to enhance its capability. COM extends its functionality by creating highly specialized sets of interfaces for dealing with all sorts of tasks.

ActiveX is a technology that uses COM components, mostly COM controls. This technology was designed to make work with controls more efficient and dynamic. This is particularly important when you handle Internet/Intranet applications, where controls must be loaded on a client computer prior to being put to use.

But the ActiveX technology is not the only COM extension. Table 9.2 presents several of the most popular COM extensions at the moment.

The techniques given in Table 9.2 by no means constitute a comprehensive list of all the available COM extensions. Updating and refining existing mechanisms of interprocess communication and introducing new and more powerful technologies will likely never stop.

TABLE 9.2 COM Extensions

COM extension	*General outline*
Automation servers	*Automation servers* are those objects that can be managed from inside other applications at runtime. Therefore, by *automation*, we mean the capability of an application to programmatically control objects located in other applications.

TABLE 9.2 COM Extensions (*Continued*)

COM extension	*General outline*
Automation controllers, COM clients	*Automation controllers* are automation server clients. They enable a developer and a user to write scenarios for managing automation servers.
ActiveX controls	*ActiveX controls* are intended for use by in-process COM servers. ActiveX elements are customarily built into a client application.
Type libraries	*Type libraries* are static data structures often saved as resource files. These libraries contain highly detailed information on objects and their interfaces. Automation controllers and ActiveX controls use this information and always treat it as available information.
Active server pages	*Active server pages* are components that enable you to develop dynamic Web pages.
Active documents	*Active documents* are objects that support linking and embedding, visual editing, and the drag-and-drop technique. Microsoft Word documents and Microsoft Excel spreadsheets belong to this category of documents.
Visual cross-process objects	*Visual cross-process objects* are visual objects that can be managed from inside other processes.

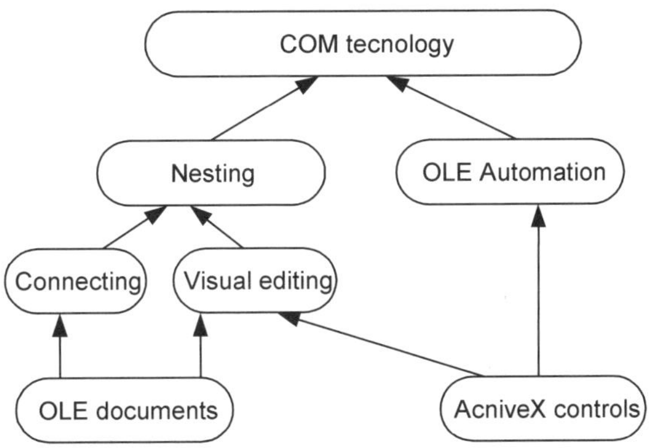

FIGURE 9.5 Technologies developed on top of COM.

Figure 9.3 shows the diagram that presents the relationship between some COM extensions and their connection with the COM technology.

In spite of the various advantages, using COM objects also has a number of drawbacks, as well as certain limitations. COM objects can be visual and non-visual. Some COM objects need to run in the same process with their client, others can run in a different process or on another computer.

Table 9.3 provides you with the essential features of the objects associated with the COM extensions shown in Figure 9.5.

TABLE 9.3 Characteristics of Various COM Objects

COM object	***Visibility***	***Process***	***Communication technique***	***Type library***
Active document	Usually visible	In-process, or local	OLE	None
Automation	Can be both visible and invisible	In-process, local, or remote	Automatic marshaling through the`IDispatch` interface	Required for implementing automatic marshaling
ActiveX control	Usually visible	In-process	Automatic marshaling through the`IDispatch` interface	Required
Custom interface object	Optional	In-process	Marshaling is not required	Recommended
Custom interface object	Optional	In-process, local, or remote	Automatic marshaling depending on type library availability; otherwise manual marshaling	Recommended

10 Creating a Simple COM Object

Delphi provides a programmer with powerful tools for creating COM objects. In order to facilitate this process, a number of wizards, which are capable of building a huge variety of COM objects, have been introduced into the Delphi environment. This chapter will outline a simple technique for creating a COM object using a wizard. You will also learn how to register and test your new object.

A COM object can be an in-process, local, or remote server. The COM Object Wizard performs the following sequence of operations:

1. Creates a new unit in the framework of the current project.
2. Defines a new class that directly descends from the `TCOMObject` class, and sets the class factory constructor.

From a developer's point of view, the whole process of building a COM object involves the following stages:

- Designing the COM object
- Creating the COM object with the COM Object Wizard
- Registering the COM object
- Testing the COM object

DESIGNING A COM OBJECT

At the design stage, you need to have a fairly good idea as to what COM interfaces your future COM object must implement. By default, the `IUnknown` interface will always be implemented by the wizard. Other than that, you are to decide what type of server you are going to use: in-process, local, or remote. If you are designing an in-process or local COM server, you must employ a type library; this will ensure automatic marshaling.

Wizards for Building COM Objects

As stated earlier in this chapter, Delphi provides a developer with a set of wizards in order to simplify the process of generating COM objects. Delphi supports wizards that can build the following objects:

- Simple COM objects
- Automation objects
- ActiveX controls
- Active Server Pages
- ActiveX forms
- ActiveX type libraries
- Property pages
- Type libraries
- Microsoft Transaction Server (MTS) objects

A wizard automates the sequence of operations involved in creating each of the above COM objects. It implements the necessary interfaces for each individual object. With a simple COM object, a wizard implements just the one required interface, `IUnknown`, that installs the interface pointer in the object.

For an automation object, the wizard builds two interfaces, `IUnknown` and `IDispatch`. The latter allows for automatic marshaling.

For an ActiveX control, the wizard implements the whole set of interfaces necessary for the successful functioning of any control: `IUnknown`, `IDispatch`, `IOleObject`, `IOleControl`, etc. (*see Figure 11.3 in Chapter 11*). The full list of interfaces associated with ActiveX controls will be covered *in Chapters 11 and 12.*

So as you can see, different wizards implement different interfaces. Thus, you need to select the wizard that builds the interfaces which you want to implement for your COM object. Table 10.1 contains the lists of interfaces provided by different wizards.

TABLE 10.1 The Interfaces Implemented by Various Wizards

Wizard	*Implemented interfaces*	*Operations performed by the wizard*
COM server	IUnknown	Exports necessary routines that implement the registration of a given server and a given class. Loads and unloads a server and class instances. Creates and manages the class factory for the objects implemented in a given server. Specifies the thread models utilized for interfaces of a given object. Provides a type library, if required.
Automation server	IUnknown, IDispatch	Performs all the operations of the COM Server Wizard, and also implements the chosen interface and automatically provides a type library.
ActiveX control	IUnknown, IDispatch, IPersistStreamInit, IOleInPlaceActiveObject, IPersistStorage, IViewObject, IOleObject, IViewObject2, IOleControl, IPerPropertyBrowsing, IOleInPlaceObject, IspecifyPropertyPages	Performs all the operations implemented by the aforementioned wizards, and in addition provides properties, methods, and events for all TActiveXControl interfaces. Enables a developer to edit objects in the **Code Editor** window.
ActiveX forms	IUnknown, IDispatch, IPersistStreamInit, IOleInPlaceActiveObject, IPersistStorage, IViewObject, IOleObject, IViewObject2, IOleControl, IPerPropertyBrowsing, IOleInPlaceObject, IspecifyPropertyPages	Operates as the ActiveX Control Wizard and lets a developer edit an application.
Active server object	IUnknown, IDispatch	Performs the same operations as the Automation Server Wizard, and in addition generates a page with the ASP extension that can be loaded on a Web browser. This wizard enables a developer to modify properties and methods of an object through the Type Library editor.
ActiveX library	None	Creates a new DLL for an ActiveX or COM server, and provides all necessary functions.

TABLE 10.1 The Interfaces Implemented by Various Wizards (*Continued*)

Wizard	*Implemented Interfaces*	*Operations performed by the wizard*
A property page	`IUnknown, IPropertyPage`	Creates a new property page that can be edited in the **Form Editor** window.
Type library	`None`	Creates a new type library and associates it with the current project.
MTS object	`IobjectControl`	Adds a new unit to the current project that contains an MTS object declaration.

It should be mentioned that if you want to build your own custom object, Delphi provides you with such a capability. You must begin the process of building a new interface by creating a descendant of the `IDispatch` interface and declaring all the methods that you will require in it. To change an already existing interface, you have to create its direct descendant, and after that modify this descendant as you choose. In other words, a developer cannot directly modify existing interfaces.

Building a COM Object Using the COM Object Wizard

This section will guide you through the whole step-by-step process of creating a new COM object with the COM Object Wizard:

1. Select File/New from Delphi's main menu, and you'll see a dialog window for adding new items to your project (Figure 10.1).
2. Select the ActiveX tab in this window.
3. Double-click the COM object icon.
4. The above operations will result in the COM Object Wizard window appearing on your screen (Figure 10.2).

The COM Object Wizard window contains several edit fields and check boxes:

- The Class Name field: Specifies the name of your new COM object
- The Instancing field: Determines the technique used to create the COM object; this field can be assigned one of the following values:
  - **Internal:** An object can be created only within a process; an external application is not capable of directly creating instances of this object. This approach to building COM objects can be illustrated by a text processor that can contain a document as an object that can be created only by calling a method of the given text processor.

- Single Instance: Allows only for a single interface for each application. This means that as soon as one application has attached to a given object, this object becomes unavailable to all other applications.
- Multiple Instance: A given object can be attached to multiple applications at the same time. Every time a client requests a server, a new instance of this server is built. For example, every time a user opens Windows Explorer, a new instance of Explorer is created.

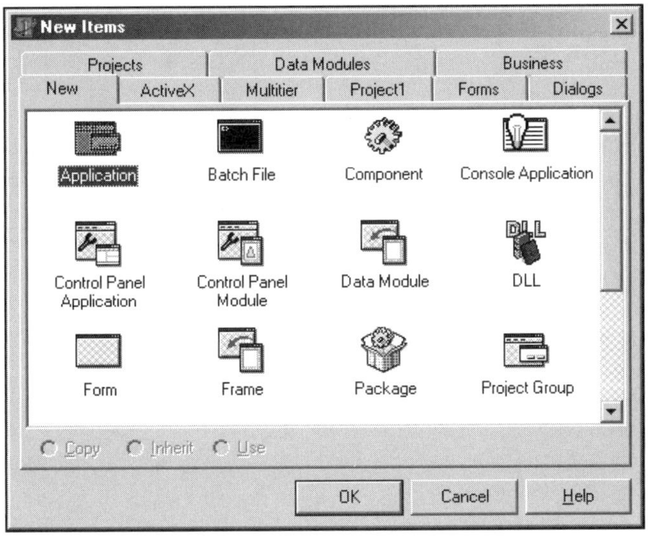

FIGURE 10.1 The dialog window for adding new items to a project.

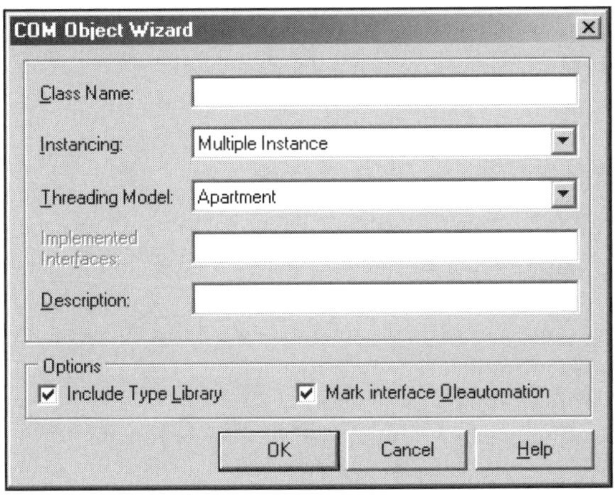

FIGURE 10.2 The **COM Object Wizard** dialog window.

NOTE

If a COM object is designated only for in-process use, the **Instancing** *field is ignored.*

- The Threading Model field: Defines how client applications can call your COM object. *Threading models will be discussed later in this chapter.*
- The Implemented Interfaces field: Specifies the names of any interfaces that the COM object can implement.
- The Description field: Provides a description of a given COM object.
- The Include Type Library check box: Select this box if you mean to build a type library for the COM object. As soon as this check box is selected, Delphi automatically enables the other check box, Mark interface Oleautomation.
- The Mark interface Oleautomation check box: Activates the marshaling code. COM knows how to implement marshaling for all objects that are compatible with the automation server, and sets proxies and stubs automatically.

Choosing the Thread Model

When creating a new COM object with the wizard, you have to choose a thread model. Choosing the correct thread model will improve the functioning of your COM object.

Table 10.2 briefly describes the thread models possible for COM objects.

TABLE 10.2 Thread models for COM Objects

Thread model	*Description*	*Advantages and disadvantages of the model*
Single	No thread support. Client queries are processed one after another.	Clients are processed in the order they stand in the line, and therefore thread support is unnecessary.
Apartment	Clients can call methods of the object only from the thread in which that object was created. Objects of the same server can be called from different threads, but each object can be called only from one thread.	While the data from the one instance is secure, global data must be protected with a critical section or in some other manner. These objects are relatively easy to write, but you might find writing the code for the client difficult. Primarily used for Web browser controls.

TABLE 10.2 Thread models for COM Objects

Thread model	***Description***	***Advantages and disadvantages of the model***
Free	Clients can call any methods of the object at any time and from any thread. The number of threads is unlimited.	You need to protect all the data in the instance, as well as the global data of the object. Local variables are unreliable due to the large number of calls. Clients are easy to write, but you might have trouble with the object's code. First used for the DCOM technology.
Both	Objects can support clients that use either the Free or Apartment model.	Maximum flexibility; may improve your work.

When the two parts of the COM application, client and server, are interacting, you'll get a message concerning which thread models they each support. COM compares these models. If both parts describe the same thread model, COM sets up a direct connection between the client and the server. If their thread models differ, COM uses marshaling to set up a connection between the application parts. Marshaling does slow down the working speed, but its advantages are clear: marshaling allows two applications that use different thread models to work together.

A thread model is used only for in-process servers. Local servers are registered as EXE applications and provide the thread model themselves.

In the next chapters, we'll look at concrete examples of the process of creating COM objects.

11 Automation Servers

Automation is the COM protocol that specifies the technique to be implemented by an application in order to get access to the objects that are contained inside another application or DLL.

An *automation server* is an application that provides certain services to client applications. Such applications as Microsoft Word, Microsoft Excel, and Microsoft Internet Explorer belong to the category of automation servers. The behavior of such applications can be managed from Delphi applications and other applications. In order to successfully work with automation servers, a developer must be familiar with the properties and methods provided by automation server objects. Comprehensive information on such properties and methods can be obtained from the developer documentation of the individual server application.

An *automation controller* (or *automation dispatcher*) is a client application that manages an automation server by using the objects supported by the `IDispatch` interface.

Automation controllers can be written in any programming language that supports COM. Most automation controllers are currently developed in such languages as C++, Object Pascal (Delphi), and Visual Basic.

In this chapter, you will learn how Delphi can help you create automation controllers and automation servers.

THE *IDISPATCH* INTERFACE

Automation objects are COM objects that use the `IDispatch` interface. This interface is declared in the `System` unit in the following way:

```
type
   IDispatch = interface (IUnknown)
   ['{00020400-0000-0000-C000-000000000046}']
   function GetTypeInfoCount(out Count: Integer): HResult; stdcall;
   function GetTypeInfo(Index, LocaleID: Integer; out TypeInfo):HResult;
            stdcall;
   function GetIDsOfNames(const IID: TGUID; Names: Pointer; NameCount,
   LocaleID: Integer;
   DispIDs: Pointer): HResult; stdcall;
   function Invoke(DispID: Integer; const IID: TGUID; LocaleID: Integer;
   Flags: Word;
   var Params; VarResult, ExceptInfo, ArgErr: Pointer): HResult;
               stdcall;
end;
```

The main function of the `IDispatch` interface is implemented by its `Invoke` method. A client application can call this method to perform certain operations on an automation server. A client application specifies the method that it needs to invoke by passing the name of this method as the `DispID` parameter when it calls the `Invoke` method. The parameter is represented by a number, referred to as a *dispatch ID*. The number indicates the method which is to execute on the server. The next parameter of the `Invoke` method, `IID`, is not currently used. The `LocaleID` parameter contains information on localization. The `Flags` parameter determines how the method will be called: for reading properties, for writing properties, or in the regular fashion. The `Params` property contains the pointer to the `TDispParams` array. This array stores the parameters to be passed to the method. The `VarResult` parameter is the pointer to `OleVariant`, which contains a return value for a given method (if there is such a value). The `ExcepInfo` parameter stores the pointer to the `TExcepInfo` record that includes information about an error when the `Invoke` method returns the `DISP_E_EXCEPTION` value. The last parameter, `ArgError`, is the pointer to an integer that is the index of an incorrect parameter in the `Params` array. In such a case, the `Invoke` method will return `DISP_E_TYPEMISMATCH` or `DISP_E_PARAMNOTFOUND`.

Another method of the IDispatch interface is GetIDsOfNames. It is used for obtaining the dispatch ID of one or several methods using the name strings of these methods. The IID parameter of this method is not used. The Names parameter is the pointer to the array of method names. This array has a PWideChar type. The NameCount parameter contains the number that indicates the number of strings in the array pointed to by the Names parameter. The LocaleID parameter contains information about localization. The DispIDs parameter is the pointer to the NameCount integer array.

The GetTypeInfo method is used to obtain information on the type of a given automation object. The Index parameter describes the information on the type and should be (as a rule) equal to zero. The LCID parameter contains information on localization. If the method has been successfully completed, then the TypeInfo parameter will contain the ITypeInfo pointer to information on the type of the automation object.

The GetTypeInfoCount method is used to obtain information on the availability of the interfaces that provide information on the type. A value is returned in the Count parameter. This parameter can contain one of two values: 0 if a given automation object does not provide runtime information on the type, and if 1 it does.

LATE BINDING VS. EARLY BINDING

There are two possible operating modes for handling automation objects: *late binding* and *early binding*.

Late binding implies that the required method of an automation server is called by a client from inside the Invoke method of the IDispatch interface. A client is forbidden to call the required method before the moment of its implementation, and the call itself can be made only through the Invoke method. At the time of compilation, a call for any method of an automation server is automatically converted to a call for the IDispatch.Invoke method. During runtime, the Invoke method invokes the required automation server method.

Early binding means that an automation server provides its methods via a custom interface, which must be a descendant of the IDispatch interface. In this case, an automation controller can directly invoke an automation server method without calling the IDispatch interface's Invoke method. Using early binding helps you speed up the performance of automation objects.

A great number of automation objects support a so-called *dual interface*. This means that such automation objects allow you to call automation server methods both from the Invoke method and from descendants of the IDispatch interface. Automation servers created with Delphi always support a dual interface. Automation dispatchers that were created with Delphi can call the required methods both directly from the user interface and indirectly, from inside the Invoke method.

CREATING AN AUTOMATION CONTROLLER

One of the simplest ways to develop an automation controller is to import the type library of an automation server. You can also use automatically generated classes for managing the automation server.

NOTE

Importing the type library of an automation server is of particular importance for those developers who design using earlier versions of Delphi. Starting with Delphi 5, the Servers *tab, where you can find icons that enable you to access all major automation servers installed on a given computer, was added to the Component palette.*

In order to import a type library, act as follows:

1. Select **Project/Import Type Library** from the Delphi main menu.
2. As soon as the dialog window appears (Figure 11.1), select the required type library from the list.

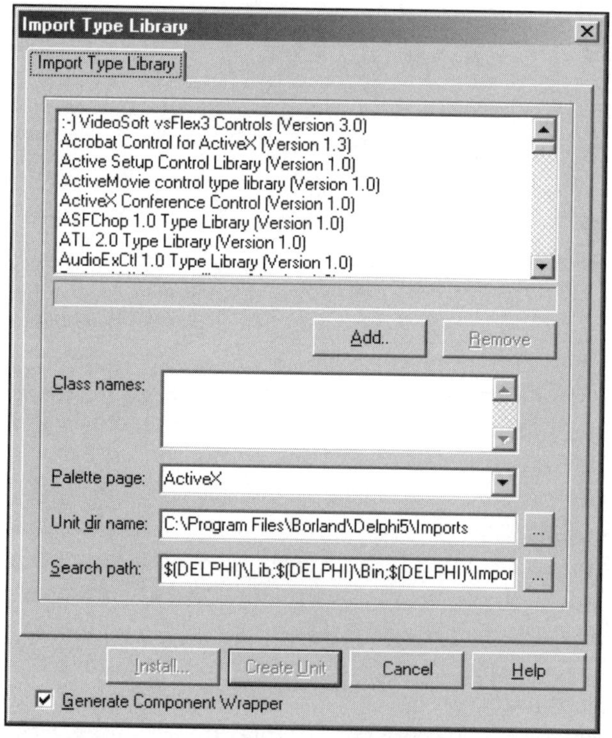

FIGURE 11.1 The dialog window for importing a type library.

> **NOTE** *The list in the dialog window for importing type libraries contains all the type libraries that have been registered with the operating system on a given computer. If you cannot find the required type library, it means that the library in question should be added to the list using the* **Add** *button. As soon as you've clicked* **Add**, *find the desired type library and append it to the list with any of the following extensions: TLB, OLB, DLL, OCX or EXE. You can also delete a type library from the list in the Import Type Library dialog window by using the* **Remove** *button. Just select the type library you want to remove and click* **Remove**.

3. From the **Palette page** drop-down list of the dialog window, select the page of the Delphi Component palette on which you are going to place the chosen automation server.
4. Make sure that the **Generate Component Wrapper** check box is selected.
5. Click the **Install** button, and follow the instructions in the dialog.

Processing Automation Controller Events

As soon as you have installed the required automation server to the Component palette, you can use **Object Inspector** to create event handlers. Events are handled the same as other Delphi components' events:

1. Find the automation server in the Component palette and place it on the form.
2. Click the component, and then open the **Events** tab in the Object Inspector window where all the events of the component will be listed.
3. Double-click across from the required event, and Delphi will generate a shell for the event handler in which you can insert your code.

When all the necessary event handlers have been written, you can get started connecting to the automation server.

CONNECTING TO AN AUTOMATION SERVER

Let's use Microsoft Word, Microsoft Excel and Microsoft Outlook (provided with the popular Microsoft Office program pack) to discuss the process of connecting to an automation server. The process that we will consider may be slightly different for other automation servers, but fundamentally, the technique is the same everywhere.

Prior to connecting to an automation server, let's consider the Microsoft Office Object Model.

There is no such concept as "inheritance" in Microsoft Office; embedding is used instead. It is embedding that lets you create new classes in Microsoft Office applications. Every Microsoft Office application has a central *base* object. In Microsoft Word, this is `Word.Application`, and in Microsoft Excel, it is `Excel.Application`. As for Microsoft Outlook, it is itself a base object and called `OutLookApplication`, but all other objects that are in turn properties of this base object are built in the `Application` object, nonetheless.

Different objects of Microsoft Office applications contain a wide variety of methods, but some of these methods can be found in every application, such as `Run`, `Activate`, etc.

NOTE

There is a distinction among the aforementioned methods. The parameters of these methods vary for different Microsoft Office applications. Additionally, methods that have the same name in different applications may perform different operations.

Figure 11.2 shows a small fragment of the Microsoft Word Object's architecture. *Comprehensive information on Microsoft Office Object architecture can be found in Microsoft Office reference materials.*

As soon as you've created a new document in a Microsoft Office application, the framework for this new document is automatically generated. This framework is essentially a set of class libraries. Instances of these classes will be available in your new document. The task of the developer who is designing the automation controller is to provide access to the root directory of a given server, to build an access chain to the built-in objects, and to ensure that correct parameters are set.

So, the `Application` object is the base object in every application. Let's now try to access it using Delphi tools.

NOTE

The following procedure will work for all Delphi versions beginning with Delphi 5.

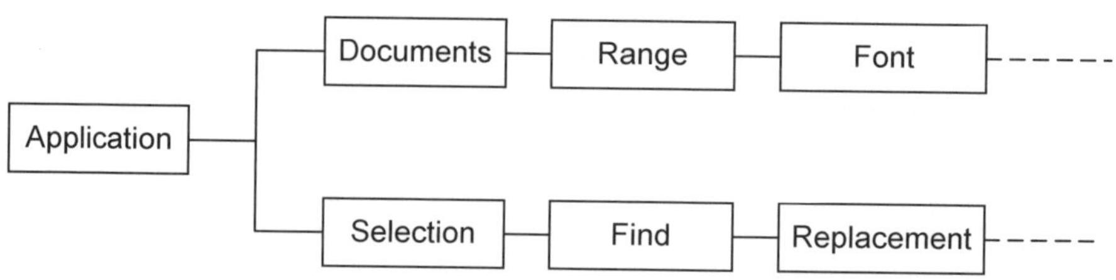

FIGURE 11.2 A fragment of the Microsoft Word Object's architecture.

Proceed as follows:

1. Create a new Delphi project via the **File/New Application** item of the main menu.
2. Place the `WordApplication` component from the Servers tab of the Component palette on your form.
3. Set the `AutoConnect` and `AutoQuit` properties of the `WordApplication` component to `true`. (These properties allow you to automatically load the automation server to memory and unload it from memory when you run your application.)
4. Start the application with the **Run/Run** item of the main menu.

As a result—although no visible changes on the form can be detected—your application has done a lot of work: it's launched the Microsoft Word automation server. In order to make sure that this is really the case, take a look at the list of tasks being performed by Windows when you run your application. Start Windows Task Manager (in Windows 9x and XP press <Ctrl>+<Alt>+<Del>; in Windows NT 4.0 and 2000 press <Ctrl>+<Alt>+<Del> and select **Task Manager** from the menu that appears). at runtime and you will see Winword.exe among the tasks being performed by Windows.

Without going into detail, let's outline the operations that have been performed by your application:

- Upon starting up your application, the `Word.Application`'s automation server was found in the Windows registry using CLSID.
- The application with the address indicated in the Windows registry was started.
- The automation server provided your application (which in fact is a simplistic automation controller) with an interface through which the application can access the Microsoft Word base object.

Now, close the application and look again at the tasks being performed by Windows. The automation server has been unloaded from the memory using the `IDispatch` interface. (This interface contains the `_ADDRef` method, which enables you to learn how many clients are currently working with the server.)

The same result can be achieved if you use the code presented in Listing 11.1. But first place two buttons on your form: **Start** and **Finish**.

LISTING 11.1

```
unit Unit1;

interface

uses
  Windows, Messages, SysUtils, Classes, Graphics, Controls,
  Forms, Dialogs, StdCtrls, COMObj;
```

```
type
  TForm1 = class(TForm)
    Start: TButton;
    Finish: TButton;
    procedure StartClick(Sender: TObject);
    procedure FinishClick(Sender: TObject);
  private
    {Private declarations}
  public
    {Public declarations}
  end;
var
  Form1: TForm1;
 wd:OleVariant;
 fileName:string;
implementation
{$R *.DFM}
procedure TForm1.StartClick(Sender: TObject);
begin
try
  fileName:=ExtractFilePath(Application.EXEName)+'report.DOC';
// Create the interface object for accessing the COM server
  wd:=CreateOleObject('Word.Application');
// A check on the availability of the methods and the validity of the
// parameters will be implemented at runtime
  wd.application.documents.add;
  wd.application.activedocument.range.insertAfter(now);
  wd.application.activedocument.saveas(fileName);
except
  on E: Exception do Application.MessageBox(E.Message),
  pChar('Some Application'),MB_OK or MB_ICONERROR);
end;
end;
procedure TForm1.FinishClick(Sender: TObject);
begin
   // Unload the server from the computer memory
  wd.application.quit(True,0);
end;
end.
```

Notice that it is absolutely essential to add the COMObj unit to the Uses clause.

As you can see, the Servers tab of the Component palette contains a lot of components. In addition to the base objects of automation servers, this tab contains a number of embedded objects, such as WordDocument, ExcelWorkbook, etc.

It should be noted that all the components contained in the Servers tab are descendants of the TOLEServer class, which in its turn descends from the TComponent class. The TOLEServer class is the base class for all COM servers. You can create it by importing the type libraries of automation servers. This class owns several properties and methods that enable it to manage the connection to a COM server. For example, it has the AutoConnect property that, once you've set it to True, automatically starts a COM server and implements the interface for connecting a server with an automation controller.

Let's now discuss a very important feature of this class: the ConnectKind property (the type of the process that you are connecting to). This property uses the Connect method that is called automatically if AutoConnect=True. Table 11.1 includes the values of the ConnectKind property.

TABLE 11.1 The Values of the ConnectKind Property

Value of ConnectKind	*Description*
ckRunningOrNew	The automation controller connects to an existing process. If no process is running, an automation controller starts one and connects to it. This kind of interaction between a controller and a server is the most common kind.
ckNewInstance	The automation controller always creates a new instance of an automation server.
ckRunningInstance	Connection can be established only with an existing automation server; if such a server is not found, then an error is generated.
ckRemote	Used for connecting to a remote automation server. If you set the ConnectKind property to this value, you must specify the name of the remote computer in the RemoteMachineName property.
ckAttachToInterface	Here, the server cannot be connected. That's why the AutoConnect property cannot be set to True. The required connection can be made using the ConnectTo method.

NOTE

If you assign the last value, ckAttachToInterface, to the ConnectKind property, you can successively attach a number of components, such as WordDocument or WordFont, to an existing interface. This value must be set when an automation controller must track down the events that occur in a given automation server.

The `ConnectKind` property can be set in the **Object Inspector** window using the drop-down list that appears as soon as you click a property.

MANAGING AN AUTOMATION SERVER

This section covers the technique of connecting and managing an automation server by using the `ConnectKind` property. This technique involves the following steps:

1. Create a new project through **File/New Application** of the main menu.
2. Place the `WordApplication` and `WordDocument` components—which can be found in the **Servers** tab—on the form.
3. Set the `AutoConnect` property and the `AutoQuit` property for the `WordApplication` component to `True`.
4. Set the `ConnectKind` property for the `WordDocument` component to `ckAttachToInterface`.
5. Select the `WordApplication` component on the form and open the **Events** tab in the **Object Inspector** window.
6. Double-click the `OnDocumentChange` event and write the code presented in Listing 11.2 to the shell of the event handler that Delphi is to generate.

LISTING 11.2

```
procedure TForm1.WordApplication1DocumentChange(Sender: TObject);
begin
// Connect to the active Microsoft Word document
   WordDocument1.ConnectTo(WordApplication1.ActiveDocument);
// Your automation controller inserts a new string in the current document
   WordDocument1.Range.InsertAfter(#13+'Move to the document '+#13+
   WordApplication1.ActiveDocument.Get_FullName+' is implemented :'+
   DateTimeToStr(Now));
end;
```

Let's see what operations will be executed by the code in Listing 11.2. First of all, a given code will be implemented every time you change your current Microsoft Word document. As soon as you change the current document (that is, switch from one Microsoft Word document to another), your automation controller attaches to the active document by using the `ConnectTo` method. Then, a new text string is inserted into the current document through the `InsertAfter` method. Moving to the next string in the document is done by inserting the line feed character (#13). The `Get_FullName` method returns the name of the current Microsoft Word document.

Write the code given in Listing 11.3 for the `Create` event of the form.

LISTING 11.3

```
procedure TForm1.FormCreate(Sender: TObject);
begin
// The automation server is displyed on the screen
   WordApplication1.Visible:=True;
end;
```

This code will display Microsoft Word on the screen, even if it has not been previously loaded.

Start your newly created automation controller through the **Run/Run** item of the main menu. As soon as the application starts, Microsoft Word will be automatically loaded. By using **File/New** of the Microsoft Word menu, create several new documents. Now, let's make sure that your automation controller works. Try to toggle between the documents using the **Window** item of the Microsoft Word menu. You will see how your automation controller adds new strings to the current document.

The same management principle is equally applicable for Microsoft Excel. When a new workbook is created in Microsoft Excel, the `OnNewWorkBook` event is generated.

CREATING AN AUTOMATION SERVER

An automation server can be represented either by an application or a DLL. Let's outline the procedure that you should perform in order to develop an automation server.

1. Create an application or DLL that will act as the automation server. You can use any of your already existing applications for this purpose, but first you need to add automation to it.
2. Using the **Automation Object Wizard**, create an automation object and add it to the project.
3. Add properties and methods to your automation object using the type library. These properties and methods are necessary so that automation controllers can use them when they call your automation server.
4. Register the application as an automation server.

Let's now discuss the above steps in more detail.

Let's create the most simplistic application, one consisting of only one form. In order to do this, start Delphi and select **File/New Application**.

Now add an automation object to your application if you want to make your application perform the functions of an automation server. Select **File/New**. This will activate the New Items dialog window, where you have to choose the **ActiveX** tab (Figure 11.3).

Select the **Automation Object** icon by double-clicking it. You will see the **Automation Object Wizard** window (Figure 11.4).

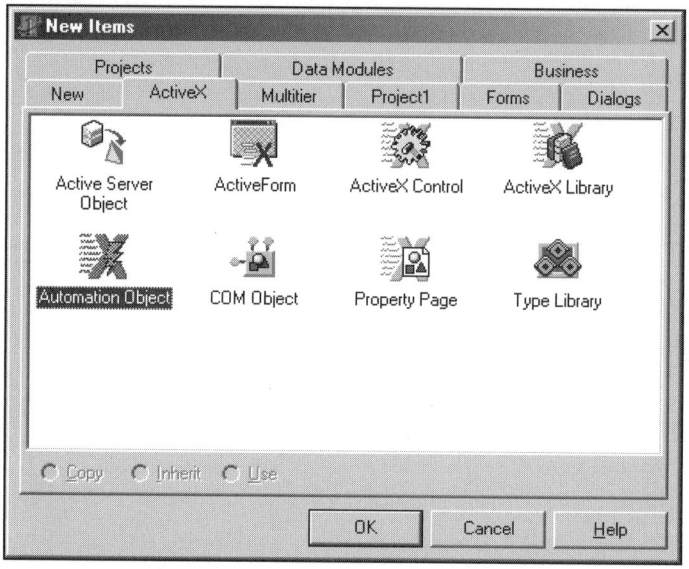

FIGURE 11.3 The **ActiveX** tab in the **New Items** dialog window.

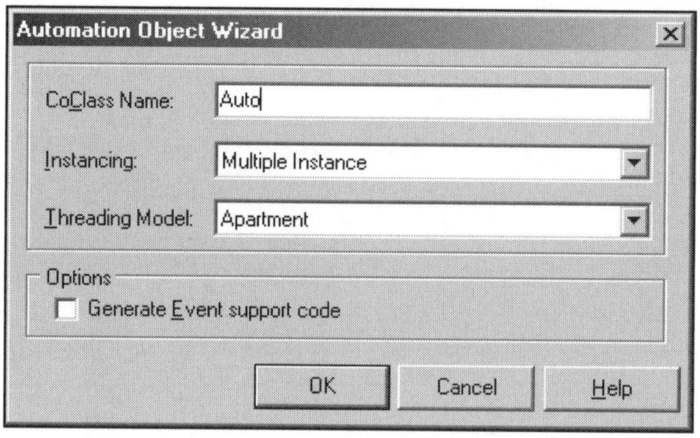

FIGURE 11.4 The **Automation Object Wizard** dialog window.

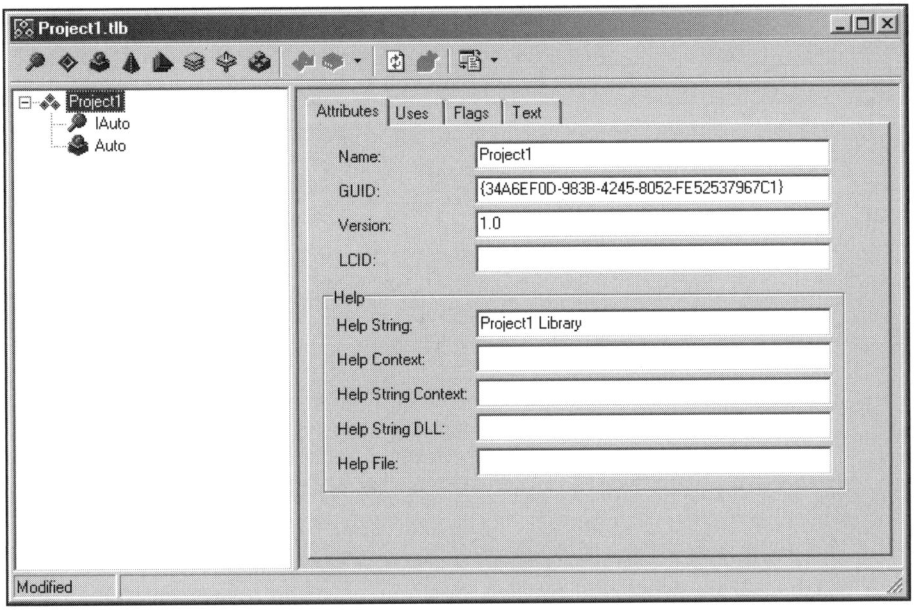

FIGURE 11.5 A new automation project in the Type Library Editor window.

Enter the `Auto` name into the **CoClass Name** field to specify the class name for your COM object. The Wizard will automatically prefix the class name with a T if you are creating an Object Pascal class for your automation object, or with an I if you are creating an interface for your automation object.

The values that can be entered in the rest of the fields have already been discussed in previous chapters.

As soon as all the settings in this dialog window are specified, Delphi builds a new type library for the project, and also adds an interface and a component class to this library. Moreover, the wizard will create a new unit in your project that will contain an implementation of the automation interface that has been added to the type library. Figure 11.5 shows the Type Library Editor window immediately after the **Automation Object Wizard** dialog window has been closed.

Listing 11.4 contains the code for the new unit that the Delphi **Automation Object Wizard** generates.

LISTING 11.4

```
unit Unit2;
interface
uses
  ComObj, ActiveX, Project1_TLB, StdVcl;
type
```

```
  TAuto = class(TAutoObject, IAuto)
  protected
    {Protected declarations}
  end;
implementation
uses ComServ;
initialization
  TAutoObjectFactory.Create(ComServer, TAuto, Class_Auto,
    ciMultiInstance, tmApartment);
end.
```

It can be inferred from the Listing 11.4 that the new automation object, `TAuto`, is a descendant class of the `TAutoObject` class. It should be mentioned that the `TAutoObject` class is the base class for all automation objects.

Now that you've included the new `TAuto` automation object to your project, you can add all the required properties and methods to the `IAuto` base interface.

Let's take on a simple task: suppose you need your automation server to change the color of your form by receiving the required color from the automation controller. Begin by adding the `Color` property to the `IAuto` interface. This can be done in the Type Library Editor in a number of ways, one of which is as follows:

1. Left-click the `IAuto` interface icon in the left part of the Type Library Editor window.
2. Since we need just to read a color from the automation controller, we can assign this property the read-only attribute. Click the small arrow to the right of the icon that represents properties in the Editor bar, and select **Write Only** (Figure 11.6).
3. Name your new property `Color`, and set its type as `OLE_COLOR` in the `Type` field.

That's it. You have just added your new property. Now click the **Refresh Implementation** button in the Editor bar to update the implementation unit of the automation object (Figure 11.7). As a result, Delphi will adjust the implementation unit so that it reflects the changes that you made in the Type Library Editor window. The code of the modified unit is presented in Listing 11.5. The `TAuto.Set_Color` procedure body has been manually inserted in the listing as well. The `uses` section has been also been modified to reference the form's unit (`Unit1`).

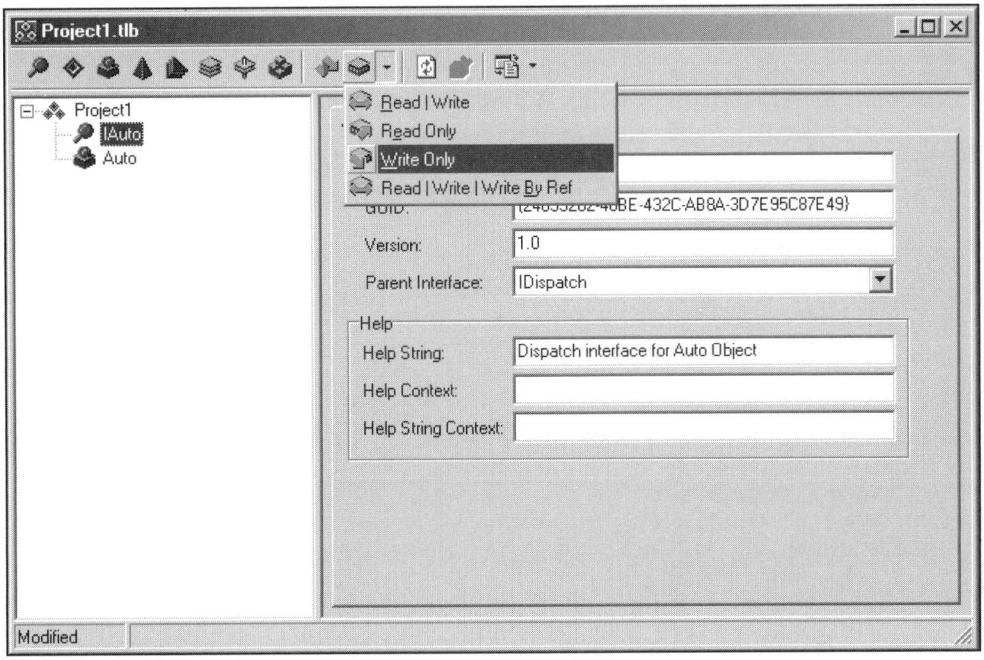

FIGURE 11.6 Adding a write-only property to the `IAuto` interface.

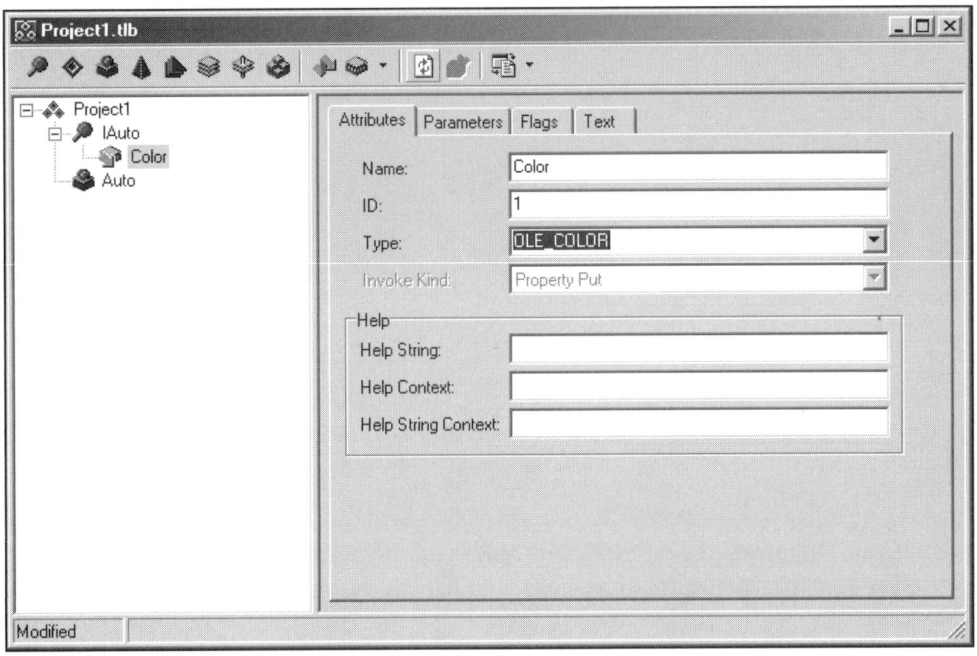

FIGURE 11.7 The complete type library.

LISTING 11.5

```
unit Unit2;
interface
uses
  ComObj, ActiveX, Test_TLB, StdVcl;
type
  TAuto = class(TAutoObject, IAuto)
  protected
    procedure Set_Color(Value: OLE_COLOR); safecall;
    {Protected declarations}
  end;
implementation
uses ComServ, Unit1;
procedure TAuto.Set_Color(Value: OLE_COLOR);
begin
  Form1.color:=Value;
end;
initialization
  TAutoObjectFactory.Create(ComServer, TAuto, Class_Auto,
    ciMultiInstance, tmApartment);
end.
```

At this point, you have to create a new folder on your hard disk and give it a name ("Automation," for example). Save your application to this folder. When saving, name your project "Test." Then run the application to get an executable file, Test.exe.

Now you have your automation server ready and can test it to make sure that it works. For this purpose you will require an automation controller. Close the current project using File/Close All, and create a new one with File/New Application. Place two buttons on the form: Connect and Change color (Figure 11.8).

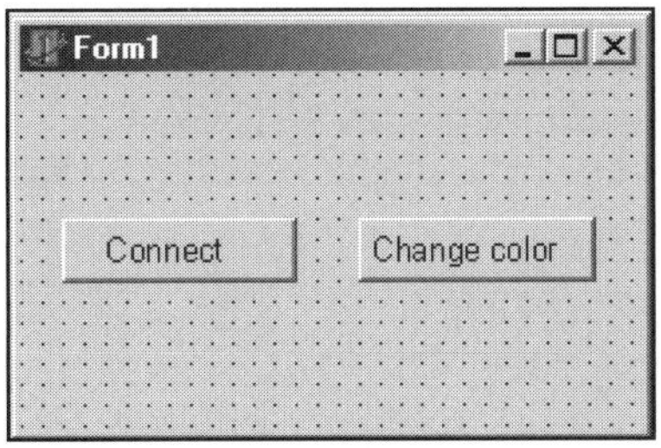

FIGURE 11.8 The appearance of a sample form of your automation controller.

Listing 11.6 below illustrates the code for your automation controller.

LISTING 11.6

```
unit Unit1;
interface
uses
  Windows, Messages, SysUtils, Classes, Graphics, Controls, Forms,
  Dialogs, StdCtrls, Test_TLB;
type
  TForm1 = class(TForm)
    Button1: TButton;
    Button2: TButton;
    procedure Button1Click(Sender: TObject);
    procedure Button2Click(Sender: TObject);
  private
    FIntf: IAuto;
    {Private declarations}
  public
    {Public declarations}
  end;
var
  Form1: TForm1;
implementation
{$R *.DFM}
procedure TForm1.Button1Click(Sender: TObject);
begin
```

```
  FIntf:=CoAuto.Create;
end;
procedure TForm1.Button2Click(Sender: TObject);
begin
  FIntf.Set_Color(clRed);
end;
end.
```

Take a closer look at the Listing 11.6. As you can see, you first need to add the `Test_TLB` type library to the `uses` clause. Then insert the `FIntf` field of the `IAuto` type in the `private` section. After that, write the `OnClick` event handler for the Connect button; the event in question creates an instance of the automation server.

As soon as you click the Connect button, the Test.exe application will start. Write the handler for the `OnClick` event for the Change color button, which will call the `Set_Color` method of the `IAuto` interface. Let's, for example, set a red color, `clRed`, for the form of the server application. Then click the Connect button and the Change color button, one after the other. You can see that the Test.exe application starts, after which its application form changes to red (see the form on the right side of Figure 11.9).

So your simple application works, and you've achieved the desired result.

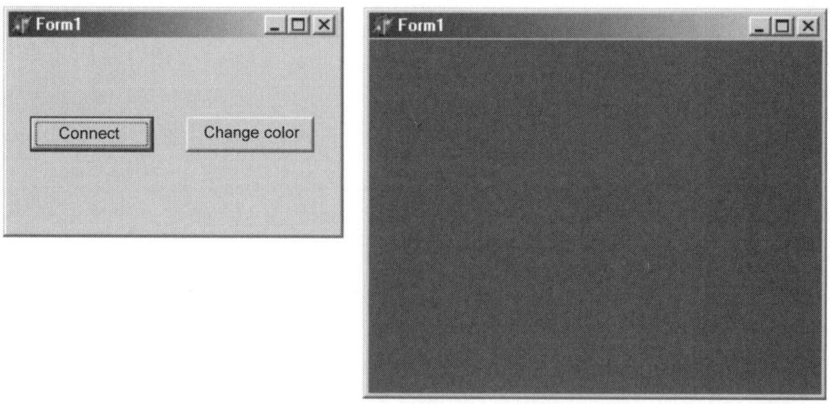

FIGURE 11.9 The result achieved by running your automation application.

12 Using ActiveX Controls in Delphi

This chapter covers the issue of using third-party ActiveX controls. You will learn what an ActiveX control is and when it can be used. Also, we'll discuss the installation of an ActiveX control into the Component palette.

WHAT IS AN ACTIVEX CONTROL?

There is no definite, clear-cut answer to this question. It all depends on the way one sees ActiveX.

From a developer's point of view, an ActiveX control is something that owns properties, events, and methods (almost like any other component). A Delphi developer may have no idea about what COM actually is, but at the same time be able to successfully use ActiveX controls in his applications.

As viewed by COM, an ActiveX control is an automation server implemented as a DLL that executes in the same process as your application. ActiveX controls support visual editing, which means that you can modify their properties and methods and write event handlers for them in the same manner as you do for other Delphi VCL components.

Strictly speaking, the idea underlying ActiveX was implemented—at least partially—some time ago. Visual Basic Extensions (VBX) were introduced as far back as in the early Microsoft Visual Basic version aimed at developing 16-bit applications. Much of the programming community embraced the idea of component development and used it to create a wide range of application development tools, including Delphi, which was created to make VBXs. This technology gradually transformed into 32-bit technology.

WHY USE ACTIVEX CONTROLS?

You may not have realized that you've been using ActiveX controls for some time for developing your applications. The thing is, quite a few ActiveX controls registered in the Windows registry have already been installed in the Delphi Component palette and outwardly do not differ from ordinary Delphi components. There is no need to elaborate here on the subject of controls and the characteristics that set them apart from other components. Instead, let's see when ActiveX controls must be used.

Typically, the necessity of using ActiveX controls arises when you need to enhance the functionality of your application at the expense of the capabilities that are already registered in the application system. For instance, if you want to create a Web browser of your own, you needn't write it from scratch. You can take advantage of the skillfully designed Web browser objectused in Microsoft Internet Explorer (SHDOCVW.DLL). You need just to connect to this object (which is an ActiveX control) and work with it.

In conclusion, it should be noted that beginning with Delphi 5, the Component palette includes the **Internet** tab, which allows a developer to design applications based on the Microsoft Internet Explorer object.

INSTALLING AN ACTIVEX CONTROL INTO THE COMPONENT PALETTE

A number of third-party ActiveX controls are supplied with Delphi, but you will most likely need to add new ActiveX controls to the Delphi Component palette on your own as well.

You must begin the process of installing an ActiveX control by selecting **Component/Import ActiveX Control** from the main menu. This will activate the dialog window (Figure 12.1) that features information on all ActiveX controls registered in the Windows registry.

Let's take a look at this dialog window.

The top part of the window lists all the ActiveX controls registered in your system. The **Class names** list box contains a list of classes that a given control contains. From Figure 12.1, you can see that the selected ActiveX control has two built-in classes, `TDHTMLEdit` and `TDHTMLSafe`.

The **Palette page** drop-down list is designed for defining the page of the Component palette on which the selected ActiveX control will be stored. By default, it will be the ActiveX page.

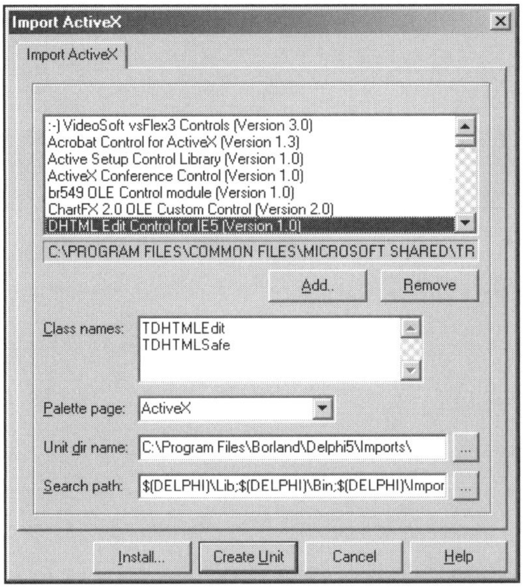

FIGURE 12.1 The dialog window for importing ActiveX controls.

The next two fields, **Unit dir name** and **Search path**, are used to specify the directory in which the ActiveX control will be placed, and to indicate the search path to this unit for a Delphi compiler.

For simplicity's sake, I recommend that you choose the same ActiveX control as the one shown in Figure 12.1. If you don't have this control, you can select any other one that you like, but we'll discuss the process of installation using this control as an example.

As soon as you've selected a control, click the **Install** button. You'll see the **Install** dialog window (Figure 12.2).

NOTE

Another button, ***Create Unit****, lets you create a so-called wrapper file. This file contains a description of the type library, as well as one for all the properties, methods, and events owned by the control. The content of a wrapper is written in Object Pascal. The name of this file consists of two parts: the first is the name of the ActiveX control, and the second is the _TLB.PAS string. By clicking the* ***Create Unit*** *button, you simply create a file, after which you can view its content. In order to continue the process of installation, you have to click the* ***Install*** *button. The window has two tabs,* ***Into existing package*** *and* ***Into new package****. You decide into which package you want the control to be installed.*

NOTE

It is recommended that you create your own new package for your ActiveX controls. This will help you save resources. However, in order not to complicate the description of the installation process here, we will not discuss creating a new package in this example.

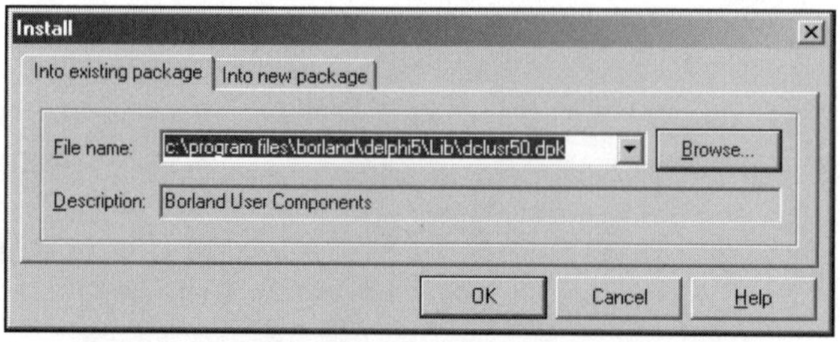

FIGURE 12.2 The dialog window for installing a control into a package.

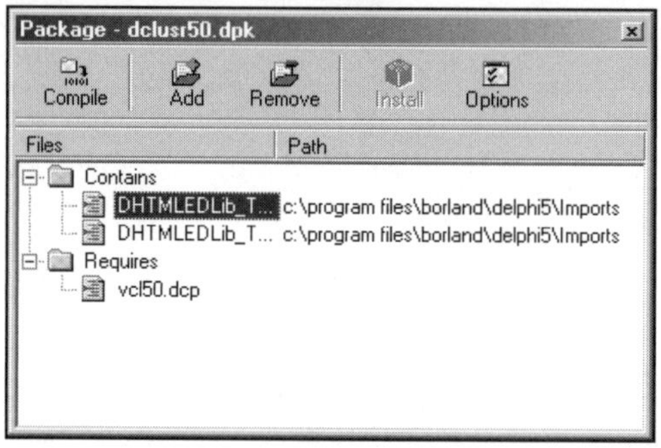

FIGURE 12.3 The content of the dclusr50.dpk package after a new ActiveX control has been installed.

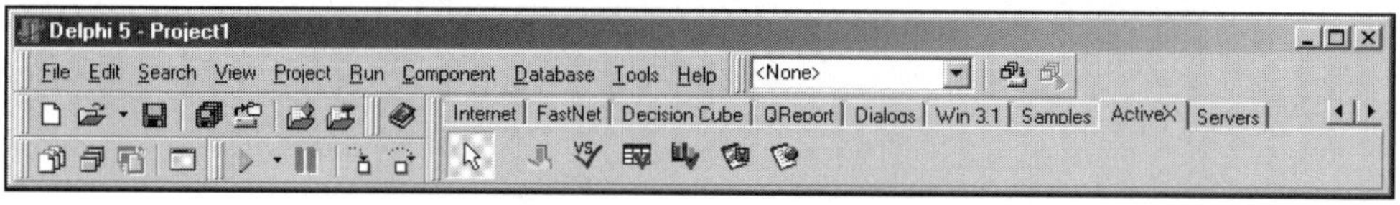

FIGURE 12.4 The content of the **ActiveX** tab.

So, add your control to the default package suggested by Delphi (dclusr50.dpk).

As soon as you've clicked the OK button in the Install dialog window, Delphi will compile the dclusr50.dpk package. Figure 12.3 shows the resulting content of a given package.

Now, move to the ActiveX tab of the Component palette in order to see the changes it has undergone (Figure 12.4).

As you can see, icons representing the two new components, `DHTMLEdit` and `DHTMLSafe`, have appeared in the tab.

From now on, you can place any of these components on your forms and use them as you use other Delphi components. That is, using Object Inspector, you can modify their properties, write event handlers, etc.

In order to uninstall an ActiveX control, open the file of the package where you've installed ActiveX, and remove all the controls that you consider unnecessary. After that, recompile the package. The controls in question will have been uninstalled from the Component palette.

13 Creating ActiveX Controls

The previous chapter discussed the issue of using ActiveX controls. Here you'll learn how to create an ActiveX control in Delphi using wizards, VCL components, and forms.

DESIGNING ACTIVEX CONTROLS

It should be noted that there are two special Delphi wizards for building ActiveX controls. A developer has to choose between the following two alternatives:

- Use the transformation wizard of any window component (a descendant of `TWinControl`) to convert this component into an ActiveX control. You can call the ActiveX Control Wizard through File/New, and then select the ActiveX Control icon in the ActiveX tab.
- Use the wizard that turns a form into an ActiveX control. Such wizards are called by selecting the ActiveForm icon in the ActiveX tab.

CREATING AN ACTIVEX CONTROL FROM EXISTING DELPHI VCL COMPONENTS

As mentioned earlier, one way of creating an ActiveX control in Delphi is to convert a Delphi VCL window component into an ActiveX control.

> *Although the **ActiveX Control Wizard** doesn't allow you to automatically create ActiveX controls from components that do not descend from `TWinControl`, a developer can build such a control himself using the Delphi ActiveX (DAX) toolkit.*

Call the **ActiveX Control Wizard**. This will activate the **ActiveX Control Wizard** window, used for converting a Delphi window component into an ActiveX control (Figure 13.1).

Then proceed as follows:

1. Select a VCL component from the VCL Class Name drop-down list.

> *As you've probably noticed, the **VCL Class Name** drop-down list doesn't contain all the VCL components. It contains only those components that satisfy the following requirements: they are in the current project you use at design time (which in turn implies that they are available from the Component palette), they descend from the `TWinControl` component, and they cannot be removed from the list by the `RegisterNonActiveX` procedure.*

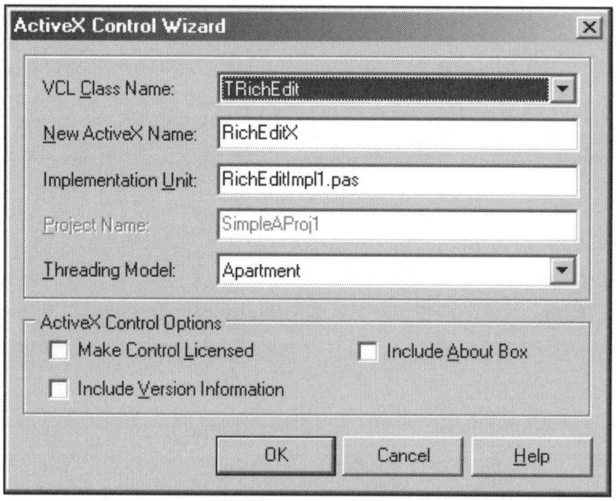

FIGURE 13.1 The **ActiveX Control Wizard** window for converting a Delphi VCL component into an ActiveX control.

NOTE

*Many components are excluded from the VCL **Class Name** list either because of their incapability of acting as ActiveX controls (for example, the `TDBGrid` component needs another VCL class, `TDataSource`, to work), or the fact that they must be manually adjusted before you start the wizard so that they'll be able to function as ActiveX controls (this applies, for instance, to the `TTreeView` component, because its nodes are very difficult to convert to ActiveX).*

2. Enter a new name for your ActiveX control into the **New ActiveX Name** field if you are not satisfied with the default value suggested by Delphi.
3. Select a name for the implementation unit of the ActiveX control under design, and enter it into the **Implementation Unit** field.
4. Enter your project name into the **Project Name** field.
5. Select the desired threading model from the **Threading Model** drop-down list.
6. Then, if you like, you can set three extra options by selecting the following check boxes:
   - **Include About Box:** This will automatically create an **About** dialog box for the control. The dialog box is a regular Delphi form.
   - **Include Version Information:** This will include information on the version of a given ActiveX control in the project. (This is required by some containers, for example, those created with Visual Basic 4.0.)
   - **Make Control Licensed:** This will create a design-time license for the control (which may be necessary if you are designing your control for commercial use). This measure will ensure that only those programmers who have the required license will be able to use this control. (This restriction applies equally to all developing environments, including Delphi, Visual Basic, etc.) When this check box is selected, a license file (LIC) is automatically generated along with the control file. In order to enable other developers to use this ActiveX control, you will need to provide them with this design-time license file together with the ActiveX control (which has an OCX extension).

As soon as you've entered the required information in the fields, the wizard will automatically generate all files necessary for supporting the given ActiveX control. These files include a project file, a type library, and an implementation unit file. Note that all controls are either DLLs or OCX files (which in fact are the same thing).

Let's see what the **ActiveX Control Wizard** is doing behind the scenes to create this ActiveX control from an existing VCL component:

- The wizard identifies the unit containing the VCL control, and passes this unit to the compiler, which then creates special character information about the properties, methods, and events of the VCL control.

- The type library for the project is generated.
- The wizard analyzes the information about the VCL control, and determines which of the methods and properties are to be added to the interface and type library being created.

NOTE

In order to determine whether a given property, method, or event should be included into the type library, the wizard checks to see if the type and parameters of a given property, as well as the return values of given events and methods, support automation. The following types are automation compatible: `Byte`, `SmallInt`, `Integer`, `Single`, `Double`, `Currency`, `TDateTime`, `WideString`, `WordBool`, `PSafeArray`, `TDecimal`, `OleVariant`, `IUnknown`, `IDispatch`*. Besides these, the* `TStrings`, `TPicture`, *and* `TFont` *type parameters are also permitted; the wizard will create intermediate objects for these types, which will allow for their encapsulation into* `IDispatch` *or* `Dispinterface`.

- The Type Library Editor builds the adjusted type library with all the added properties, methods, and events.
- The wizard generates the implementation file for the ActiveX control. This file contains the `TActiveXControl` control. The wizard also automatically creates so-called *forwarders* for the interface properties and methods. These forwarders direct calls for methods from the ActiveX control to the VCL control, and also pass events from the VCL control to the ActiveX control.

Listing 13.1 contains the code of the project file for an ActiveX control that was created from the `TRichEdit` component.

LISTING 13.1

```
library RichEditXControl1;
uses
  ComServ,
  RichEditXControl1_TLB in 'RichEditXControl1_TLB.pas',
  RichEditImpl1 in 'RichEditImpl1.pas' {RichEditX: CoClass};
{$E ocx}
exports
  DllGetClassObject,
  DllCanUnloadNow,
  DllRegisterServer,
  DllUnregisterServer;
```

```
{$R *.TLB}
{$R *.RES}
begin
end.
```

Listing 13.1 should be self-explanatory.

Listing 13.2 contains the implementation code for the ActiveX control.

LISTING 13.2

```
unit RichEditImpl1;
interface
uses
  Windows, ActiveX, Classes, Controls, Graphics, Menus, Forms, StdCtrls,
  ComServ, StdVCL, AXCtrls, RichEditXControl1_TLB, ComCtrls;
type
  TRichEditX = class(TActiveXControl, IRichEditX)
  private
    {Private declarations}
    FDelphiControl: TRichEdit;
    FEvents: IRichEditXEvents;
    procedure ChangeEvent(Sender: TObject);
    procedure KeyPressEvent(Sender: TObject; var Key: Char);
    procedure ProtectChangeEvent(Sender: TObject; StartPos, EndPos: Integer;
      var AllowChange: Boolean);
    procedure SaveClipboardEvent(Sender: TObject; NumObjects,
      NumChars: Integer; var SaveClipboard: Boolean);
    procedure SelectionChangeEvent(Sender: TObject);
  protected
    {Protected declarations}
    procedure DefinePropertyPages(DefinePropertyPage:
        TDefinePropertyPage); override;
    procedure EventSinkChanged(const EventSink: IUnknown); override;
    procedure InitializeControl; override;
    function Get_Alignment: TxAlignment; safecall;
```

```
function Get_BorderStyle: TxBorderStyle; safecall;
function Get_CanUndo: WordBool; safecall;
function Get_Color: OLE_COLOR; safecall;
function Get_Ctl3D: WordBool; safecall;
function Get_Cursor: Smallint; safecall;
function Get_DoubleBuffered: WordBool; safecall;
function Get_DragCursor: Smallint; safecall;
function Get_DragMode: TxDragMode; safecall;
function Get_Enabled: WordBool; safecall;
function Get_Font: IFontDisp; safecall;
function Get_HideScrollBars: WordBool; safecall;
function Get_HideSelection: WordBool; safecall;
function Get_ImeMode: TxImeMode; safecall;
function Get_ImeName: WideString; safecall;
function Get_Lines: IStrings; safecall;
function Get_MaxLength: Integer; safecall;
function Get_Modified: WordBool; safecall;
function Get_ParentColor: WordBool; safecall;
function Get_ParentCtl3D: WordBool; safecall;
function Get_PlainText: WordBool; safecall;
function Get_ReadOnly: WordBool; safecall;
function Get_ScrollBars: TxScrollStyle; safecall;
function Get_SelLength: Integer; safecall;
function Get_SelStart: Integer; safecall;
function Get_SelText: WideString; safecall;
function Get_Text: WideString; safecall;
function Get_Visible: WordBool; safecall;
function Get_VisibleDockClientCount: Integer; safecall;
function Get_WantReturns: WordBool; safecall;
function Get_WantTabs: WordBool; safecall;
function Get_WordWrap: WordBool; safecall;
procedure _Set_Font(const Value: IFontDisp); safecall;
procedure Set_Alignment(Value: TxAlignment); safecall;
procedure Set_BorderStyle(Value: TxBorderStyle); safecall;
```

```
    procedure Set_Color(Value: OLE_COLOR); safecall;
    procedure Set_Ctl3D(Value: WordBool); safecall;
    procedure Set_Cursor(Value: Smallint); safecall;
    procedure Set_DoubleBuffered(Value: WordBool); safecall;
    procedure Set_DragCursor(Value: Smallint); safecall;
    procedure Set_DragMode(Value: TxDragMode); safecall;
    procedure Set_Enabled(Value: WordBool); safecall;
    procedure Set_Font(var Value: IFontDisp); safecall;
    procedure Set_HideScrollBars(Value: WordBool); safecall;
    procedure Set_HideSelection(Value: WordBool); safecall;
    procedure Set_ImeMode(Value: TxImeMode); safecall;
    procedure Set_ImeName(const Value: WideString); safecall;
    procedure Set_Lines(const Value: IStrings); safecall;
    procedure Set_MaxLength(Value: Integer); safecall;
    procedure Set_Modified(Value: WordBool); safecall;
    procedure Set_ParentColor(Value: WordBool); safecall;
    procedure Set_ParentCtl3D(Value: WordBool); safecall;
    procedure Set_PlainText(Value: WordBool); safecall;
    procedure Set_ReadOnly(Value: WordBool); safecall;
    procedure Set_ScrollBars(Value: TxScrollStyle); safecall;
    procedure Set_SelLength(Value: Integer); safecall;
    procedure Set_SelStart(Value: Integer); safecall;
    procedure Set_SelText(const Value: WideString); safecall;
    procedure Set_Text(const Value: WideString); safecall;
    procedure Set_Visible(Value: WordBool); safecall;
    procedure Set_WantReturns(Value: WordBool); safecall;
    procedure Set_WantTabs(Value: WordBool); safecall;
    procedure Set_WordWrap(Value: WordBool); safecall;
  end;
implementation
uses ComObj;
{ TRichEditX }
procedure TRichEditX.DefinePropertyPages(DefinePropertyPage:
          TDefinePropertyPage);
begin
```

```
  {TODO: Specify the property pages here. It can be done by calling the
  DefinePropertyPage method along with the class identifier. For example,
  DefinePropertyPage(Class_RichEditXPage);}
end;
procedure TRichEditX.EventSinkChanged(const EventSink: IUnknown);
begin
  FEvents := EventSink as IRichEditXEvents;
end;
procedure TRichEditX.InitializeControl;
begin
  FDelphiControl := Control as TRichEdit;
  FDelphiControl.OnChange := ChangeEvent;
  FDelphiControl.OnKeyPress := KeyPressEvent;
  FDelphiControl.OnProtectChange := ProtectChangeEvent;
  FDelphiControl.OnSaveClipboard := SaveClipboardEvent;
  FDelphiControl.OnSelectionChange := SelectionChangeEvent;
end;
function TRichEditX.Get_Alignment: TxAlignment;
begin
  Result := Ord(FDelphiControl.Alignment);
end;
function TRichEditX.Get_BorderStyle: TxBorderStyle;
begin
  Result := Ord(FDelphiControl.BorderStyle);
end;
function TRichEditX.Get_CanUndo: WordBool;
begin
  Result := FDelphiControl.CanUndo;
end;
function TRichEditX.Get_Color: OLE_COLOR;
begin
  Result := OLE_COLOR(FDelphiControl.Color);
end;
function TRichEditX.Get_Ctl3D: WordBool;
begin
```

```
  Result := FDelphiControl.Ctl3D;
end;
function TRichEditX.Get_Cursor: Smallint;
begin
  Result := Smallint(FDelphiControl.Cursor);
end;
function TRichEditX.Get_DoubleBuffered: WordBool;
begin
  Result := FDelphiControl.DoubleBuffered;
end;
function TRichEditX.Get_DragCursor: Smallint;
begin
  Result := Smallint(FDelphiControl.DragCursor);
end;
function TRichEditX.Get_DragMode: TxDragMode;
begin
  Result := Ord(FDelphiControl.DragMode);
end;
function TRichEditX.Get_Enabled: WordBool;
begin
  Result := FDelphiControl.Enabled;
end;
function TRichEditX.Get_Font: IFontDisp;
begin
  GetOleFont(FDelphiControl.Font, Result);
end;
function TRichEditX.Get_HideScrollBars: WordBool;
begin
  Result := FDelphiControl.HideScrollBars;
end;
function TRichEditX.Get_HideSelection: WordBool;
begin
  Result := FDelphiControl.HideSelection;
end;
function TRichEditX.Get_ImeMode: TxImeMode;
```

```
begin
  Result := Ord(FDelphiControl.ImeMode);
end;
function TRichEditX.Get_ImeName: WideString;
begin
  Result := WideString(FDelphiControl.ImeName);
end;
function TRichEditX.Get_Lines: IStrings;
begin
  GetOleStrings(FDelphiControl.Lines, Result);
end;
function TRichEditX.Get_MaxLength: Integer;
begin
  Result := FDelphiControl.MaxLength;
end;
function TRichEditX.Get_Modified: WordBool;
begin
  Result := FDelphiControl.Modified;
end;
function TRichEditX.Get_ParentColor: WordBool;
begin
  Result := FDelphiControl.ParentColor;
end;
function TRichEditX.Get_ParentCtl3D: WordBool;
begin
  Result := FDelphiControl.ParentCtl3D;
end;
function TRichEditX.Get_PlainText: WordBool;
begin
  Result := FDelphiControl.PlainText;
end;
function TRichEditX.Get_ReadOnly: WordBool;
begin
  Result := FDelphiControl.ReadOnly;
end;
```

```
function TRichEditX.Get_ScrollBars: TxScrollStyle;
begin
  Result := Ord(FDelphiControl.ScrollBars);
end;
function TRichEditX.Get_SelLength: Integer;
begin
  Result := FDelphiControl.SelLength;
end;
function TRichEditX.Get_SelStart: Integer;
begin
  Result := FDelphiControl.SelStart;
end;
function TRichEditX.Get_SelText: WideString;
begin
  Result := WideString(FDelphiControl.SelText);
end;
function TRichEditX.Get_Text: WideString;
begin
  Result := WideString(FDelphiControl.Text);
end;
function TRichEditX.Get_Visible: WordBool;
begin
  Result := FDelphiControl.Visible;
end;
function TRichEditX.Get_VisibleDockClientCount: Integer;
begin
  Result := FDelphiControl.VisibleDockClientCount;
end;
function TRichEditX.Get_WantReturns: WordBool;
begin
  Result := FDelphiControl.WantReturns;
end;
function TRichEditX.Get_WantTabs: WordBool;
begin
  Result := FDelphiControl.WantTabs;
```

```
end;
function TRichEditX.Get_WordWrap: WordBool;
begin
  Result := FDelphiControl.WordWrap;
end;
procedure TRichEditX._Set_Font(const Value: IFontDisp);
begin
  SetOleFont(FDelphiControl.Font, Value);
end;
procedure TRichEditX.ChangeEvent(Sender: TObject);
begin
  if FEvents <> nil then FEvents.OnChange;
end;
procedure TRichEditX.KeyPressEvent(Sender: TObject; var Key: Char);
var
  TempKey: Smallint;
begin
  TempKey := Smallint(Key);
  if FEvents <> nil then FEvents.OnKeyPress(TempKey);
  Key := Char(TempKey);
end;
procedure TRichEditX.ProtectChangeEvent(Sender: TObject; StartPos,
  EndPos: Integer; var AllowChange: Boolean);
var
  TempAllowChange: WordBool;
begin
  TempAllowChange := WordBool(AllowChange);
  if FEvents <> nil then FEvents.OnProtectChange(StartPos, EndPos,
     TempAllowChange);
  AllowChange := Boolean(TempAllowChange);
end;
procedure TRichEditX.SaveClipboardEvent(Sender: TObject; NumObjects,
  NumChars: Integer; var SaveClipboard: Boolean);
var
  TempSaveClipboard: WordBool;
```

```
begin
  TempSaveClipboard := WordBool(SaveClipboard);
  if FEvents <> nil then FEvents.OnSaveClipboard(NumObjects, NumChars,
     TempSaveClipboard);
  SaveClipboard := Boolean(TempSaveClipboard);
end;
procedure TRichEditX.SelectionChangeEvent(Sender: TObject);
begin
  if FEvents <> nil then FEvents.OnSelectionChange;
end;
procedure TRichEditX.Set_Alignment(Value: TxAlignment);
begin
  FDelphiControl.Alignment := TAlignment(Value);
end;
procedure TRichEditX.Set_BorderStyle(Value: TxBorderStyle);
begin
  FDelphiControl.BorderStyle := TBorderStyle(Value);
end;
procedure TRichEditX.Set_Color(Value: OLE_COLOR);
begin
  FDelphiControl.Color := TColor(Value);
end;
procedure TRichEditX.Set_Ctl3D(Value: WordBool);
begin
  FDelphiControl.Ctl3D := Value;
end;
procedure TRichEditX.Set_Cursor(Value: Smallint);
begin
  FDelphiControl.Cursor := TCursor(Value);
end;
procedure TRichEditX.Set_DoubleBuffered(Value: WordBool);
begin
  FDelphiControl.DoubleBuffered := Value;
end;
procedure TRichEditX.Set_DragCursor(Value: Smallint);
```

```
begin
  FDelphiControl.DragCursor := TCursor(Value);
end;
procedure TRichEditX.Set_DragMode(Value: TxDragMode);
begin
  FDelphiControl.DragMode := TDragMode(Value);
end;
procedure TRichEditX.Set_Enabled(Value: WordBool);
begin
  FDelphiControl.Enabled := Value;
end;
procedure TRichEditX.Set_Font(var Value: IFontDisp);
begin
  SetOleFont(FDelphiControl.Font, Value);
end;
procedure TRichEditX.Set_HideScrollBars(Value: WordBool);
begin
  FDelphiControl.HideScrollBars := Value;
end;
procedure TRichEditX.Set_HideSelection(Value: WordBool);
begin
  FDelphiControl.HideSelection := Value;
end;
procedure TRichEditX.Set_ImeMode(Value: TxImeMode);
begin
  FDelphiControl.ImeMode := TImeMode(Value);
end;
procedure TRichEditX.Set_ImeName(const Value: WideString);
begin
  FDelphiControl.ImeName := TImeName(Value);
end;
procedure TRichEditX.Set_Lines(const Value: IStrings);
begin
  SetOleStrings(FDelphiControl.Lines, Value);
```

```
end;
procedure TRichEditX.Set_MaxLength(Value: Integer);
begin
  FDelphiControl.MaxLength := Value;
end;
procedure TRichEditX.Set_Modified(Value: WordBool);
begin
  FDelphiControl.Modified := Value;
end;
procedure TRichEditX.Set_ParentColor(Value: WordBool);
begin
  FDelphiControl.ParentColor := Value;
end;
procedure TRichEditX.Set_ParentCtl3D(Value: WordBool);
begin
  FDelphiControl.ParentCtl3D := Value;
end;
procedure TRichEditX.Set_PlainText(Value: WordBool);
begin
  FDelphiControl.PlainText := Value;
end;
procedure TRichEditX.Set_ReadOnly(Value: WordBool);
begin
  FDelphiControl.ReadOnly := Value;
end;
procedure TRichEditX.Set_ScrollBars(Value: TxScrollStyle);
begin
  FDelphiControl.ScrollBars := TScrollStyle(Value);
end;
procedure TRichEditX.Set_SelLength(Value: Integer);
begin
  FDelphiControl.SelLength := Value;
end;
procedure TRichEditX.Set_SelStart(Value: Integer);
```

```
begin
  FDelphiControl.SelStart := Value;
end;
procedure TRichEditX.Set_SelText(const Value: WideString);
begin
  FDelphiControl.SelText := String(Value);
end;
procedure TRichEditX.Set_Text(const Value: WideString);
begin
  FDelphiControl.Text := TCaption(Value);
end;
procedure TRichEditX.Set_Visible(Value: WordBool);
begin
  FDelphiControl.Visible := Value;
end;
procedure TRichEditX.Set_WantReturns(Value: WordBool);
begin
  FDelphiControl.WantReturns := Value;
end;
procedure TRichEditX.Set_WantTabs(Value: WordBool);
begin
  FDelphiControl.WantTabs := Value;
end;
procedure TRichEditX.Set_WordWrap(Value: WordBool);
begin
  FDelphiControl.WordWrap := Value;
end;
initialization
  TActiveXControlFactory.Create(
    ComServer,
    TRichEditX,
    TRichEdit,
    Class_RichEditX,
    1,
```

```
    '',
    0,
    tmApartment);
end.
```

The `TRichEditX` class from the Listing 13.2 is a descendant of `TActiveXControl`. This class is used to establish a relationship between the Delphi `TRichEdit` component and the containers that will accommodate the control being designed.

Figure 13.2 shows the Type Library Editor window for the given ActiveX control. Listing 13.3 contains the code for the type library file.

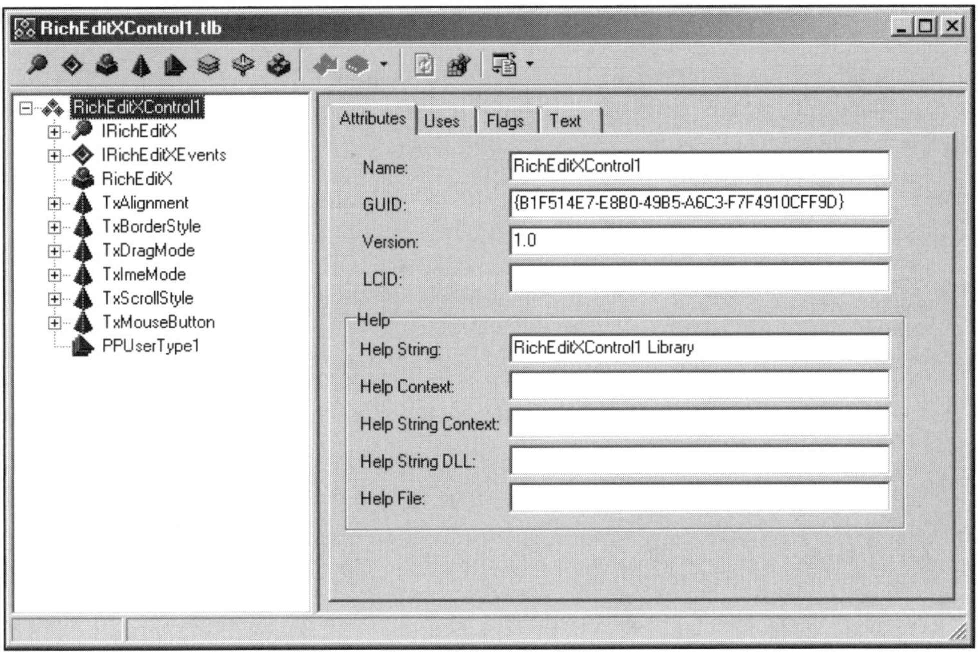

FIGURE 13.2 The `RichEdit` control in the Type Library Editor.

LISTING 13.3

```
unit RichEditXControl1_TLB;

*************************************************************************

// Warning

// The types declared in this file were generated from data
```

```
// read from the type library. If this type library is explicitly or
// indirectly (through another type library that refers to this type
// library) re-imported, or if it was activated using the 'Refresh'
// command of the Type
// Library Editor while editing the type library, the
// content of this file will be regenerated and all manual changes may
// be lost.
**********************************************************************
// PASTLWTR : $Revision:   1.88  $
// This file was created on 02.15.2001 at 18:30:46 from the type library
// described below.
**********************************************************************
// Type Lib: C:\Program Files\Borland\Delphi5\Projects\!!!\RichEditXControl1.tlb (1)
// IID\LCID: {B1F514E7-E8B0-49B5-A6C3-F7F4910CFF9D}\0
// Helpfile:
// DepndLst:
//   (1) v2.0 stdole, (C:\WINDOWS\SYSTEM\stdole2.tlb)
//   (2) v4.0 StdVCL, (C:\WINDOWS\SYSTEM\STDVCL40.DLL)
**********************************************************************
{$TYPEDADDRESS OFF} // This unit must be compiled without checking the
// types of the identifiers
interface
uses Windows, ActiveX, Classes, Graphics, OleServer, OleCtrls, StdVCL;
******************************************************************//
// The GUIDS are declared in the TypeLibrary. The following prefixes are
// used:
//   Type Libraries     : LIBID_xxxx
//   CoClasses          : CLASS_xxxx
//   DISPInterfaces     : DIID_xxxx
//   Non-DISP interfaces: IID_xxxx
******************************************************************//
const
  RichEditXControl1MajorVersion = 1;
  RichEditXControl1MinorVersion = 0;
```

```
  LIBID_RichEditXControl1: TGUID = '{B1F514E7-E8B0-49B5-A6C3-F7F4910CFF9D}';
  IID_IRichEditX: TGUID = '{86F5C46C-CDA6-4279-8BF4-F69F1A051ED7}';
  DIID_IRichEditXEvents: TGUID = '{21AB5F94-7D87-4FC0-AB5A-9BCE1D05AF8B}';
  CLASS_RichEditX: TGUID = '{7C731EE0-D98D-4040-8FE1-E0CB9E54C58B}';
*******************************************************************//
// Declaration of the enumerations declared in the type
// library
*******************************************************************//
// The constants for TxAlignment
type
  TxAlignment = TOleEnum;
const
  taLeftJustify = $00000000;
  taRightJustify = $00000001;
  taCenter = $00000002;
// The constants for TxBorderStyle
type
  TxBorderStyle = TOleEnum;
const
  bsNone = $00000000;
  bsSingle = $00000001;
// The constants for TxDragMode
type
  TxDragMode = TOleEnum;
const
  dmManual = $00000000;
  dmAutomatic = $00000001;
// The constants for TxImeMode
type
  TxImeMode = TOleEnum;
const
  imDisable = $00000000;
  imClose = $00000001;
  imOpen = $00000002;
  imDontCare = $00000003;
```

```
  imSAlpha = $00000004;
  imAlpha = $00000005;
  imHira = $00000006;
  imSKata = $00000007;
  imKata = $00000008;
  imChinese = $00000009;
  imSHanguel = $0000000A;
  imHanguel = $0000000B;
// The constants for TxScrollStyle
type
  TxScrollStyle = TOleEnum;
const
  ssNone = $00000000;
  ssHorizontal = $00000001;
  ssVertical = $00000002;
  ssBoth = $00000003;
// The constants for TxMouseButton
type
  TxMouseButton = TOleEnum;
const
  mbLeft = $00000000;
  mbRight = $00000001;
  mbMiddle = $00000002;
type
**********************************************************************//
// A preliminary declaration of the types described in the
// type library
**********************************************************************//
  IRichEditX = interface;
  IRichEditXDisp = dispinterface;
  IRichEditXEvents = dispinterface;
**********************************************************************//
// Declaration of CoClasses declared in the type library
**********************************************************************//
```

```
  RichEditX = IRichEditX;
*******************************************************************//
// Declaration of structures and unions
*******************************************************************//
  PPUserType1 = ^IFontDisp; {*}
*******************************************************************//
// Interface: IRichEditX
// Flags:     (4416) Dual OleAutomation Dispatchable
// GUID:      {86F5C46C-CDA6-4279-8BF4-F69F1A051ED7}
*******************************************************************//
  IRichEditX = interface(IDispatch)
    ['{86F5C46C-CDA6-4279-8BF4-F69F1A051ED7}']
    function  Get_Alignment: TxAlignment; safecall;
    procedure Set_Alignment(Value: TxAlignment); safecall;
    function  Get_BorderStyle: TxBorderStyle; safecall;
    procedure Set_BorderStyle(Value: TxBorderStyle); safecall;
    function  Get_Color: OLE_COLOR; safecall;
    procedure Set_Color(Value: OLE_COLOR); safecall;
    function  Get_Ctl3D: WordBool; safecall;
    procedure Set_Ctl3D(Value: WordBool); safecall;
    function  Get_DragCursor: Smallint; safecall;
    procedure Set_DragCursor(Value: Smallint); safecall;
    function  Get_DragMode: TxDragMode; safecall;
    procedure Set_DragMode(Value: TxDragMode); safecall;
    function  Get_Enabled: WordBool; safecall;
    procedure Set_Enabled(Value: WordBool); safecall;
    function  Get_Font: IFontDisp; safecall;
    procedure _Set_Font(const Value: IFontDisp); safecall;
    procedure Set_Font(var Value: IFontDisp); safecall;
    function  Get_HideSelection: WordBool; safecall;
    procedure Set_HideSelection(Value: WordBool); safecall;
    function  Get_HideScrollBars: WordBool; safecall;
    procedure Set_HideScrollBars(Value: WordBool); safecall;
    function  Get_ImeMode: TxImeMode; safecall;
```

```
procedure Set_ImeMode(Value: TxImeMode); safecall;
function  Get_ImeName: WideString; safecall;
procedure Set_ImeName(const Value: WideString); safecall;
function  Get_Lines: IStrings; safecall;
procedure Set_Lines(const Value: IStrings); safecall;
function  Get_MaxLength: Integer; safecall;
procedure Set_MaxLength(Value: Integer); safecall;
function  Get_ParentColor: WordBool; safecall;
procedure Set_ParentColor(Value: WordBool); safecall;
function  Get_ParentCtl3D: WordBool; safecall;
procedure Set_ParentCtl3D(Value: WordBool); safecall;
function  Get_PlainText: WordBool; safecall;
procedure Set_PlainText(Value: WordBool); safecall;
function  Get_ReadOnly: WordBool; safecall;
procedure Set_ReadOnly(Value: WordBool); safecall;
function  Get_ScrollBars: TxScrollStyle; safecall;
procedure Set_ScrollBars(Value: TxScrollStyle); safecall;
function  Get_Visible: WordBool; safecall;
procedure Set_Visible(Value: WordBool); safecall;
function  Get_WantTabs: WordBool; safecall;
procedure Set_WantTabs(Value: WordBool); safecall;
function  Get_WantReturns: WordBool; safecall;
procedure Set_WantReturns(Value: WordBool); safecall;
function  Get_WordWrap: WordBool; safecall;
procedure Set_WordWrap(Value: WordBool); safecall;
function  Get_CanUndo: WordBool; safecall;
function  Get_Modified: WordBool; safecall;
procedure Set_Modified(Value: WordBool); safecall;
function  Get_SelLength: Integer; safecall;
procedure Set_SelLength(Value: Integer); safecall;
function  Get_SelStart: Integer; safecall;
procedure Set_SelStart(Value: Integer); safecall;
function  Get_SelText: WideString; safecall;
procedure Set_SelText(const Value: WideString); safecall;
function  Get_Text: WideString; safecall;
```

```
procedure Set_Text(const Value: WideString); safecall;
function  Get_DoubleBuffered: WordBool; safecall;
procedure Set_DoubleBuffered(Value: WordBool); safecall;
function  Get_VisibleDockClientCount: Integer; safecall;
function  Get_Cursor: Smallint; safecall;
procedure Set_Cursor(Value: Smallint); safecall;
property Alignment: TxAlignment read Get_Alignment write Set_Alignment;
property BorderStyle: TxBorderStyle read Get_BorderStyle write
         Set_BorderStyle;
property Color: OLE_COLOR read Get_Color write Set_Color;
property Ctl3D: WordBool read Get_Ctl3D write Set_Ctl3D;
property DragCursor: Smallint read Get_DragCursor write Set_DragCursor;
property DragMode: TxDragMode read Get_DragMode write Set_DragMode;
property Enabled: WordBool read Get_Enabled write Set_Enabled;
property Font: IFontDisp read Get_Font write _Set_Font;
property HideSelection: WordBool read Get_HideSelection write
         Set_HideSelection;
property HideScrollBars: WordBool read Get_HideScrollBars write
         Set_HideScrollBars;
property ImeMode: TxImeMode read Get_ImeMode write Set_ImeMode;
property ImeName: WideString read Get_ImeName write Set_ImeName;
property Lines: IStrings read Get_Lines write Set_Lines;
property MaxLength: Integer read Get_MaxLength write Set_MaxLength;
property ParentColor: WordBool read Get_ParentColor write
         Set_ParentColor;
property ParentCtl3D: WordBool read Get_ParentCtl3D write
         Set_ParentCtl3D;
property PlainText: WordBool read Get_PlainText write Set_PlainText;
property ReadOnly: WordBool read Get_ReadOnly write Set_ReadOnly;
property ScrollBars: TxScrollStyle read Get_ScrollBars write
         Set_ScrollBars;
property Visible: WordBool read Get_Visible write Set_Visible;
property WantTabs: WordBool read Get_WantTabs write Set_WantTabs;
property WantReturns: WordBool read Get_WantReturns write
         Set_WantReturns;
property WordWrap: WordBool read Get_WordWrap write Set_WordWrap;
```

```
    property CanUndo: WordBool read Get_CanUndo;
    property Modified: WordBool read Get_Modified write Set_Modified;
    property SelLength: Integer read Get_SelLength write Set_SelLength;
    property SelStart: Integer read Get_SelStart write Set_SelStart;
    property SelText: WideString read Get_SelText write Set_SelText;
    property Text: WideString read Get_Text write Set_Text;
    property DoubleBuffered: WordBool read Get_DoubleBuffered write
             Set_DoubleBuffered;
    property VisibleDockClientCount: Integer read
             Get_VisibleDockClientCount;
    property Cursor: Smallint read Get_Cursor write Set_Cursor;
  end;
*****************************************************************//
// DispIntf:  IRichEditXDisp
// Flags:     (4416) Dual OleAutomation Dispatchable
// GUID:      {86F5C46C-CDA6-4279-8BF4-F69F1A051ED7}
*****************************************************************//
  IRichEditXDisp = dispinterface
    ['{86F5C46C-CDA6-4279-8BF4-F69F1A051ED7}']
    property Alignment: TxAlignment dispid 1;
    property BorderStyle: TxBorderStyle dispid 2;
    property Color: OLE_COLOR dispid -501;
    property Ctl3D: WordBool dispid 3;
    property DragCursor: Smallint dispid 4;
    property DragMode: TxDragMode dispid 5;
    property Enabled: WordBool dispid -514;
    property Font: IFontDisp dispid -512;
    property HideSelection: WordBool dispid 6;
    property HideScrollBars: WordBool dispid 7;
    property ImeMode: TxImeMode dispid 8;
    property ImeName: WideString dispid 9;
    property Lines: IStrings dispid 10;
    property MaxLength: Integer dispid 11;
    property ParentColor: WordBool dispid 12;
```

```
    property ParentCtl3D: WordBool dispid 13;
    property PlainText: WordBool dispid 14;
    property ReadOnly: WordBool dispid 15;
    property ScrollBars: TxScrollStyle dispid 16;
    property Visible: WordBool dispid 17;
    property WantTabs: WordBool dispid 18;
    property WantReturns: WordBool dispid 19;
    property WordWrap: WordBool dispid 20;
    property CanUndo: WordBool readonly dispid 34;
    property Modified: WordBool dispid 35;
    property SelLength: Integer dispid 36;
    property SelStart: Integer dispid 37;
    property SelText: WideString dispid 38;
    property Text: WideString dispid -517;
    property DoubleBuffered: WordBool dispid 39;
    property VisibleDockClientCount: Integer readonly dispid 40;
    property Cursor: Smallint dispid 49;
  end;
*******************************************************************//
// DispIntf:  IRichEditXEvents
// Flags:     (0)
// GUID:      {21AB5F94-7D87-4FC0-AB5A-9BCE1D05AF8B}
*******************************************************************//
  IRichEditXEvents = dispinterface
    ['{21AB5F94-7D87-4FC0-AB5A-9BCE1D05AF8B}']
    procedure OnChange; dispid 1;
    procedure OnKeyPress(var Key: Smallint); dispid 8;
    procedure OnProtectChange(StartPos: Integer; EndPos: Integer;
    var AllowChange: WordBool); dispid 16;
    procedure OnSaveClipboard(NumObjects: Integer; NumChars: Integer;
    var SaveClipboard: WordBool); dispid 18;
    procedure OnSelectionChange; dispid 19;
  end;
*******************************************************************//
```

```
// Declaration of the OLE Control Proxy class
// Control Name     : TRichEditX
// Help String      : RichEditX Control
// Default Interface: IRichEditX
// Def. Intf. DISP? : No
// Event   Interface: IRichEditXEvents
// TypeFlags        : (34) CanCreate Control
*********************************************************************//
  TRichEditXOnKeyPress = procedure(Sender: TObject; var Key: Smallint)
                     of object;
  TRichEditXOnProtectChange = procedure(Sender: TObject; StartPos:
                          Integer; EndPos: Integer;
var AllowChange: WordBool) of object;
  TRichEditXOnSaveClipboard = procedure(Sender: TObject; NumObjects:
                          Integer; NumChars: Integer;
var SaveClipboard: WordBool) of object;
  TRichEditX = class(TOleControl)
  private
    FOnChange: TNotifyEvent;
    FOnKeyPress: TRichEditXOnKeyPress;
    FOnProtectChange: TRichEditXOnProtectChange;
    FOnSaveClipboard: TRichEditXOnSaveClipboard;
    FOnSelectionChange: TNotifyEvent;
    FIntf: IRichEditX;
    function  GetControlInterface: IRichEditX;
  protected
    procedure CreateControl;
    procedure InitControlData; override;
    function  Get_Lines: IStrings;
    procedure Set_Lines(const Value: IStrings);
  public
    property  ControlInterface: IRichEditX read GetControlInterface;
    property  DefaultInterface: IRichEditX read GetControlInterface;
    property CanUndo: WordBool index 34 read GetWordBoolProp;
```

```
  property Modified: WordBool index 35 read GetWordBoolProp write
           SetWordBoolProp;
  property SelLength: Integer index 36 read GetIntegerProp write
           SetIntegerProp;
  property SelStart: Integer index 37 read GetIntegerProp write
           SetIntegerProp;
  property SelText: WideString index 38 read GetWideStringProp write
           SetWideStringProp;
  property Text: WideString index -517 read GetWideStringProp write
           SetWideStringProp;
  property DoubleBuffered: WordBool index 39 read GetWordBoolProp
           write SetWordBoolProp;
  property VisibleDockClientCount: Integer index 40 read GetIntegerProp;
published
  property Alignment: TOleEnum index 1 read GetTOleEnumProp write
           SetTOleEnumProp stored False;
  property BorderStyle: TOleEnum index 2 read GetTOleEnumProp write
           SetTOleEnumProp stored False;
  property Color: TColor index -501 read GetTColorProp write
           SetTColorProp stored False;
  property Ctl3D: WordBool index 3 read GetWordBoolProp write
           SetWordBoolProp stored False;
  property DragCursor: Smallint index 4 read GetSmallintProp write
           SetSmallintProp stored False;
  property DragMode: TOleEnum index 5 read GetTOleEnumProp write
           SetTOleEnumProp stored False;
  property Enabled: WordBool index -514 read GetWordBoolProp write
           SetWordBoolProp stored False;
  property Font: TFont index -512 read GetTFontProp write SetTFontProp
           stored False;
  property HideSelection: WordBool index 6 read GetWordBoolProp write
           SetWordBoolProp stored False;
  property HideScrollBars: WordBool index 7 read GetWordBoolProp write
           SetWordBoolProp stored False;
  property ImeMode: TOleEnum index 8 read GetTOleEnumProp write
           SetTOleEnumProp stored False;
  property ImeName: WideString index 9 read GetWideStringProp write
           SetWideStringProp stored False;
```

```
    property Lines: IStrings read Get_Lines write Set_Lines stored False;
    property MaxLength: Integer index 11 read GetIntegerProp write
             SetIntegerProp stored False;
    property ParentColor: WordBool index 12 read GetWordBoolProp write
             SetWordBoolProp stored False;
    property ParentCtl3D: WordBool index 13 read GetWordBoolProp write
             SetWordBoolProp stored False;
    property PlainText: WordBool index 14 read GetWordBoolProp write
             SetWordBoolProp stored False;
    property ReadOnly: WordBool index 15 read GetWordBoolProp write
             SetWordBoolProp stored False;
    property ScrollBars: TOleEnum index 16 read GetTOleEnumProp write
             SetTOleEnumProp stored False;
    property Visible: WordBool index 17 read GetWordBoolProp write
             SetWordBoolProp stored False;
    property WantTabs: WordBool index 18 read GetWordBoolProp write
             SetWordBoolProp stored False;
    property WantReturns: WordBool index 19 read GetWordBoolProp write
             SetWordBoolProp stored False;
    property WordWrap: WordBool index 20 read GetWordBoolProp write
             SetWordBoolProp stored False;
    property Cursor: Smallint index 49 read GetSmallintProp write
             SetSmallintProp stored False;
    property OnChange: TNotifyEvent read FOnChange write FOnChange;
    property OnKeyPress: TRichEditXOnKeyPress read FOnKeyPress write
             FOnKeyPress;
    property OnProtectChange: TRichEditXOnProtectChange read
             FOnProtectChange write FOnProtectChange;
    property OnSaveClipboard: TRichEditXOnSaveClipboard read
             FOnSaveClipboard write FOnSaveClipboard;
    property OnSelectionChange: TNotifyEvent read FOnSelectionChange
             write FOnSelectionChange;
  end;
procedure Register;
implementation
uses ComObj;
procedure TRichEditX.InitControlData;
```

```
const
  CEventDispIDs: array [0..4] of DWORD = (
    $00000001, $00000008, $00000010, $00000012, $00000013);
  CTFontIDs: array [0..0] of DWORD = (
    $FFFFFE00);
  CControlData: TControlData2 = (
    ClassID: '{7C731EE0-D98D-4040-8FE1-E0CB9E54C58B}';
    EventIID: '{21AB5F94-7D87-4FC0-AB5A-9BCE1D05AF8B}';
    EventCount: 5;
    EventDispIDs: @CEventDispIDs;
    LicenseKey: nil (*HR:$80040154*);
    Flags: $0000002D;
    Version: 401;
    FontCount: 1;
    FontIDs: @CTFontIDs);
begin
  ControlData := @CControlData;
  TControlData2(CControlData).FirstEventOfs := Cardinal(@@FOnChange)-Cardinal(Self);
end;
procedure TRichEditX.CreateControl;
  procedure DoCreate;
  begin
    FIntf := IUnknown(OleObject) as IRichEditX;
  end;
begin
  if FIntf = nil then DoCreate;
end;
function TRichEditX.GetControlInterface: IRichEditX;
begin
  CreateControl;
  Result := FIntf;
end;
function  TRichEditX.Get_Lines: IStrings;
```

```
begin
  Result := DefaultInterface.Get_Lines;
end;
procedure TRichEditX.Set_Lines(const Value: IStrings);
begin
  DefaultInterface.Set_Lines(Value);
end;
procedure Register;
begin
  RegisterComponents('ActiveX',[TRichEditX]);
end;
end.
```

As you can see, these listings are rather bulky. But the fact that Delphi takes such a large amount of work upon itself ensures that even novices and amateurs can develop ActiveX controls using powerful wizards. The wizard generates a full-fledged ActiveX control, complete with relevant interfaces, events, and a type library, so that a developer doesn't need to worry about writing a single string of code!

In order to install a control into the Delphi Component palette, you need to:

1. Compile the project using the **Project/Compile <Project Name>** command of the main menu; this will create the OCX library.
2. Open the window for importing your new ActiveX control using the **Component/Import ActiveX Control** item of the main menu.
3. Click the **Add** button in the **Import ActiveX Control** window, go to the directory that contains the newly created OCX file, and select it by double-clicking it. The new control will then appear in the list in the dialog window.
4. Select the control from the list and click the **Install** button.
5. Select a package file and click **OK**.

Once you've completed this procedure, your new ActiveX control will be installed in the Delphi Component palette.

However, it should be noted that creating ActiveX controls from standard components is a rather uncommon practice. You can apply this technique of converting a component into an ActiveX control to your own custom component in order to enhance its functionality and enable other developers to use your component in various programming environments.

CREATING ACTIVEX CONTROLS WITH AN ACTIVEFORM

This technique—which is referred to as `ActiveForms` — enables you to develop an ActiveX control using a form from your application.

In order to create an ActiveX control from a form, do the following:

1. Call the **ActiveForm Wizard**. You can do this by selecting **File/New** from the main menu, and then opening the **ActiveX** tab and selecting the **ActiveForm** icon. The wizard window will be activated (Figure 13.3).

   At first glance, this wizard seems very similar to the wizard that converts Delphi VCL components into ActiveX controls. However, there is one difference that is not easy to miss: the **ActiveForm Wizard** automatically sets the value of `TActiveForm` in the **VCL Class Name** field.
2. Enter a name for your ActiveX control into the **New ActiveX Name** field. In this example, let's name it `MyForm`. This operation will automatically produce corresponding changes in the other fields (these changes were already described when we discussed the **ActiveX Control Wizard**).
3. As soon as you've clicked **OK**, the wizard will create all necessary shells for your ActiveX control (in almost the same way as in the previous case). The space within `MyForm` becomes your working space. You can place various components into it, declare methods and events for components and the form itself, and set their properties.

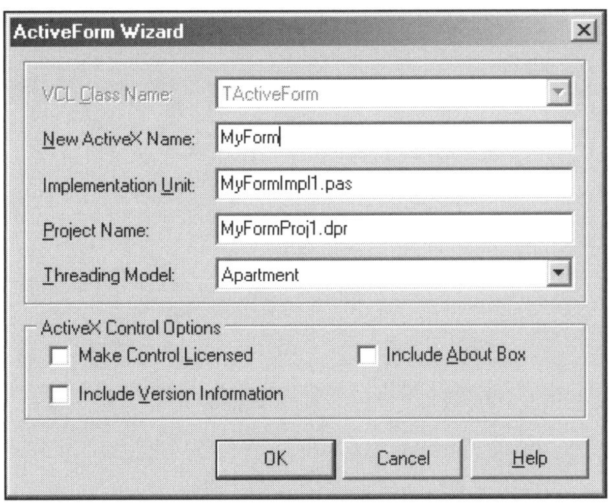

FIGURE 13.3 The **ActiveForm Wizard** dialog box.

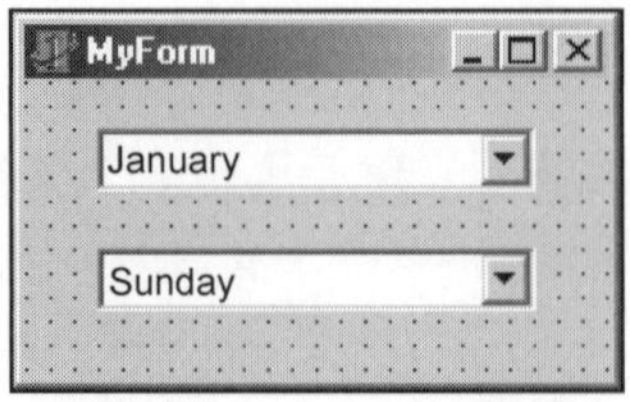

FIGURE 13.4 The **MyForm** form.

Let's place two `ComboBox` components in the `MyForm` form, as shown in Figure 13.4.

Enter the values that correspond to the names of months from January through December into the `Items` property for the first `ComboBox` component. Then set the values that correspond to the names of days of a week, from Sunday through Saturday, for the `Items` property of the second `ComboBox` component. Now if you click the button of the first component, you will see the name of the month, and if you click the second component's button, you will get the name of the day of the week.

Generally speaking, you've already created your ActiveX control. But the control is still useless, since you haven't yet passed the selected values from the lists to your users. To do this, you need to create an interface with the control's user.

Performing this task requires adding two new properties to the `IMyForm` interface in the type library for a given control. Let's call them `Month` and `Day`, respectively. Open the Type Library Editor using **View/Type Library** from the main menu. You already know how to operate this tool, and shouldn't find it too difficult to add the `Month` and `Day` properties to the `IMyForm` interface (Figure 13.5).

Now you have to refresh the `MyFormImpl1` implementation unit. Press the **Refresh Implementation** button in the top toolbar of the Type Library Editor window. The declarations of the new properties will appear in both project files, and the following skeleton code will be added to the implementation file (Listing 13.4).

LISTING 13.4

```
function TMyForm.Get_Day: Integer;
begin
end;
function TMyForm.Get_Month: Integer;
begin
end;
procedure TMyForm.Set_Day(Value: Integer);
```

```
begin
end;
procedure TMyForm.Set_Month(Value: Integer);
begin
end;
```

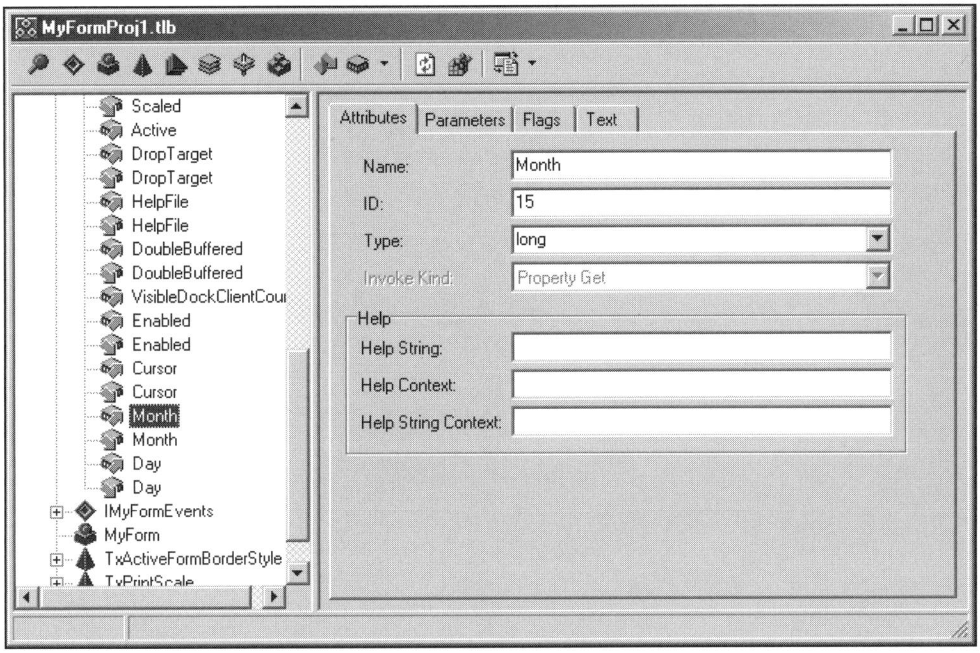

FIGURE 13.5 Adding the `IMyForm` interface and the `Month` and `Day` properties to the Type Library Editor.

As you can see, two pieces of skeleton code for the `Get` functions and another two blocks of skeleton code for the `Set` procedures have been added. The `Get` functions are used for returning a value to the program that called the function in question. The `Set` procedures enable you to set parameters.

Let's fill these code shells as follows (Listing 13.5).

LISTING 13.5

```
function TMyForm.Get_Day: Integer;
begin
 Result:=ComboBox2.ItemIndex;
end;
```

```
function TMyForm.Get_Month: Integer;
begin
 Result:=ComboBox1.ItemIndex;
end;
procedure TMyForm.Set_Day(Value: Integer);
begin
 ComboBox2.ItemIndex:=value;
end;
procedure TMyForm.Set_Month(Value: Integer);
begin
 ComboBox1.ItemIndex:=value;
end;
```

In this example, it is assumed that the values that are set to and read from the `Day` and `Month` properties have an `Integer` type, but you could have assigned some other type to these properties when you were designing them in the Type Library Editor.

That's it. You've built an ActiveX control from your form. Now just compile your project and install your newborn control into the Component palette. (This operation was covered in detail at the end of the previous section.)

It's now time to test your new ActiveX control in your application. Create a new project. Place the `MyForm` ActiveX control on it. In addition, place four buttons and two edit boxes on the same form (Figure 13.6).

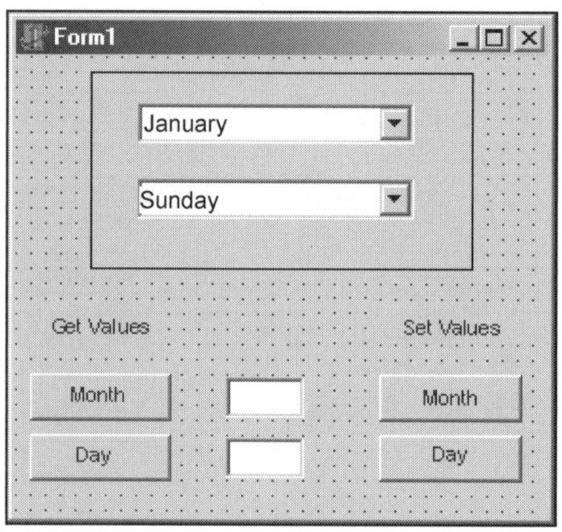

FIGURE 13.6 The appearance of an application that uses the `MyForm` ActiveX control.

Listing 13.6 contains the code for the application shown in Figure 13.6.

LISTING 13.6

```
unit Unit1;
interface
uses
  Windows, Messages, SysUtils, Classes, Graphics, Controls, Forms,
  Dialogs, StdCtrls, OleCtrls, MyFormProj1_TLB;
type
  TForm1 = class(TForm)
    MyForm1: TMyForm;
    GetMonth: TButton;
    Edit1: TEdit;
    GetDay: TButton;
    Edit2: TEdit;
    SetMonth: TButton;
    SetDay: TButton;
    Label1: TLabel;
    Label2: TLabel;
    procedure GetMonthClick(Sender: TObject);
    procedure GetDayClick(Sender: TObject);
    procedure SetMonthClick(Sender: TObject);
    procedure SetDayClick(Sender: TObject);
  private
    {Private declarations}
  public
    {Public declarations}
  end;
var
  Form1: TForm1;
implementation
{$R *.DFM}
procedure TForm1.GetMonthClick(Sender: TObject);
begin
 Edit1.Text:=IntToStr(MyForm1.Month+1);
end;
```

```
procedure TForm1.GetDayClick(Sender: TObject);
begin
 Edit2.Text:=IntToStr(MyForm1.Day+1);
end;
procedure TForm1.SetMonthClick(Sender: TObject);
begin
 MyForm1.Month:=StrToInt(Edit1.Text)-1;
end;
procedure TForm1.SetDayClick(Sender: TObject);
begin
 MyForm1.Day:=StrToInt(Edit2.Text)-1;
end;
end.
```

When you click either of the buttons located in the left part of the form (`GetMonth` or `GetDay`), the ordering number of a value from the required list of the `MyForm` component will appear in the relevant edit field. (Due to the fact that the items in the `ComboBox` list are numbered beginning with zero, you need to increase the returned value by one.) Accordingly, when you click either of the buttons located in the right part of a given form (`SetMonth` or `SetDay`), you give the value contained in the appropriate edit field to the ActiveX control. The relevant property of the `MyForm` element is set to a new value at the same time.

Figure 13.7 illustrates such an application in operation.

FIGURE 13.7 Running an application that uses the ActiveX control.

14 Creating MTS Components

Microsoft Transaction Server is an add-on technology that is built on top of COM and serves as an enhanced client-server solution. The core services of MTS include transaction management and ensuring data security. MTS can be used with the Windows NT and Windows 98 operating systems. Delphi enables a developer to create MTS components by using a built-in wizard.

This chapter provides you with a brief overview of the capabilities of MTS components. It will also show you how to develop MTS components using a Delphi wizard.

MTS COMPONENTS

MTS components provide the following low-level services:

- Handling system resources—including processes, threads, and multiple user support—when users connect simultaneously to a single database
- Automatic transaction management
- Creating, implementing, and removing server components
- Implementing your application security by employing the role-based authorization scheme

Delphi allows you to use stand-alone applications and active forms as MTS clients.

MTS components are in-process COM servers that are contained within DLLs. They differ from other COM components in that they execute in a special MTS environment. MTS components are implemented in Delphi the same way as in all other classes.

As a rule, MTS servers are rather small objects that are used for performing a wide range of business functions. For example, MTS components can provide business rules in a given application, and implement various states and state transition for applications. Consider a typical application used in clinics and hospitals, where they need to store a huge amount of various types of information such as medical records on every patient. MTS components allow for such records to be updated in real time, so that these records reflect the most recent changes (for example, a new patient being admitted, getting test results, etc.).

As shown in Figure 14.1, an MTS object can be viewed as any other COM object, except for an MTS object's capability of supporting a number of its own MTS interfaces in addition to COM interfaces.

Besides COM interfaces, Figure 14.1 shows an `IObjectControl` interface. Just as all COM objects have the `IUnknown` interface as their base interface, `IObjectControl` is the base interface for all MTS objects. This interface contains methods for activating and terminating an MTS object, as well as methods for managing resources.

A client that is located within the MTS environment is referred to as a *base client.* From the point of view of such a base client, a COM object in an MTS environment looks the same as any other COM object. MTS objects are placed in DLLs that are attached to an executable MTS file.

In their operation, MTS objects are similar to the traditional COM objects we discussed in previous chapters.

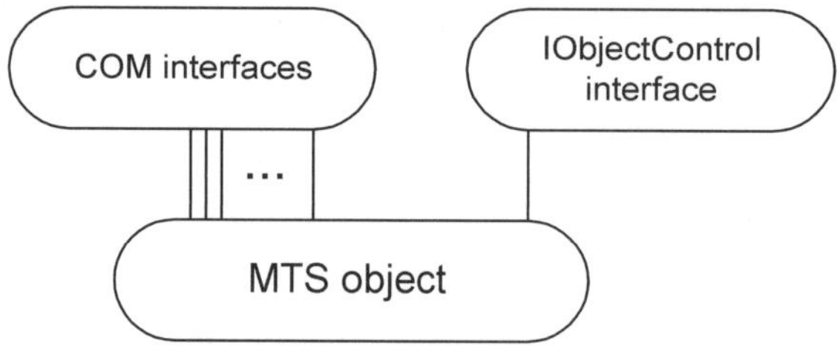

FIGURE 14.1 A simple MTS object.

REQUIREMENTS FOR MTS COMPONENTS

In addition to all the fundamental requirements that should be met by every COM object, MTS components must comply with the following rules:

- MTS components, when they are created by using the wizard, must have their own class factory that Delphi will automatically provide.
- MTS components must export the standard `DllGetClassObject` method.
- All the interfaces and `CoClasses` of an MTS component must be declared in its type library, which in turn is also built by the MTS Object Wizard.
- MTS components must export interfaces that use standard COM marshaling.
- MTS components must export the `DllRegisterServer` function and enable the independent interfaces and type libraries registration (`CLSID`, `ProgID`).
- An MTS component that is running in an MTS process cannot aggregate components that are not running in MTS.

CREATING AN MTS OBJECT USING THE WIZARD

To create a simple MTS object, perform the following procedure:

1. Use the MTS Object wizard to build an MTS component.
2. Add the necessary properties and methods via the Type Library Editor.
3. Test and debug your MTS component.
4. Install your MTS component into either an existing package or a new one.
5. Manage the MTS environment using the MTS Explorer.

Using the MTS Object Wizard

Before adding an MTS object to a project, the project must be an ActiveX library. In order to start the MTS Object wizard:

1. Select **File/New** from the main menu.
2. Select the **Multitier** tab in the activated dialog window.
3. Double-click the **MTS Object** icon (Figure 14.2).

The above operations will launch the MTS Object wizard (Figure 14.3).

Enter a name for your MTS class in the **CoClass Name** field: MyMTS, for example. Select the required type of threading model for your MTS object from the **Threading Model** drop-down list (threading models were covered in previous chapters). Then select the required transaction model by selecting the relevant **Transaction Model** radio button.

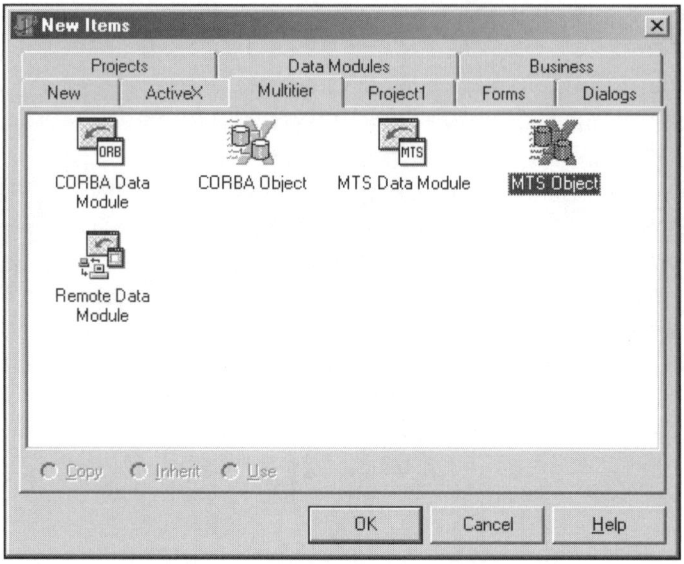

FIGURE 14.2 Creating a new MTS object.

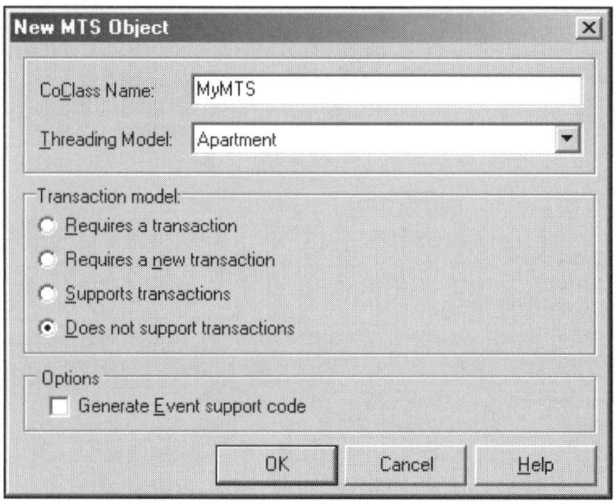

FIGURE 14.3 The MTS Object wizard.

At this point, elaboration on the subject of transaction models is called for. Every MTS object must possess a *transaction attribute*, which is written to an MTS directory. An MTS directory also contains information on components, packages, and roles. A developer can manage an MTS directory by using the MTS Explorer.

A transaction attribute can be set to one of four values:

- **Requires a transaction:** The MTS object must execute within the scope of a transaction. Every newly created MTS object inherits the transaction from the client. If the client does not contain transactions, MTS automatically builds a new transaction for the MTS object.
- **Requires a new transaction:** The MTS object must execute within its own transaction. MTS automatically builds a new transaction for every newly created MTS object, regardless of whether or not the client contains transactions. This object never executes within the scope of the client's transaction. The system always creates new transactions for new objects.
- **Supports transactions:** The MTS object can execute within the scope of a client transaction. A newly created object inherits the client transactions. If the client has no transactions, the MTS object will also be created without transactions.
- **Does not support transactions:** The MTS object does not function within the scope of a transaction. Every new MTS object is built without transactions, no matter whether the client has transactions or not. This value can be set if you create COM objects that support MTS.

The **Generate Event support code** option is set if you mean to use your own interface for managing the events for your MTS object.

As soon as you've clicked OK, a new unit will be added to your project in the MTS Object wizard window, which contains a declaration of the new MTS object (Listing 14.1).

LISTING 14.1

```
uses
  ActiveX, MtsObj, Mtx, ComObj, Project2_TLB, StdVcl;
type
  TMyMTS = class(TMtsAutoObject, IMyMTS)
  protected
    {Protected declarations}
  end;
implementation
uses ComServ;
initialization
  TAutoObjectFactory.Create(ComServer, TMyMTS, Class_MyMTS,
    ciMultiInstance, tmApartment);
end.
```

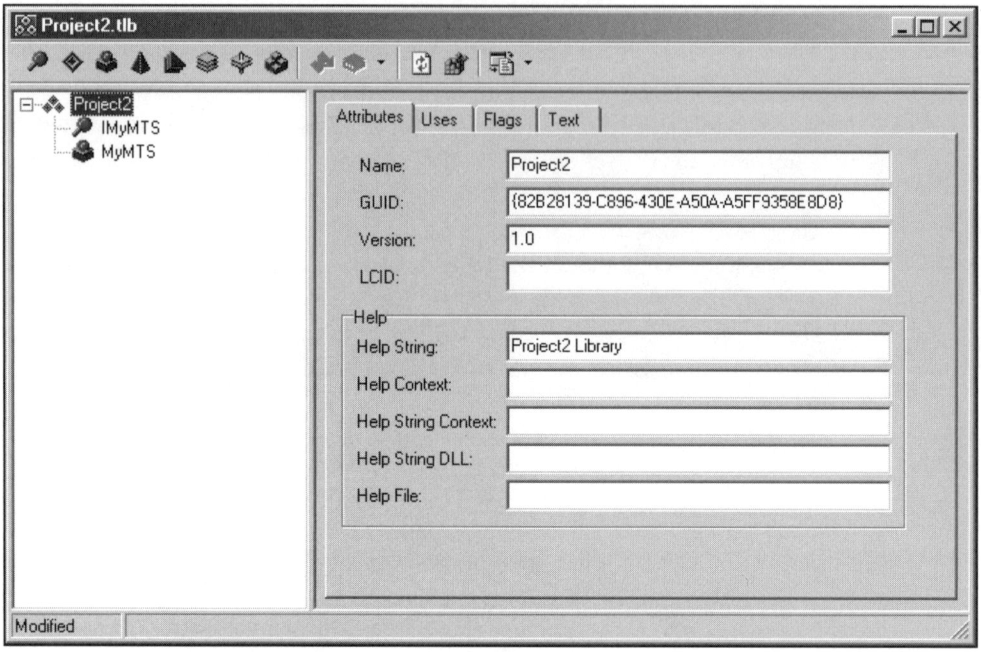

FIGURE 14.4 The Type Library Editor and an MTS object.

Also, the wizard will add information to the project type library and open the Type Library Editor window (Figure 14.4).

Adding Properties and Methods

The technique of adding properties and methods to an MTS object is identical to that of adding properties and methods to any traditional COM object.

Installing an MTS Object into an MTS Package

To install your MTS object into an MTS package, act as follows:

1. Select Run/Install MTS Object from the main menu.
2. Make sure that the MTS object has been successfully installed.

Appendix
Win32 API Error Messages

Exceptions were covered in detail in *Chapter 2*. This appendix deals with Win32 API system errors. The code of such an error can be returned by the `GetLastError` function. Table A.1 lists the constants that are returned by the `GetLastError` function along with their values and descriptions.

TABLE A.1 Win32 API Errors

Constant	***Value***	***Description***
`ERROR_SUCCESS`	0	The operation was successfully completed.
`ERROR_INVALID_FUNCTION`	1	Invalid function.
`ERROR_FILE_NOT_FOUND`	2	The required file was not found.
`ERROR_PATH_NOT_FOUND`	3	The specified path was not found.
`ERROR_TOO_MANY_OPEN_FILES`	4	Cannot open a file.
`ERROR_ACCESS_DENIED`	5	Access denied.
`ERROR_INVALID_HANDLE`	6	Invalid handle.
`ERROR_ARENA_TRASHED`	7	Control memory blocks have been corrupted.

TABLE A.1 Win32 API Errors *(Continued)*

Constant	*Value*	*Description*
ERROR_NOT_ENOUGH_MEMORY	8	The available amount of memory is insufficient for performing a given operation.
ERROR_INVALID_BLOCK	9	Invalid address for a control memory block.
ERROR_BAD_ENVIRONMENT	10	Environment error.
ERROR_BAD_FORMAT	11	Invalid file format.
ERROR_INVALID_ACCESS	12	Invalid access code.
ERROR_INVALID_DATA	13	Invalid data.
ERROR_OUTOFMEMORY	14	The available amount of memory is insufficient for completing the operation.
ERROR_INVALID_DRIVE	15	Cannot find the specified disk.
ERROR_CURRENT_DIRECTORY	16	Cannot delete the directory.
ERROR_NOT_SAME_DEVICE	17	Cannot move the file to another disk.
ERROR_NO_MORE_FILES	18	There are no more files.
ERROR_WRITE_PROTECT	19	This is a write protected disk.
ERROR_BAD_UNIT	20	Cannot find the specified device.
ERROR_NOT_READY	21	The device is not ready.
ERROR_BAD_COMMAND	22	The device cannot identify the command.
ERROR_CRC	23	Cyclic Redundancy Check error.
ERROR_BAD_LENGTH	24	The length of a given command exceeds the specified limit.
ERROR_SEEK	25	Cannot find the specified track or sector on the disk.
ERROR_NOT_DOS_DISK	26	The disk cannot be accessed.
ERROR_SECTOR_NOT_FOUND	27	Cannot find the specified sector on the given disk.
ERROR_OUT_OF_PAPER	28	The printer is out of paper.
ERROR_WRITE_FAULT	29	Cannot write to given device.
ERROR_READ_FAULT	30	Cannot read from given device.
ERROR_GEN_FAILURE	31	The system device has failed to work.
ERROR_SHARING_VIOLATION	32	This process cannot access the file because another process is currently working with it.

TABLE A.1 Win32 API Errors *(Continued)*

Constant	***Value***	***Description***
ERROR_LOCK_VIOLATION	33	This process cannot access the file because a part of this file is locked by another process.
ERROR_WRONG_DISK	34	Wrong disk in the drive.
ERROR_SHARING_BUFFER_EXCEEDED	36	Too many active shared files.
ERROR_HANDLE_EOF	38	The end of the file has been reached.
ERROR_HANDLE_DISK_FULL	39	The disk is full.
ERROR_NOT_SUPPORTED	50	The particular network query is not supported.
ERROR_REM_NOT_LIST	51	The remote computer is unreachable.
ERROR_DUP_NAME	52	There are duplicate names in the network.
ERROR_BAD_NETPATH	53	Invalid network path.
ERROR_NETWORK_BUSY	54	The network is busy.
ERROR_DEV_NOT_EXIST	55	The network resource or device has become unavailable.
ERROR_TOO_MANY_CMDS	56	The number of NetBIOS commands exceeds the specified limit.
ERROR_ADAP_HDW_ERR	57	A network adapter hardware error.
ERROR_BAD_NET_RESP	58	The server cannot perform the required operation.
ERROR_UNEXP_NET_ERR	59	An unexpected network error.
ERROR_BAD_REM_ADAP	60	An incompatible remote adapter.
ERROR_PRINTQ_FULL	61	The print queue is full.
ERROR_NO_SPOOL_SPACE	62	There is no free spool space on the server for the file that you need to print.
ERROR_PRINT_CANCELLED	63	The print command for a file in the print queue has been cancelled.

TABLE A.1 Win32 API Errors *(Continued)*

Constant	*Value*	*Description*
ERROR_NETNAME_DELETED	64	The specified network name has been deleted.
ERROR_NETWORK_ACCESS_DENIED	65	Cannot access the network.
ERROR_BAD_DEV_TYPE	66	Invalid network resource type.
ERROR_BAD_NET_NAME	67	The given network name cannot be found.
ERROR_TOO_MANY_NAMES	68	The number of names that are used in the network adapter exceeds the specified limit.
ERROR_TOO_MANY_SESS	69	The number of NetBIOS sessions exceeds the specified limit.
ERROR_SHARING_PAUSED	70	The network server has either been stopped or is currently in the process of restarting.
ERROR_REQ_NOT_ACCEP	71	Cannot connect to the remote computer because the maximum number of connections has been reached.
ERROR_REDIR_PAUSED	72	The functioning of the given device has been suspended.
ERROR_FILE_EXISTS	80	That file exists.
ERROR_CANNOT_MAKE	82	Cannot create a file or a directory.
ERROR_FAIL_I24	83	Improper call for the INT 24 interrupt.
ERROR_OUT_OF_STRUCTURES	84	The available amount of memory is insufficient for processing the query.
ERROR_ALREADY_ASSIGNED	85	This device name is already being used.
ERROR_INVALID_PASSWORD	86	Invalid network password.
ERROR_INVALID_PARAMETER	87	Invalid parameter.
ERROR_NET_WRITE_FAULT	88	The attempt to write to the network has failed.

TABLE A.1 Win32 API Errors *(Continued)*

Constant	*Value*	*Description*
ERROR_NO_PROC_SLOTS	89	Cannot start another process.
ERROR_TOO_MANY_SEMAPHORES	100	Cannot create another system semaphore.
ERROR_EXCL_SEM_ALREADY_OWNED	101	This exclusive semaphore is already owned by another process.
ERROR_SEM_IS_SET	102	The semaphore has been installed and cannot be closed.
ERROR_TOO_MANY_SEM_REQUESTS	103	The semaphore cannot be set repeatedly.
ERROR_INVALID_AT_INTERRUPT_TIME	104	Cannot query an exclusive semaphore at interrupt time.
ERROR_SEM_OWNER_DIED	105	The semaphore is no longer owned by the process that has used it.
ERROR_SEM_USER_LIMIT	106	The number of semaphore users has reached the specified limit.
ERROR_DISK_CHANGE	107	There is an incorrect disk in the drive.
ERROR_DRIVE_LOCKED	108	The drive is busy or locked.
ERROR_BROKEN_PIPE	109	The pipe is closed.
ERROR_OPEN_FAILED	110	Cannot open the specified device or file.
ERROR_BUFFER_OVERFLOW	111	A buffer overflow.
ERROR_DISK_FULL	112	There is no free space on the disk.
ERROR_NO_MORE_SEARCH_HANDLES	113	There are no more file search handles.
ERROR_INVALID_TARGET_HANDLE	114	Invalid file handle.
ERROR_INVALID_CATEGORY	117	Invalid function call.
ERROR_INVALID_VERIFY_SWITCH	118	Invalid parameter for the operation of verifying data records on a disk.
ERROR_BAD_DRIVER_LEVEL	119	Cannot process the given command.

TABLE A.1 Win32 API Errors *(Continued)*

Constant	*Value*	*Description*
ERROR_CALL_NOT_IMPLEMENTED	120	Win16 does not support this function call.
ERROR_SEM_TIMEOUT	121	The time for waiting for the semaphore has elapsed.
ERROR_INSUFFICIENT_BUFFER	122	Insufficient buffer area.
ERROR_INVALID_NAME	123	Invalid name for a file, directory, or volume label.
ERROR_INVALID_LEVEL	124	Invalid level for a system call.
ERROR_NO_VOLUME_LABEL	125	The disk has no volume label.
ERROR_MOD_NOT_FOUND	126	The unit cannot be found.
ERROR_PROC_NOT_FOUND	127	The procedure cannot be found.
ERROR_WAIT_NO_CHILDREN	128	There are no child processes that need to be completed.
ERROR_CHILD_NOT_COMPLETE	129	The child process was not completed.
ERROR_DIRECT_ACCESS_HANDLE	130	An attempt was made to use a handle to a file to open a disk and perform an operation other than an input/output operation.
ERROR_NEGATIVE_SEEK	131	An attempt was made to place the pointer to a file before this file.
ERROR_SEEK_ON_DEVICE	132	The file pointer cannot be set to the specified file.
ERROR_IS_JOIN_TARGET	133	The JOIN command cannot be used for drives that contain joined drives.
ERROR_IS_JOINED	134	An attempt was made to use either the JOIN or SUBST command for a disk that has already been included into a set of joined drives.
ERROR_IS_SUBSTED	135	An attempt was made to use either the JOIN or SUBST command for a drive that has already been substituted.

TABLE A.1 Win32 API Errors (*Continued*)

Constant	*Value*	*Description*
ERROR_NOT_JOINED	136	The drive has not been joined.
ERROR_NOT_SUBSTED	137	Cannot revoke signs of substitution from a drive that has not been substituted.
ERROR_JOIN_TO_JOIN	138	Cannot join a drive to a directory that is located in a joined drive.
ERROR_SUBST_TO_SUBST	139	Cannot substitute a drive for a directory in a substituted drive.
ERROR_JOIN_TO_SUBST	140	Cannot join a given drive to a directory that is located in a substituted drive.
ERROR_SUBST_TO_JOIN	141	Cannot substitute a directory that is located in a joined drive with a drive.
ERROR_BUSY_DRIVE	142	The drive is busy; neither the JOIN nor SUBST command can be performed.
ERROR_SAME_DRIVE	143	Incorrect attempt to perform the JOIN or SUBST command for the same drive.
ERROR_DIR_NOT_ROOT	144	This directory is not the root directory.
ERROR_DIR_NOT_EMPTY	145	The directory is not empty.
ERROR_IS_SUBST_PATH	146	The specified path is used for a substituted drive.
ERROR_IS_JOIN_PATH	147	The specified path is used for a joined drive.
ERROR_PATH_BUSY	148	The path is busy.
ERROR_IS_SUBST_TARGET	149	Cannot join or substitute the drive because its directory is already being used for substitution.
ERROR_SYSTEM_TRACE	150	Program trace is not allowed.

TABLE A.1 Win32 API Errors *(Continued)*

Constant	*Value*	*Description*
ERROR_INVALID_EVENT_COUNT	151	An invalid semaphore event count is specified for the DosMuxSemWait procedure.
ERROR_TOO_MANY_MUXWAITERS	152	Too many semaphores are set for the DosMuxSemWait procedure.
ERROR_INVALID_LIST_FORMAT	153	Incorrect call for the DosMuxSemWait procedure.
ERROR_LABEL_TOO_LONG	154	The volume label is too long.
ERROR_TOO_MANY_TCBS	155	The number of threads exceeds the maximum permissible limit.
ERROR_SIGNAL_REFUSED	156	The signal was refused by the receiving process.
ERROR_DISCARDED	157	Cannot lock a released segment.
ERROR_NOT_LOCKED	158	The segment is not locked.
ERROR_BAD_THREADID_ADDR	159	An invalid address for the thread ID was specified.
ERROR_BAD_ARGUMENTS	160	An invalid argument was passed to the DosExecPrgm procedure.
ERROR_BAD_PATHNAME	161	An invalid path is set.
ERROR_SIGNAL_PENDING	162	The signal is undergoing processing now.
ERROR_MAX_THRDS_REACHED	164	Cannot create extra threads.
ERROR_LOCK_FAILED	167	Cannot revoke a given file lock.
ERROR_BUSY	170	The requested resource is busy.
ERROR_CANCEL_VIOLATION	173	A lock request is bound to a specified area.
ERROR_ATOMIC_LOCKS_NOT_SUPPORTED	174	The file system doesn't support this change to a lock type.

TABLE A.1 Win32 API Errors (*Continued*)

Constant	*Value*	*Description*
ERROR_INVALID_SEGMENT_NUMBER	180	Invalid segment number.
ERROR_INVALID_ORDINAL	182	Invalid order.
ERROR_ALREADY_EXIST	183	The file already exists.
ERROR_INVALID_FLAG_NUMBER	186	Invalid number for a flag.
ERROR_SEM_NOT_FOUND	187	The semaphore cannot be found.
ERROR_INVALID_STARTING_CODESEG	188	An invalid starting code page was specified.
ERROR_INVALID_STACKSEG	189	Invalid stack segment.
ERROR_INVALID_MODULETYPE	190	Invalid module type.
ERROR_INVALID_EXE_SIGNATURE	191	Invalid name for an EXE file.
ERROR_EXE_MARKED_INVALID	192	The EXE file is incorrectly marked.
ERROR_BAD_EXE_FORMAT	193	Invalid format for an EXE file.
ERROR_ITERATED_DATA_EXCEEDS_64K	194	A data block size must not exceed 64 KB.
ERROR_INVALID_MINALLOCSIZE	195	Invalid minimum file size.
ERROR_DYNLINK_FROM_INVALID_RING	196	Invalid dynamic link.
ERROR_IOPL_NOT_ENABLED	197	Cannot run the application under the given operating system.
ERROR_INVALID_SEGDPL	198	Invalid segment.
ERROR_AUTODATASEG_EXCEEDS_64K	199	The code segment must not exceed 64 KB.
ERROR_ENVVAR_NOT_FOUND	203	Cannot find the specified parameter.
ERROR_NO_SIGNAL_SENT	205	No process can process the signal.
ERROR_FILENAME_EXCED_RANGE	206	The length of the filename or file extension exceeds the maximum limit.
ERROR_RING2_STACK_IN_USE	207	The stack is busy.

TABLE A.1 Win32 API Errors *(Continued)*

Constant	*Value*	*Description*
`ERROR_MATA_EXPANSION_TOO_LONG`	208	An invalid template for a file name has been specified.
`ERROR_INVALID_SIGNAL_NUMBER`	209	Invalid signal.
`ERROR_THREAD_1_INACTIVE`	210	Cannot set a signal handler.
`ERROR_LOCKED`	212	A given segment is locked and cannot be moved.
`ERROR_TOO_MANY_MODULES`	214	The maximum limit of modules that can be attached to a given program or unit has been exceeded.
`ERROR_NESTING_NOT_ALLOWED`	215	Calls for the `LoadModule` procedure cannot be nested.
`ERROR_BAD_PIPE`	230	Invalid state of the pipe.
`ERROR_PIPE_BUSY`	231	The pipe is busy.
`ERROR_NO_DATA`	232	The pipe is in the process of closing.
`ERROR_PIPE_NOT_CONNECTED`	233	The pipe is not connected to any process.
`ERROR_MORE_DATA`	234	Extra data is needed.
`ERROR_VC_DISCONNECTED`	240	The session has been aborted.
`ERROR_INVALID_EA_NAME`	254	Invalid name for an extra attribute.
`ERROR_EA_LIST_INCONSISTENT`	255	Conflicting extra attributes.
`ERROR_NO_MORE_ITEMS`	259	There are no more items.
`ERROR_CANNOT_COPY`	266	Cannot use the API Copy interface.
`ERROR_DIRECTORY`	267	Invalid directory name.
`ERROR_EAS_DIDN'T_FIT`	275	The extra attributes don't fit into the buffer.
`ERROR_EA_FILE_CORRUPT`	276	The extra attribute file is corrupted.
`ERROR_EA_TABLE_FULL`	277	The extra attribute file is full.

TABLE A.1 Win32 API Errors *(Continued)*

Constant	*Value*	*Description*
ERROR_INVALID_EA_HANDLE	278	An invalid handle was specified for an extra attribute.
ERROR_EAS_NOT_SUPPORTED	282	The file system doesn't support extra attributes.
ERROR_NOT_OWNER	288	A synchronization object is freed from a process that doesn't own this object.
ERROR_TOO_MANY_POSTS	298	Too many events for a given semaphore.
ERROR_PARTIAL_COPY	299	A read/write query has been processed only partially.
ERROR_MR_MID_NOT_FOUND	317	Cannot find the given message in the message file.
ERROR_INVALID_ADDRESS	487	Invalid address.
ERROR_ARITHMETIC_OVERFLOW	534	The result of an arithmetic operation exceeds 32 bits.
ERROR_PIPE_CONNECTED	535	The pipe is already busy with another process.
ERROR_PIPE_LISTENING	536	The pipe is waiting for a process to open it.
ERROR_EA_ACCESS_DENIED	994	Access to additional attributes is denied.
ERROR_OPERATION_ABORTED	995	An input/output operation has been discontinued.
ERROR_IO_INCOMPLETE	996	An input/output operation is incomplete.
ERROR_IO_PENDING	997	An input/output event is taking place.
ERROR_NOACCESS	998	Invalid attempt to access memory address.
ERROR_SWAPERROR	999	Invalid operation on a page.
ERROR_STACK_OVERFLOW	1001	A stack overflow.
ERROR_INVALID_MESSAGE	1002	Cannot process a message.

TABLE A.1 Win32 API Errors (*Continued*)

Constant	*Value*	*Description*
ERROR_CAN_NOT_COMPLETE	1003	Cannot complete processing a function.
ERROR_INVALID_FLAGS	1004	Invalid flags.
ERROR_UNRECOGNIZED_VOLUME	1005	Cannot identify the file system installed on a given volume.
ERROR_FILE_INVALID	1006	The file is invalid.
ERROR_FULLSCREEN_MODE	1007	Cannot perform the given operation in full-screen mode.
ERROR_NO_TOKEN	1008	The element does not exist.
ERROR_BADDB	1009	The database has been corrupted.
ERROR_BADKEY	1010	Invalid registry key.
ERROR_CANTOPEN	1011	Cannot open the given registry key.
ERROR_CANTREAD	1012	Cannot read from the given registry key.
ERROR_CANTWRITE	1013	Cannot write to the given registry key.
ERROR_REGISTRY_RECOVERED	1014	One of the registry files has been successfully recovered.
ERROR_REGISTRY_CORRUPT	1015	The registry is corrupted.
ERROR_REGISTRY_IO_FAILED	1016	Cannot read from/write to a file that contains the system image.
ERROR_NOT_REGISTRY_FILE	1017	Cannot find the registry file, or it has an invalid format.
ERROR_KEY_DELETED	1018	The registry key has been deleted.
ERROR_NO_LOG_SPACE	1019	Cannot allocate space in the registry log.
ERROR_KEY_HAS_CHILDREN	1020	Cannot create a symbolic link to a key that already has child keys or values.

TABLE A.1 Win32 API Errors *(Continued)*

Constant	*Value*	*Description*
ERROR_CHILD_MUST_BE_VOLATILE	1021	Cannot create a static child key for a volatile parent key.
ERROR_NOTIFY_ENUM_DIR	1022	Data has not been returned to the buffer of a calling procedure.
ERROR_DEPENDENT_SERVICES_RUNNING	1051	The stop instruction has been issued for a service on which other services depend.
ERROR_INVALID_SERVICE_CONTROL	1052	Invalid instruction for the given service.
ERROR_SERVICE_REQUEST_TIMEOUT	1053	The time to wait for a service response has run out.
ERROR_SERVICE_NO_THREAD	1054	Cannot create the instruction thread for the given service.
ERROR_SERVICE_DATABASE_LOCKED	1055	The database of the given service is locked.
ERROR_SERVICE_ALREADY_RUNNING	1056	This service is already running.
ERROR_INVALID_SERVICE_ACCOUNT	1057	The account name is invalid or does not exist.
ERROR_SERVICE_DISABLED	1058	The specified service is disabled.
ERROR_CIRCULAR_DEPENDENCY	1059	Cannot set a circular dependency between the services.
ERROR_SERVICE_DOES_NOT_EXIST	1060	The service has not been installed.
ERROR_SERVICE_CANNOT_ACCEPT_CTRL	1061	The service cannot accept commands.
ERROR_SERVICE_NOT_ACTIVE	1062	The service is not running.
ERROR_FAILED_SERVICE_CONTROLLER	1063	A process of the given service cannot connect to the service controller.
ERROR_EXCEPTION_IN_SERVICE	1064	An exception has occurred in the service while processing a command.
ERROR_DATABASE_DOES_NOT_EXIST	1065	The specified database does not exist.

TABLE A.1 Win32 API Errors *(Continued)*

Constant	***Value***	***Description***
ERROR_SERVICE_SPECIFIC_ERROR	1066	The service returned a specific error code.
ERROR_PROCESS_ABORTED	1067	The process was aborted.
ERROR_SERVICE_DEPENDENCY_FAIL	1068	Unable to run a dependent service.
ERROR_SERVICE_LOGON_FAILED	1069	The service did start because of a logon failure.
ERROR_SERVICE_START_HANG	1070	The service hung at start.
ERROR_INVALID_SERVICE_LOCK	1071	Improper lock on the database of the specified service.
ERROR_SERVICE_MARKED_FOR_DELETE	1072	The service was marked for deletion.
ERROR_SERVICE_EXISTS	1073	The service already exists.
ERROR_ALREADY_RUNNING_LKG	1074	The system is running on the last known good configuration.
ERROR_SERVICE_DEPENDENCY_DELETED	1075	The specified dependent service does not exist or has been marked for deletion.
ERROR_BOOT_ALREADY_ACCEPTED	1076	The current configuration has already been used as the source of the last known good parameter set.
ERROR_SERVICE_NEVER_STARTED	1077	The service never started.
ERROR_DUPLICATE_SERVICE_NAME	1078	This service name already exists.
ERROR_END_OF_MEDIA	1100	The end of a streaming tape has been detected.
ERROR_FILEMARK_DETECTED	1101	The file label has been detected.
ERROR_BEGINNING_OF_MEDIA	1102	The beginning of a streaming tape has been detected.
ERROR_SETMARK_DETECTED	1103	The end of a file set has been detected.
ERROR_NO_DATA_DETECTED	1104	No data was detected on the streaming tape.

TABLE A.1 Win32 API Errors (*Continued*)

Constant	*Value*	*Description*
ERROR_PARTITION_FAILURE	1105	Cannot partition the streaming tape.
ERROR_INVALID_BLOCK_LENGTH	1106	Invalid block length while referencing a new tape from a multivolume partition.
ERROR_DEVICE_NOT_PARTITIONED	1107	The device is not partitioned.
ERROR_UNABLE_TO_LOCK_MEDIA	1108	Cannot lock the mechanism for unloading a media tape.
ERROR_UNABLE_TO_UNLOAD_MEDIA	1109	Cannot unload media tape.
ERROR_MEDIA_CHANGED	1110	The tape in the device has been changed.
ERROR_BUS_RESET	1111	The input/output bus has been reset.
ERROR_NO_MEDIA_IN_DRIVE	1112	There is no tape in the drive.
ERROR_NO_UNICODE_TRANSLATION	1113	Unable to translate a Unicode character.
ERROR_DLL_INIT_FAILED	1114	DLL initialization has failed.
ERROR_SHUTDOWN_IN_PROGRESS	1115	System shutdown is in progress.
ERROR_NO_SHUTDOWN_IN_PROGRESS	1116	Cannot stop system shutdown because it has not been initialized.
ERROR_IO_DEVICE	1117	An input/output error.
ERROR_SERIAL_NO_DEVICE	1118	Serial devices are not initialized.
ERROR_IRQ_BUSY	1119	The given interrupt request (IRQ) is already being used by another device.
ERROR_MORE_WRITES	1120	A serial input/output operation was terminated as a result of writing to a serial port.
ERROR_COUNTER_TIMEOUT	1121	A serial input/output operation was terminated as soon as the specified period of waiting had come to an end.

TABLE A.1 Win32 API Errors (*Continued*)

Constant	*Value*	*Description*
ERROR_FLOPPY_ID_MARK_NOT_FOUND	1122	No identifier label is detected on the floppy disk.
ERROR_FLOPPY_WRONG_CYLINDER	1123	The identifier field of a given floppy disk sector and the address of a given controller track are incompatible.
ERROR_FLOPPY_UNKNOWN_ERROR	1124	An unknown error has been returned by a floppy disk controller.
ERROR_FLOPPY_BAD_REGISTERS	1125	Incorrect register values have been returned by a floppy dick controller.
ERROR_DISK_RECALIBRATE_FAILED	1126	Multiple failures in the check operation on the hard disk.
ERROR_DISK_OPERATION_FAILED	1127	Multiple failures in the operation on the hard disk.
ERROR_DISK_RESET_FAILED	1128	Cannot reset the hard disk controller.
ERROR_EOM_OVERFLOW	1129	The physical end of a given device is detected.
ERROR_NOT_ENOUGH_SERVER_MEMORY	1130	The amount of free memory on a given server is not enough to process this command.
ERROR_POSSIBLE_DEADLOCK	1131	A possible deadlock is detected.
ERROR_MAPPED_ALIGNMENT	1132	The address map is improperly aligned.
ERROR_SET_POWER_STATE_VETOED	1140	The attempt to change the power state has been locked by another application.
ERROR_SET_POWER_STATE_FAILED	1141	BIOS has failed in the process of changing the power state.
ERROR_OLD_WIN_VERSION	1150	The functioning of the program requires a more recent version of Windows.

TABLE A.1 Win32 API Errors (*Continued*)

Constant	*Value*	*Description*
ERROR_APP_WRONG_OS	1151	The program is not a Windows or MS-DOS application.
ERROR_SINGLE_INSTANCE_APP	1152	Cannot run more that one copy of the given program.
ERROR_RMODE_APP	1153	The program uses real-time mode.
ERROR_INVALID_DLL	1154	A DLL file that is necessary for running this application is corrupted.
ERROR_NO_ASSOCIATION	1155	The specified file is not associated with any application for performing this operation.
ERROR_DDE_FAIL	1156	The system has failed to pass a given command to the application.
ERROR_DLL_NOT_FOUND	1157	One of the DLL files that are necessary for running this application was not found.
ERROR_BAD_DEVICE	1200	Invalid device name.
ERROR_CONNECTION_UNAVAIL	1201	The device is not connected.
ERROR_DEVICE_ALREADY_REMEMBERED	1202	The data on the given device has already been remembered by the system.
ERROR_NO_NET_OR_BAD_PATH	1203	Either there is no connection to the network or the specified network path is incorrect.
ERROR_BAD_PROVIDER	1204	Invalid provider name is specified.
ERROR_CANNOT_OPEN_PROFILE	1205	Cannot open the profile configuration for connecting to the network.
ERROR_BAD_PROFILE	1206	The profile for connecting to the network is corrupted.

TABLE A.1 Win32 API Errors *(Continued)*

Constant	***Value***	***Description***
ERROR_NOT_CONTAINER	1207	Cannot use enumerations for objects that are not containers.
ERROR_EXTENDED_ERROR	1208	An error.
ERROR_INVALID_GROUPNAME	1209	Invalid format for a group name.
ERROR_INVALID_COMPUTERNAME	1210	Invalid format for a computer name.
ERROR_INVALID_EVENTNAME	1211	Invalid format for an event name.
ERROR_INVALID_DOMAINNAME	1212	Invalid format for a domain name.
ERROR_INVALID_SERVICENAME	1213	Invalid format for a service name.
ERROR_INVALID_NETNAME	1214	Invalid format for a network name.
ERROR_INVALID_SHARENAME	1215	Invalid format for a shared resource name.
ERROR_INVALID_PASSWORDNAME	1216	Invalid format for a password.
ERROR_INVALID_MESSAGENAME	1217	Invalid format for a message name.
ERROR_INVALID_MESSAGEDEST	1218	Invalid format for a message recipient address.
ERROR_SESSION_CREDENTIAL_CONFLIC	1219	Conflicting specified and actual credentials.
ERROR_REMOTE_SESSION_LIMIT_EXCEE	1220	There are too many sessions running on the server.
ERROR_DUP_DOMAINNAME	1221	This domain name/workgroup name already exists and is used by another computer on the network.
ERROR_NO_NETWORK	1222	There is no network.
ERROR_CANCELLED	1223	The operation has been cancelled by a user.
ERROR_USER_MAPPED_FILE	1224	The operation cannot be performed on a file with one of its sections opened.

TABLE A.1 Win32 API Errors (*Continued*)

Constant	*Value*	*Description*
ERROR_CONNECTION_REFUSED	1225	The remote system denied the request for a network connection.
ERROR_GRACEFUL_DISCONNECT	1226	The network connection has been closed.
ERROR_ADDRESS_ALREADY_ASSOCIATED	1227	The end point of the network transport is already associated with a certain address.
ERROR_ADDRESS_NOT_ASSOCIATED	1228	The end point of the network transport has not been associated with any address.
ERROR_CONNECTION_INVALID	1229	The connection is invalid.
ERROR_CONNECTION_ACTIVE	1230	Invalid operation for an active network connection.
ERROR_NETWORK_UNREACHABLE	1231	The remote network is inaccessible.
ERROR_HOST_UNREACHABLE	1232	The network transport cannot provide for your accessing a remote system.
ERROR_PROTOCOL_UNREACHABLE	1233	The remote system does not support a given transport protocol.
ERROR_PORT_UNREACHABLE	1234	No service is running on the remote system.
ERROR_REQUEST_ABORTED	1235	Processing of the request has been aborted.
ERROR_CONNECTION_ABORTED	1236	The connection has been aborted.
ERROR_RETRY	1237	Couldn't complete the operation. A second attempt to start it must be made.
ERROR_CONNECTION_COUNT_LIMIT	1238	The limit of permissible concurrent connections has been reached for the given account name.
ERROR_LOGIN_TIME_RESTRICTION	1239	The given user cannot log ontothe network at any time other than the one specified in the account.

TABLE A.1 Win32 API Errors (*Continued*)

Constant	*Value*	*Description*
ERROR_LOGIN_WKSTA_RESTRICTION	1240	The given user cannot log onto the network from that particular work station.
ERROR_INCORRECT_ADDRESS	1241	Cannot use a network address for the given operation.
ERROR_ALREADY_REGISTERED	1242	This service is already registered.
ERROR_SERVICE_NOT_FOUND	1243	This service was not found.
ERROR_NOT_AUTHENTICATED	1244	A given user was not registered.
ERROR_NOT_LOGGED_ON	1245	A given user has not logged onto the network.
ERROR_CONTINUE	1246	The operation in progress must be continued.
ERROR_ALREADY_INITIALIZED	1247	Initialization has already been performed.
ERROR_NO_MORE_DEVICES	1248	There are no more local devices.
ERROR_NOT_ALL_ASSIGNED	1300	The access rights of the user are limited.
ERROR_SOME_NOT_MAPPED	1301	Some user names and security IDs are not consistent.
ERROR_NO_QUOTAS_FOR_ACCOUNT	1302	There are no system quotas for the given account name.
ERROR_LOCAL_USER_SESSION_KEY	1303	The encryption key is unavailable.
ERROR_NULL_LM_PASSWORD	1304	The given Windows NT password is too complicated and cannot be converted to a LAN Manager password. An empty string has been returned instead of the LAN Manager password.
ERROR_UNKNOWN_REVISION	1305	An unknown version.
ERROR_REVISION_MISMATCH	1306	Mismatching versions.

TABLE A.1 Win32 API Errors (*Continued*)

Constant	*Value*	*Description*
ERROR_INVALID_OWNER	1307	The given security code is invalid for the owner of the given object.
ERROR_INVALID_PRIMARY_GROUP	1308	The given security code is invalid for the object's primary group.
ERROR_NO_IMPERSONATION_TOKEN	1309	An improper attempt was made to use a stream of commands that do not represent the client.
ERROR_CANT_DISABLE_MANDATORY	1310	The group cannot be disabled.
ERROR_NO_LOGON_SERVERS	1311	There are no network servers that can process logons.
ERROR_NO_SUCH_LOGON_SESSION	1312	The specified logon session does not exist.
ERROR_NO_SUCH_PRIVILEGE	1313	The specified privilege does not exist.
ERROR_PRIVILEGE_NOT_HELD	1314	The client doesn't have the necessary privileges.
ERROR_INVALID_ACCOUNT_NAME	1315	Invalid account name.
ERROR_USER_EXISTS	1316	Another user with this name already exists.
ERROR_NO_SUCH_USER	1317	No user with this name was found.
ERROR_GROUP_EXISTS	1318	The specified group already exists.
ERROR_NO_SUCH_GROUP	1319	The specified group doesn't exist.
ERROR_MEMBER_IN_GROUP	1320	The specified user is already a member of the given group.
ERROR_MEMBER_NOT_IN_GROUP	1321	The specified user is not a member of the given group.
ERROR_LAST_ADMIN	1322	The last account name in the administration group cannot be deleted or disabled.

TABLE A.1 Win32 API Errors *(Continued)*

Constant	*Value*	*Description*
ERROR_WRONG_PASSWORD	1323	An incorrect value for the old password was specified in the process of changing the password.
ERROR_ILL_FORMED_PASSWORD	1324	The new password contains forbidden characters.
ERROR_PASSWORD_RESTRICTION	1325	One of the rules for renewing a password has been violated.
ERROR_LOGON_FAILURE	1326	The user name and password were not identified.
ERROR_ACCOUNT_RESTRICTION	1327	Due to certain account limitations, the user has not been logged on.
ERROR_INVALID_LOGON_HOURS	1328	The account name does not permit the user to log on at this time.
ERROR_INVALID_WORKSTATIONDELETE ME	1329	The user is not permitted to log on from this computer.
ERROR_PASSWORD_EXPIRED	1330	The password has expired.
ERROR_ACCOUNT_DISABLED	1331	The account name has been disabled.
ERROR_NONE_MAPPED	1332	Users' names are not mapped on security IDs.
ERROR_TOO_MANY_LUIDS_REQUESTED	1333	Too many local user IDs have been requested.
ERROR_LUIDS_EXHAUSTED	1334	Extra local user IDs are unavailable.
ERROR_INVALID_SUB_AUTHORITY	1335	Part of a given security ID is invalid.
ERROR_INVALID_ACL	1336	The access control list (ACL) has an invalid structure.
ERROR_INVALID_SID	1337	The given security ID (SID) is invalid.
ERROR_INVALID_SECURITY_DESCR	1338	Invalid security descriptor.

TABLE A.1 Win32 API Errors *(Continued)*

Constant	*Value*	*Description*
ERROR_BAD_INHERITANCE_ACL	1340	Cannot create the access control list or an element for this list.
ERROR_SERVER_DISABLED	1341	The server is disabled.
ERROR_SERVER_NOT_DISABLED	1342	The server is activated.
ERROR_INVALID_ID_AUTHORITY	1343	Invalid value for a security ID.
ERROR_ALLOTTED_SPACE_EXCEEDED	1344	Too little free memory space to update security Ids.
ERROR_INVALID_GROUP_ATTRIBUTES	1345	The specified attributes are invalid or inconsistent with the group attributes.
ERROR_BAD_IMPERSONATION_LEVEL	1346	Incorrect impersonation level.
ERROR_CANT_OPEN_ANONYMOUS	1347	Cannot open an anonymous security element (which has an unknown impersonation level).
ERROR_BAD_VALIDATION_CLASS	1348	An incorrect validation class has been requested.
ERROR_BAD_TOKEN_TYPE	1349	The element type is inconsistent with the given operation.
ERROR_NO_SECURITY_ON_OBJECT	1350	A data security operation cannot be performed for an insecure object.
ERROR_CANT_ACCESS_DOMAIN_INFO	1351	The domain controller is unreachable, or the objects located inside the domain are secure.
ERROR_INVALID_SERVER_STATE	1352	The security controller or a local server couldn't perform the given operation.
ERROR_INVALID_DOMAIN_STATE	1353	The operation cannot be performed while the domain is in its current state.
ERROR_INVALID_DOMAIN_ROLE	1354	The given operation is specified only for the domain primary controller.
ERROR_NO_SUCH_DOMAIN	1355	The specified domain does not exist.

TABLE A.1 Win32 API Errors *(Continued)*

Constant	*Value*	*Description*
ERROR_DOMAIN_EXISTS	1356	The specified domain already exists.
ERROR_DOMAIN_LIMIT_EXCEEDED	1357	The number of domains exceeds the limit specified for the server.
ERROR_INTERNAL_DB_CORRUPTION	1358	Cannot complete the operation due to the corruption of an internal database on the given disk.
ERROR_INTERNAL_ERROR	1359	The security database contains internal inconsistencies.
ERROR_GENERIC_NOT_MAPPED	1360	An access mask must be mapped on generic types.
ERROR_BAD_DESCRIPTION_FORMAT	1361	Invalid format for a security descriptor.
ERROR_NOT_LOGON_PROCESS	1362	A given action can be used only during a logon session.
ERROR_LOGON_SESSION_EXISTS	1363	A new logon cannot be implemented.
ERROR_NO_SUCH_PACKAGE	1364	Unknown package of password validating programs.
ERROR_BAD_LOGON_SESSION_STATE	1365	Cannot perform the given operation while the logon session is in the current state.
ERROR_LOGON_SESSION_COLLISION	1366	The given ID is already being used in a given session.
ERROR_INVALID_LOGON_TYPE	1367	Invalid logon type.
ERROR_CANNOT_IMPERSONATE	1368	Cannot implement impersonation.
ERROR_RXACT_INVALID_STATE	1369	Invalid operation for the given registry key.
ERROR_RXACT_COMMIT_FAILURE	1370	The security database has been corrupted.
ERROR_SPECIAL_ACCOUNT	1371	A special account is required to perform the given operation.
ERROR_SPECIAL_GROUP	1372	The operation requires a special user group.
ERROR_SPECIAL_USER	1373	The given operation requires a special user.

TABLE A.1 Win32 API Errors (*Continued*)

Constant	*Value*	*Description*
ERROR_MEMBERS_PRIMARY_GROUP	1374	Cannot remove a user from a primary group.
ERROR_TOKEN_ALREADY_IN_USE	1375	The element is already in use.
ERROR_NO_SUCH_ALIAS	1376	The specified local group does not exist.
ERROR_MEMBER_NOT_IN_ALIAS	1377	The specified user is not a member of a local group.
ERROR_MEMBER_IN_ALIAS	1378	The specified user is already a member of a local group.
ERROR_ALIAS_EXISTS	1379	The given local group already exists.
ERROR_LOGON_NOT_GRANTED	1380	The selected logon mode is not granted to a given user.
ERROR_TOO_MANY_SECRETS	1381	Too many secure resources for one system.
ERROR_SECRET_TOO_LONG	1382	The protected data is too long.
ERROR_INTERNAL_DB_ERROR	1383	Internal inconsistency in a local security database has been detected.
ERROR_TOO_MANY_CONTEXT_IDS	1384	Too many security IDs for a given logon session.
ERROR_LOGON_TYPE_NOT_GRANTED	1385	The selected logon type is not granted to the user.
ERROR_NT_CROSS_ENCRYPTION_REQUI	1386	An encrypted password is required in order to change a current password.
ERROR_NO_SUCH_MEMBER	1387	No new member can be added to the given local group.
ERROR_INVALID_MEMBER	1388	Cannot add a new member to the given local group because he has an invalid account name
ERROR_TOO_MANY_SIDS	1389	Too many security IDs have been specified.

TABLE A.1 Win32 API Errors *(Continued)*

Constant	*Value*	*Description*
ERROR_LM_CROSS_ENCRYPTION_REQUIR	1390	An encrypted password is required in order to change a current password.
ERROR_NO_INHERITANCE	1391	The access control list does not contain inherited components.
ERROR_FILE_CORRUPT	1392	The file or folder has been corrupted and cannot be written to or read from.
ERROR_DISK_CORRUPT	1393	The disk has been corrupted.
ERROR_NO_USER_SESSION_KEY	1394	There is no user session key for the given logon session.
ERROR_LICENSE_QUOTA_EXCEEDED	1395	The quota for permissible connections to a given service has been exceeded.
ERROR_INVALID_WINDOW_HANDLE	1400	Invalid window handle.
ERROR_INVALID_MENU_HANDLE	1401	Invalid menu handle.
ERROR_INVALID_CURSOR_HANDLE	1402	Invalid cursor handle.
ERROR_INVALID_ACCEL_HANDLE	1403	Invalid handle to the shortcut key table.
ERROR_INVALID_HOOK_HANDLE	1404	Invalid hook handle.
ERROR_INVALID_DWP_HANDLE	1405	Invalid handle to a given multi-window structure.
ERROR_TLW_WITH_WSCHILD	1406	Cannot create a child window.
ERROR_CANNOT_FIND_WND_CLASS	1407	The window class was not found.
ERROR_WINDOW_OF_OTHER_THREAD	1408	The given window belongs to another thread.
ERROR_HOTKEY_ALREADY_REGISTERED	1409	The hotkey value is already registered.
ERROR_CLASS_ALREADY_EXIST	1410	The class already exists.
ERROR_CLASS_DOES_NOT_EXIST	1411	The class does not exist.
ERROR_CLASS_HAS_WINDOWS	1412	The class has active windows.

TABLE A.1 Win32 API Errors *(Continued)*

Constant	*Value*	*Description*
ERROR_INVALID_INDEX	1413	Invalid index.
ERROR_INVALID_ICON_HANDLE	1414	Invalid icon handle.
ERROR_PRIVATE_DIALOG_INDEX	1415	Improper use of the keywords relevant to dialog windows of the private type.
ERROR_LISTBOX_ID_NOT_FOUND	1416	The ID of a given list box was not found.
ERROR_NO_WILDCARD_CHARACTERS	1417	Wildcard characters were not found.
ERROR_CLIPBOARD_NOT_OPEN	1418	The clipboard is not open.
ERROR_HOTKEY_NOT_REGISTERED	1419	The given shortcut is not registered.
ERROR_WINDOW_NOT_DIALOG	1420	The given window is not a dialog.
ERROR_CONTROL_ID_NOT_FOUND	1421	The ID of the given control was not found.
ERROR_INVALID_COMBOBOX_MESSAGE	1422	Invalid combo box message.
ERROR_WINDOW_NOT_COMBOBOX	1423	The given window is not a combo box.
ERROR_INVALID_EDIT_HEIGHT	1424	The maximum edit field height must be 256.
ERROR_DC_NOT_FOUND	1425	Invalid handle for the device context (DC).
ERROR_INVALID_HOOK_FILTER	1426	Invalid hook type.
ERROR_INVALID_FILTER_PROC	1427	Invalid filter procedure.
ERROR_HOOK_NEEDS_HMOD	1428	Cannot install a global hook without the handle to the given module.
ERROR_GLOBAL_ONLY_HOOK	1429	The given hook can be only global.
ERROR_JOURNAL_HOOK_SET	1430	The given journal hook is already installed.
ERROR_HOOK_NOT_INSTALLED	1431	The given journal hook is not installed.
ERROR_INVALID_LB_MESSAGE	1432	Invalid list box message.
ERROR_SETCOUNT_ON_BAD_LB	1433	The LB_SETCOUNT parameter is specified for a list of invalid type.

TABLE A.1 Win32 API Errors (*Continued*)

Constant	*Value*	*Description*
ERROR_LB_WITHOUT_TABSTOPS	1434	The given list box is not included into the tab stop list.
ERROR_DESTROY_OBJECT_OF_OTHER_TH	1435	Cannot delete an object that was created by another thread.
ERROR_CHILD_WINDOW_MENU	1436	Child windows cannot contain menus.
ERROR_NO_SYSTEM_MENU	1437	The given window has no menu.
ERROR_INVALID_MSGBOX_STYLE	1438	Invalid type for a message window.
ERROR_INVALID_SPI_VALUE	1439	Invalid value for a system parameter.
ERROR_SCREEN_ALREADY_LOCKED	1440	The screen is already locked.
ERROR_HWNDS_HAVE_DIFF_PARENT	1441	Window handles of a multi-window structure must have a common parent descriptor.
ERROR_NOT_CHILD_WINDOW	1442	This window is not a child window.
ERROR_INVALID_GW_COMMAND	1443	Invalid system command.
ERROR_INVALID_THREAD_ID	1444	Invalid thread ID.
ERROR_NON_MDICHILD_WINDOW	1445	The window is not a component of a multi-window interface.
ERROR_POPUP_ALREADY_ACTIVE	1446	The given pop-up menu is already active.
ERROR_NO_SCROLLBARS	1447	The window doesn't have scroll bars.
ERROR_INVALID_SCROLLBAR_RANGE	1448	Invalid value for a scroll bar (it must fall within the range from 0 to 7FFF).
ERROR_INVALID_SHOWWIN_COMMAND	1449	Cannot show or hide a window in this way.
ERROR_EVENTLOG_FILE_CORRUPT	1500	The event log file has been corrupted.
ERROR_EVENTLOG_CANT_START	1501	Cannot find the event log file
ERROR_LOG_FILE_FULL	1502	The event log file is full.
ERROR_EVENTLOG_FILE_CHANGED	1503	The event log file has been modified between two read operations.

TABLE A.1 Win32 API Errors *(Continued)*

Constant	*Value*	*Description*
ERROR_INVALID_USER_BUFFER	1784	An invalid user buffer.
ERROR_UNRECOGNIZED_MEDIA	1785	Cannot identify the type of the disk.
ERROR_NO_TRUST_LSA_SECRET	1786	The work group cannot participate in a trust relationship.
ERROR_NO_TRUST_SAM_ACCOUNT	1787	The Windows NT server doesn't contain the trust relationship account for the given computer.
ERROR_TRUSTED_DOMAIN_FAILURE	1788	Couldn't establish a trust relationship between the main domain and the given trusted domain.
ERROR_TRUSTED_RELATIONSHIP_FAILURE	1789	Couldn't establish a trust relationship between the given computer and the main domain.
ERROR_TRUST_FAILURE	1790	Logon has failed.
ERROR_NETLOGON_NOT_STARTED	1792	A network logon service was disabled.
ERROR_ACCOUNT_EXPIRED	1793	The given account name has expired.
ERROR_REDIRECTOR_HAS_OPEN_HANDLE	1794	The redirector is busy and cannot be disabled.
ERROR_PRINTER_DRIVER_ALREADY_INST	1795	The printer driver has already been installed.
ERROR_UNKNOWN_PORT	1796	An attempt has been made to connect a non-existent port.
ERROR_UNKNOWN_PRINTER_DRIVER	1797	Unknown printer driver.
ERROR_UNKNOWN_PRINTPROCESSOR	1798	Unknown print processor.
ERROR_INVALID_SEPARATOR_FILE	1799	Invalid separator file.
ERROR_INVALID_PRIORITY	1800	Invalid priority setting.
ERROR_INVALID_PRINTER_NAME	1801	Invalid printer name.
ERROR_PRINTER_ALREADY_EXISTS	1802	The specified printer already exits.
ERROR_INVALID_PRINTER_COMMAND	1803	Invalid printer command.

TABLE A.1 Win32 API Errors *(Continued)*

Constant	*Value*	*Description*
ERROR_INVALID_DATATYPE	1804	Invalid data type.
ERROR_INVALID_ENVIRONMENT	1805	Invalid environment.
ERROR_INVALID_PRINTER_STATE	1906	Invalid printer state.
ERROR_PASSWORD_MUST_CHANGE	1907	The given password must be changed.
ERROR_DOMAIN_CONTROLLER_NOT_FOUND	1908	The domain controller was not found.
ERROR_ACCOUNT_LOCKED_OUT	1909	The account name of a given user is locked.
ERROR_INVALID_PIXEL_FORMAT	2000	Invalid pixel format.
ERROR_BAD_DRIVER	2001	Invalid driver.
ERROR_INVALID_WINDOW_STYLE	2002	The given window style attribute is invalid.
ERROR_METAFILE_NOT_SUPPORTED	2003	The given operation on metafiles is not supported.
ERROR_TRANSFORM_NOT_SUPPORTED	2004	The given transformation operation is not supported.
ERROR_CLIPPING_NOT_SUPPORTED	2005	The given clipping operation is not supported.
ERROR_BAD_USERNAME	2202	Invalid user name.
ERROR_NOT_CONNECTED	2250	There is no active connection.
ERROR_OPEN_FILES	2401	There are open files or queries on the connected device waiting to be processed.
ERROR_ACTIVE_CONNECTIONS	2402	There are active connections running.
ERROR_DEVICE_IN_USE	2404	The device is currently in use and cannot be deactivated.
ERROR_UNKNOWN_PRINT_MONITOR	3000	The print monitor is unknown.
ERROR_PRINTER_DRIVER_IN_USE	3001	The printer driver is already being used.
ERROR_SPOOL_FILE_NOT_FOUND	3002	The spool file was not found.
ERROR_NO_BROWSER_SERVERS_FOUND	6118	A list of servers for the given work group is not available.

Index

A

B

C

T

U

V

W

Z